W9-BHS-332

NEVADA

The Great Rotten Borough

1859–1964

NEVADA

The Great Rotten Borough 1859–1964

Gilman M. Ostrander

NEW YORK: ALFRED · A · KNOPF

1966

LIBRARY
FLORIDA STATE UNIVERSITY
TALLAHASSEE, FLORIDA

L. C. catalog card number: 66–10747

THIS IS A BORZOI BOOK,
PUBLISHED BY ALFRED A. KNOPF, INC.

Copyright © 1966 by Gilman M. Ostrander. All rights reserved. No part of this book may be reproduced in any form without permission in writing from the publisher, except by a reviewer, who may quote brief passages in a review to be printed in a magazine or newspaper. Manufactured in the United States of America, and distributed by Random House, Inc. Published simultaneously in Toronto, Canada, by Random House of Canada, Limited.

FIRST EDITION

Introduction

Much has been written about the Great Compromise in the Constitutional Convention in 1787, but not enough attention has been paid to the results of it. The Great Compromise discarded the holy principle of proportional representation, so far as the proposed upper house of the national legislature was concerned, and gave equal representation to all states, regardless of the disparity of their populations. At the time, many of the founding fathers thought it a shocking thing to do, but once the new nation had taken form under the new Constitution, it was accepted as the wise decision of the sages and patriots who had founded the republic. It was especially so accepted by the citizens of Delaware, who were the first to ratify the Constitution, and it was later approved, in like manner, by such other underpopulated states as Arizona, Montana, and Nevada. These states have clearly been the beneficiaries of small-state statesmanship in the United States Senate, but it is not so clear that the nation as a whole has benefited.

The question of the degree of sovereignty to be enjoyed by the several states was less controversial in 1787. The convention had been summoned mainly to deal with the troubles caused by state tariffs and state money issues, and these were prohibited, as a matter of course. Otherwise, the states were left in possession of the right to do as they wished, on the condition that their acts did not contravene other specific injunctions laid down in the Constitution. Later, the tenth amendment reserved to the states all of the rights not granted to the federal government, but the founders had already denied the states the right to do all of the things they had been doing which, at the time, were of national consequence. Hamilton supposed, hopefully, that the states would all but atrophy, for the lack of anything to do. This has, of course, not proved to be the case at all. The states, taken as a whole, have consistently outdistanced the federal government bureaucratically, and they have found ways which the eighteenth-century founders could not have imagined, to affect people outside their borders.

Nevada: The Great Rotten Borough is a historical study of the one state which, throughout its history, has been the extreme example of the oddest aspects of federalism, as that system rather accidentally emerged in America. During almost all of its history, Nevada has possessed the smallest population of any state in the Union, although at the present time it is—as it takes every opportunity to point out—the fastest-growing state in the Union, proportionally, and no longer rests on the bottom of the list. Economically, furthermore, it has tended to be absentee-owned, by mine operators, railroads, ranching corporations, and gambling syndicates.

In this, again, Nevada presents an extreme example, but, except for the factor of legalized gambling, it has been by no means a unique one. A historical study of the political economies of any of the lightly populated Western states would reveal a somewhat similar pattern of absentee economic and political control and a similar tendency on the part of the citizens to see the general welfare of the nation as a whole in the light of their own narrowly provincial concerns.

The impact of most small-state senators upon the legislative history of the nation has been rather slight. This is not to be explained on the ground that they represent fewer people than do their colleagues, for the rules and customs of the Senate make no such distinctions. The Senate does take meticulously into account the vested interests of the state for which the individual senator speaks. As a general rule a senator from Nevada does not expect to exert as much influence upon enactments that do not greatly affect his state, such as those dealing with agriculture, manufacturing and labor, as does a colleague from a state where these activities are important. In such areas as mining law, land reclamation, and monetary policy concerning silver, however, his arguments may become very weighty.

In the case of legislation affecting the nation as a whole, such as the establishment of a Federal Trade Commission or of a restrictive immigration law (to cite two examples where the Senate followed the lead of Nevada senators), a senator's influence is not diminished in the least by the fact that he represents, comparatively speaking, only a handful of people. He is not given less consideration on this account when appointments are made to the Commerce Committee, the Judiciary Committee, or the Foreign Relations Committee, each of which has been chaired by a Nevadan. The relative lack of statesmanship of small-state senators throughout American history is therefore not due to any lack of opportunity to assert their influence. The likelier explanation is that their horizons are narrowed in accordance with the narrowness of their constituencies. This has been the rule with Nevada senators.

There have, of course, been exceptions to this rule. Francis Newlands and Pat McCarran of Nevada each took the fullest advantage of his senatorial authority, and each, by doing so, measurably altered the course of national affairs. They remain exceptions. No other Nevada senator has ever demonstrated any real interest in legislative matters which did not directly concern the Sagebrush State. This was true even of

Key Pittman, from 1933 to 1940, when he served as chairman of the Foreign Relations Committee.

Other exceptions to the rule can readily be cited in the cases of other relatively underpopulated states, but generally the furthering of local interest is the prime concern of a senator. The Great Compromise was an unhappy arrangement which served to dilute the quality of the upper branch of the national legislature.

The anomaly of this superfluity of small-state representation in the Senate is in some respects matched by the states' rights anomaly of autonomous jurisdictions, individually retained and resolutely defended by the several states, in matters affecting the nation as a whole. The tenth amendment to the Constitution was passed during an ancient age, when local control of local affairs followed logically from the circumstances of a rural, small-town nation, made up of rather isolated and self-contained local societies. The railroad and automobile and the industrial revolution and the rise of finance capitalism changed all this, without, of course, altering the wording of the pre-industrial Constitution.

Inevitably, the Constitution came to take on new meanings, as it was used to interpret a rapidly changing society. Even where old constitutional construction continued to be applied in a new context, the results of its application could hardly have been conceived of by the founding fathers. In the gasoline age Nevada became the most conspicuous travesty of the Jeffersonian dream. During the first half century of Nevada's existence, the ideal of local autonomy had meant for it the enrichment of San Franciscans through the exploitation of its resources and the political advantage to San Franciscans of representation in the Senate by their ability virtually to purchase the Nevada senatorships for themselves.

During the second half century Nevadans reacted violently against this carpetbagger domination. Home rule in politics was insisted upon and achieved. Then Nevada went on the offensive and implemented the states' rights provisions of the Constitution in order to take money from non-Nevadans in general and Californians in particular by means of a variety of legal devices. It would be unthinkable, if it were not so commonplace, that a corporation operating in one state could arbitrarily place itself under the jurisdiction of another. The Constitution permits it, however, and, while Nevada cannot claim credit for devising the method, it followed eagerly where other small states led in the late nineteenth century.

Probably no other state has done better than Nevada in freeing its citizens of the tyranny of taxation, on the one hand, and in levying taxes from strangers, on the other. This tax policy has served the further purpose of bringing businesses to Nevada which, except for unusual tax benefits, would have no business being there. It has also brought millionaire "tax dodgers," as the Nevadans call them, who build expensive houses and spend much money in other ways.

These tax and incorporation laws have helped a state which is so poor in natural resources and so small in population that it benefits economically from the least activity. Much more lucrative, however, were the quick-divorce and quick-marriage businesses, which by the early years of the Great Depression had developed themselves into an economic mainstay of the state. By that time other states had entered into competition for the divorce trade, and California had passed retaliatory laws that sharply limited the profits from easy incorporation and tax laws, profits which in Nevada had been taken mainly from the Golden State.

Then in 1931, at the bottom of the depression, Nevada hit states' rights pay dirt with the legalizing of gambling. It was as slow to show a big profit as the Comstock Lode had been, but, unlike the Comstock Lode, the bonanza continued. During the 1950s Nevada was the fastest growing state of the union, proportionally, and it was enjoying the highest per capita income of any state. All of this was made possible by the gambling laws which permitted Nevadans to have "fun in the sun," as the advertisements put it, under the terms of the Constitution.

Nevada's economy is now based upon gambling and the allied "tourism," for mining and ranching are now a relatively insignificant part of it. Until the mid-forties, it seemed that Nevada, with legalized gambling, had at last developed a home-owned industry from which it could live in a state of proud self-reliance. Then the national crime syndicates moved in and began to take over, especially in Las Vegas, where local gambling enterprise had not firmly established itself by the close of World War II, as it had in the Reno area. The extent to which Nevada gambling is controlled by nation-wide crime mergers has yet to be clearly analyzed. Nevertheless, the Nevada gambling industry since the advent of Benjamin "Bugsy" Siegel at the end of World War II has provided another example of the difficulty of retaining local control of a local industry in an economy which has become nationalized, even in its criminal activities.

From the mining economy of the first years to the gambling economy of the last, the simplicity of Nevada's economic life allows for an engagingly simple study of the interaction of business and politics in American life. This book was not written in order to debunk the American democratic system; nor did I suppose at the outset that the result would be as severely critical of Nevada's role in the nation's history as it appears here. Initially, the tentative title for the study was *The Great Pocket Borough*, but I changed it under the accumulating weight of evidence. Furthermore, this study was not undertaken as an attempt to turn American business history back fifty years to the days of business-baiting writers such as

Gustavus Myers. Yet there are some astonishingly naïve interpretations of American history currently receiving wide credence, and my work may do something to correct them.

There is the still fairly new school of business historians, which, bracing itself against a previous generation of unopposed onslaughts upon American business, has created the pompous thesis of American industrial statesmanship. It is no great exaggeration to say that these historians think that the leading business figures of the late nineteenth century were trying, first of all, to bring order out of economic chaos and so prepare America to meet the challenges of the twentieth century.

It would be characteristic of this school of history, for instance, to argue that the purpose of the plunder of the Comstock Lode was to provide the gold and silver bullion needed to win the war which was being waged to preserve the Union and to rid the nation of slavery. It would also be characteristic of this school to ascribe those idealistic motives to the speculators and mine operators who, by successfully accumulating fortunes running into the tens of millions of dollars, presumably demonstrated forever their business sagacity and foresight.

I have found that the guiding purpose of the prominent entrepreneurs of Nevada to this day has been to make as much money as possible, and the devil take the hindmost. There are exceptions to this rule, and the man who struck it richest of all in Nevada's history, John W. Mackay, was perhaps the most distinguished one. The rule nevertheless holds, and it is amply supported by the correspondence and other evidence of the activities of leading businessmen.

The other dominant historical trend which it has become my ambition to deflect in some measure is one that has been with us ever since Captain John Smith wrote our first history. This is the standard American school of political history—and, even more, of political biography—which persists in recording American politics, and the careers of American politicians, in the terms of the dull annals of statesmanship. Disraeli once referred to his rise to political eminence in England as the climbing of the greasy pole. Presumably, the political biographer cannot avoid noticing that in American politics also the footing is slippery; but the tendency among many American political biographers has nevertheless been to treat the protagonist as an idealistic boy in Keds who somehow managed to tread forthrightly up the greasy pole to whatever heights were necessary for whatever degree of statesmanship he had in mind.

Actually, almost everybody knows that businessmen are out to make money and that politicians are out to gain office and that much history has been made in this nation by businessmen and politicians helping each other out. What follows this introduction is, in part, a study of these mutually beneficial exchanges as they occurred historically in a remarkably simple context.

The research for this book was done in a wide variety of pleasant surroundings: the Nevada Historical Society, the Nevada Room of the University of Nevada Library, the Nevada Historical Museum, the Huntington Library, the Library of Congress, the Sterling Library at Yale University, and, mainly, the Bancroft Library at the University of California, Berkeley. From members of the staffs of all of these libraries I received perceptive and patient assistance. The manuscript was read by Stuart Bruchey and Vernon Carstensen, and the sometimes devastating criticisms contained in their politely written critiques rescued the author from his ignorance in many places. The completion of the research for this book was made possible by an American Philosophical Society summer research grant and by a leave for research granted by Michigan State University.

Contents

NEVADA

The Great Rotten Borough

1859–1964

CHAPTER I

A State of Nature

Northeast from San Francisco, across the fertile fields of the Sacramento, the Sierra Nevadas rise gradually through the rugged, pine-green California gold mining country, two miles into the sky above Lake Tahoe; then drop more than a mile to the sands of Nevada's Carson Valley, at the rim of the Great American Desert. A half day's walk beyond, past brackish Washoe Lake, Sun Mountain looms above the valley floor, a massive barrier of rock, studded with runty pinion pines, covered with a scraggly growth of desert weeds and created by nature for coyotes, jack rabbits, rattlesnakes, horned toads, and spotted lizards.

Sun Mountain was avoided by the neighboring Paiute Indians, and with good reason; for, at its summit, it was almost as bleak and arid as the moon, although billions of gallons of water seethed and steamed beneath its surface. Also beneath its surface, under the farther slope, was the Comstock Lode, four miles long by 3,000 feet wide by 3,000 feet down to its fiery depth—the richest treasure of silver and gold ever discovered anywhere on earth in so concentrated an area.[1]

Discovered in 1859,[2] the Comstock yielded more than $300 million of bullion during the first two decades of operation. In 1881, the last of the bonanza mines was almost played out and in flames. The lode was by then a honeycomb of deserted shafts and tunnels, and the former boom towns of Gold Hill and Virginia City already were becoming shadows of the past, although the milling of low-grade ore continued profitably into the twentieth century. In San Francisco, meanwhile, the millionaire class of nabobs had established itself. It was estimated that there was a greater proportion of millionaires and multimillionaires in San Francisco than in any other city in the nation, and the majority of their fortunes had been made possible by the Comstock.

The mines of California were much richer, taken as a whole, than were those of the Comstock, and they were also much closer to San Francisco. It would be logical to suppose that they created the San Francisco fortunes. The illogical fact is that they did not. Those richer California gold regions were geographically equalitarian in that the gold was widely dispersed and easy to come by in beautiful rivers and streams. Comstock bullion, by contrast, was hard in the heart of a desert mountain, and much capital and equipment were required to extract it. The California mining region was destined to be democratic by force of geological determinism. The Comstock was destined to be autocratic for geological reasons.

The free and easy miners from California came to Nevada and became a mining proletariat (the most affluent proletariat, it is true, to be found anywhere in the world). They brought with them their California experience and the mining laws which had grown out of that experience. These laws had been silly enough when applied to the California Mother Lode. They were ruinously ridiculous when applied to the Comstock. The result was that the first men to strike it rich on the

Comstock were the lawyers, who reaped large rewards from the misapplication of the California experience in the field of law.

Most of those Comstock miners had known as little about gold mining when they had arrived in California in 1849 as they knew about silver mining when they joined "the rush to Washoe", as western Nevada was called, in 1859, but in the case of California gold, that ignorance had put them to little disadvantage.[3] Initially, there had been opportunities for all comers along the 120-mile stretch of the California Mother Lode and then in various other gold-rich areas north into Oregon. The precious metal was to be found in the sand and gravel along the banks of rivers and streams, and the lucky miner needed nothing more than a pan for equipment. Most of the California miners had been Americans, ignorant of their new trade, but they had been able to pick up effective methods easily from more experienced foreigners: the Mexicans, the Cornish, and the Germans.

A simply constructed and highly effective device for separating gold from gravel was an open-ended box on rockers. Wooden strips were nailed across the floor of the box to catch the gold, with its heavier specific gravity, as the sand and gravel was rocked and washed away. Somewhat more ambitious was the long tom and then the sluice, both of them simply long troughs subjected to a continuous flow of water. Quicksilver was in general use in 1849 to amalgamate with the gold and reject other minerals. One of the few important sources of quicksilver in North America was discovered nearby, south of San Francisco.

For the first three or four flush years there had been circumstances that had favored the individual enterpriser and had hindered corporate effort. Foreign companies had been organized to exploit the opportunities, only to have their workers desert them upon arriving in San Francisco, to strike out for themselves. Quartz mining, which was attempted in the early years, required capital for heavy, expensive equipment to crush the quartz and remove the ore. The quartz-mining operators did not know what they were doing, however, and the machinery proved largely useless. The consequence was a series of bankruptcies in 1853 which discouraged such efforts thereafter. Some quartz-mining continued in California, and the experience acquired there later proved of great importance to the Comstock Lode; for it was the California quartz miners, primitive though their methods were, who were best equipped to deal with the problems of the Comstock. Nevertheless, it has been estimated that by 1860 the technologically simpler placer mining had accounted for about 99 per cent of the gold yield in California.[4]

All of the early successful methods could have been used by miners who had no capital and worked in partnership with only two or more men, but by the mid-fifties that day was largely over. Because the river banks no longer offered easy rewards, the miners organized companies which diverted streams and rivers so that they could mine the beds of the rivers. Most importantly of all, they used increasingly large-scale and expensive hydraulic mining techniques to apply powerful jets of water to tear gold-bearing veins of gravel from the hillsides. This was a distinctively California process. At the outset of the gold rush a competent miner might, with fair confidence, have expected to make twenty dollars a day, and he might not unreasonably have hoped to strike a rich vein which would return him as much as a thousand dollars daily for a time. By 1851, however, five dollars was considered to be a fair daily yield, and the situation naturally tended to worsen. By 1859 many miners in California were driven to becoming day laborers in large mines for as little as $1.50 per day,[5] and the more hopeful were scouring the adjacent territories for new bonanzas.

The Federal military authorities who ruled California at the start of the gold rush confirmed the squatters in their rights on the ground that nothing else could be done about it.[6] The widely dispersed, relatively small deposits gave all a chance and none a monopoly. The miners, for their part, tended to be so genially optimistic about the opportunities open to all that they felt no great pressure of competition and no sense of permanent property ownership. If things did not go their way, they would be off to another mining district where there was news of better diggings. There they would take their chances under elective local governments of their own devising. Undeniably there was murder and theft and chicanery and oppression of minorities, especially the Mexicans and the Chinese, throughout the mining areas. Nevertheless, among the Americans, democracy prevailed by force of the environment. "Class distinctions," wrote the California historian H. H. Bancroft, "suffered above all a ruthless levelling. Never existed a varied community with such equality among its members socially and politically. . . ."[7]

Sun Mountain provided no such verdant environment for democracy. Richer than any similar extent of the Mother Lode, the Comstock was nothing like the easy pickings that the California mines had been. It was, to begin with, primarily a silver-mining operation. Although the lode produced more than $100 million of gold, the ore averaged twenty-one parts silver to one part gold. Silver mining had been unknown in the United States until the Comstock. Much expensive experimentation therefore was necessary before effective mining and milling methods were established, and these, for obvious reasons, proved much more costly in relation to the value of the bullion than had the gold-mining techniques in California.

The Comstock was a quartz-mining operation, of the sort that had not been well understood or highly profitable in California. Initially, it was supposed that the ores were contained in more or less parallel ledges dipping westward on the eastern slope of the mountain. What proved to be the case after a half dozen years of ruinously expensive tunneling and drifting and litigation and counterlitigation, was that the lode was one great fissure of ore slanting eastward. Its form was generally V-shaped, the ledges tending to join together below the 1600-foot level. The ore-bearing ledges together made up about 1/500th of the lode, and no very good way was ever devised to predict closely where the veins would run. John W. Mackay, who was generally considered the best miner on the Comstock and who operated by far its richest mines, observed that the results could never be clearly predicted more than two days in advance.[8] Experts agreed that the mining operations were usually characterized by much ignorance and much needless extravagance, but the difficulties and the expenses involved in finding that elusive 1/500th of meandering and often disappearing veins of ore 3,000 feet downward through rock are manifest.

The quality of the ore, while generally rich, varied greatly, but the Comstock was notable for the quantity of its ore rather than the quality, and milling ores were the rule. Everything therefore depended upon developing milling methods superior to those practiced in California. Systems used in other parts of the world, such as the then fairly well-known Mexican patio method, depended on local conditions and were not satisfactory in Nevada. The errors which accompanied the trials were extremely costly.[9] The two most productive mines of the early period, the Ophir and the Gould & Curry, spent $500,000 and $900,000 respectively on mills which were later abandoned as unprofitable. By 1863 the cost of mill construction had reached $5 million. Quicksilver was required in huge amounts and was expensive.

As the veins of ore widened underground, their increasing richness became the source of an additional cost. The Ophir was the first to encounter the sad experience of veins so rich and extensive that extraction of the ore was prevented by continual cave-ins. The operators found the solution for this in the square-set system of timbering, afterwards adopted by all of the other principal mines. As the vein was opened, timbers, generally a foot square and about six feet in length, were formed into the frame of a cube, inside of which the miner worked. As the size of the excavation increased, square-sets were added to each other like blocks and continued to hold the walls and ceiling in place with a sturdy and ever-growing network of timber.

Put to this use, the timbers of the Carson Valley area were used up in short order, and lumber companies were formed to cut wood high in the Sierras to be carried in V-flumes to the valley floor. From there, until the construction of the Virginia & Truckee Railroad, the timber was dragged to the mines by mule teams. At the height of mining activity 72 million feet of lumber were consumed in timbering the lode, during a single year, at a cost of roughly $1.5 million, in addition to 320,000 cords of firewood. At one time an average of 45 trains a day were running over the Virginia & Truckee Railroad to bring in supplies and lumber and to carry out ore.[10]

The problems of supplying the lode with water were similarly difficult. In the early days a sufficient quantity of water was obtained from abandoned tunnels in the lode, although the need was always pressing. As the mines penetrated deeper, however, the water became nauseating and impure, and water had to be brought instead from the High Sierras by a twenty-five-mile system of pipes, constructed at a cost of $2,200,000. Beyond that, virtually all of the other necessities of life were imported to the Comstock from California along two main toll roads cut through the Sierras, one by way of Placerville and the other through Nevada City. In brisk times, it was said, the Placerville road was traveled by 3,000 teams numbering 25,000 mules, and it was serviced by 94 hotels, all adding to the upkeep of the Comstock.[11]

As the mines deepened, the problems increased and the

costs multiplied. Continual changes were necessary in the hoisting apparatus, the operation of which cost as much as $1,000 per mine per month.[12] Even more serious and more expensive were the problems of heat and water encountered at the lower depths. When a miner in the Ophir thoughtlessly struck his pick through a seam of clay, a stream of water broke through which continued to flow for more than five months and which flooded out that area of the mine for two years, despite continuous pumping at full capacity. In an extreme case, two adjoining mines, in a period of two and a half years, pumped out 450 million gallons of water in order to continue operations.

The problem of heat increased with depth even more surely than the problem of water. It was quite common for miners to be obliged to work in temperatures of 130 degrees on ore that was still hotter. At the 3,000-foot level the heat rose to as much as 170 degrees. Under such conditions it was impossible for miners to work for long periods and survive; so they were constantly shifted about. Nearly naked, they were protected by canvas sheets held in front of them and by pailfuls of ice water doused on them from the rear; then they were rushed to the ice rooms maintained on all of the lower levels. During 1875 the miners on the lower levels of the Consolidated Virginia and California mines consumed an average of 95 pounds of ice per man daily. In 1877 the Consolidated Virginia mine alone purchased 3,439,980 pounds of ice.[13] Finally, the cost of the labor, which necessarily became so inefficient at the lower levels, was prodigiously high for those days, even in mining areas. The average wage for common miners in California in 1874 was from $1.50 to $2.00 per day; the minimum wage for any kind of work underground on the Comstock was $4.00 for an eight-hour shift.[14]

The four-dollar wage of the Comstock miner was thought by contemporary observers to be exorbitant even by the standards of the extravagant Comstock, but it was not seen in this light by members of the miners' union. They were obliged to provide much of their own equipment, and their cost of living was unquestionably higher than that of any other workman in the world. Worst of all, they were reduced to working for wages by the mountain, which had attracted them by its untold riches. They had reason to concur with a contemporary expert, who wrote: "Viewed as a whole, then, there are many discouragements to persons of limited means resorting to the Washoe country for the purpose of gold or silver mining; and the few rich discoveries already made there should not betray this class, or any other being profitably employed, into a hasty departure for the region."[15]

There were other mining regions by the dozen in Nevada, and the well-paid Comstock miners departed for them again and again. Silver ledges were discovered in the Esmeralda Mining District in August 1860, and a great rush followed from Carson City and Virginia City, thus creating the murderous town of Aurora. The rush to the Humboldt River region took place the next spring. In 1862 Comstockers flocked to the Reese River area and built up the dangerous town of Austin. In the winter of 1863–4, an Indian showed rich ore to prospectors, and before long the town of Pioche sprang up, settled mainly by Comstockers. By 1873 it had a population of 6,000. These areas produced rich mines, but they were quartz ledges, quickly taken up, and all of them together did not begin to compare with the Comstock Lode, to which the miners generally returned for comparative security and a four-dollar wage.[16]

To those early Comstockers who had had any experience in quartz mining, it was apparent from the beginning that the rewards of the lode would be available only to large-scale enterprises. Accordingly, by the close of 1859 the Ophir Mining Company was organized in San Francisco, and within a few months all of the main claims on the lode were in the possession of newly formed San Francisco corporations. The business community moved aggressively to snake out the silver and gold as fast as possible and bring it to the city, amid the cheering of the populace. The popular view appeared to be that after everybody had been made rich by Comstock silver, there would be enough left over to pave the streets. Symbolically, Sun Mountain was renamed Mt. Davidson, after a San Francisco banker who was a director of the Ophir Mining Company.

II

At any time during the Comstock excitement of the sixties the most casual reading of the San Francisco *Mining and Scientific Press* would have demonstrated that the stockholding owners of the mines were, of all those connected with such ventures, the least likely to make money and the most likely to lose a great deal of it. During the early years, when expenses were enormous, production was disappointingly small: about $1 million in 1860; $2.5 million in 1861; $6 million in 1862; and $12.4 million in 1863.[17] At no time during this period was the output sufficient to defray the expenses of the lode, and it was necessary constantly to levy assessments upon the stockholders to finance continued operation. Dividends were declared in some instances, but none of those paid by the major early mines equaled the assessments.

Under these circumstances, it might be supposed that the stockholders would have become disheartened and sold out, that the stocks would have become virtually worthless, that assessments would no longer have been forthcoming, and that production would have come to a halt. There were periods, indeed, when such a situation did very nearly come to pass, but these were followed, during the first two decades of the Comstock, by recurrent waves of optimism, when stocks skyrocketed once again at the news of fresh discoveries.

In part this phenomenon was pathological. The Comstock fever was a disease much discussed in the press during those years and long afterwards. The vision of a whole mountain of gold and silver overwhelmed the senses of thousands of investors and brought them to financial ruin. This was true of miners on the Comstock, of day-workers in the city, and also of many otherwise prudent and capable businessmen. Like intelligent alcoholics they might understand their problem and yet succumb all over again the next time. But the time never came for those who were down with the fever when the profits from the rise in stock prices were sufficient to justify selling out.

A somewhat, although not much more, rational reason for the continued, feverishly optimistic gambling in Comstocks was the ever-present thought that a killing could be made on the stock market, regardless of the value of the properties in question. In theory, at least, this certainly was the case; for the price of stocks fluctuated wildly throughout the Comstock era. Ophir, which sold at $60 a share in 1860, rose to $2,500 in July 1863; then dropped to $250 in December 1865. During the same period the Gould and Curry stock rose from $75 a share to $6,000 and then fell to $800. The total value of the Comstock rose to $40 million in 1863, slumped below $4 million two years later, rose to $275 million in 1875, and declined to less than $30 million two years after that.[18]

These listings included only the comparatively gilt-edged Comstocks, representing but a small fraction of the San Francisco mining companies. Mining companies were organized and stock was issued for hundreds of claims throughout Nevada and elsewhere for speculative purposes only, without the least thought of prospecting for ore. "Our citizens," commented the *Alta California* in October 1863, "own silver stock to the value of about $25,000,000. . . . 2,000 mining companies have been incorporated in this city within three years—one for every ten men. . . . But the era for which we especially long is that when our mining stocks will be worth par in the market. Then we shall be worth about $500,000,000 more than we are now." Three years later, in spite of depressed conditions in the Nevada mines, an official report on United States mineral resources noted that the nominal capital of the San Francisco mining companies was $1 billion; yet their actual market value had never exceeded $60 million. Not one company in fifty, it added, owned a claim of the least value.[19]

Very likely, the first Comstock companies had been organized originally for the purpose of making profits through the extraction of ore from the mines. As overwhelming technological problems arose and expenses mounted, however, this mode of operation was soon abandoned. If quick profits were to be made, they were evidently to be realized in stocks and not in bullion. Accordingly, in September 1862, the San Francisco Stock and Exchange Board was organized, the first of its kind in the nation, and it was joined within a few years by additional mining exchanges in Virginia City and in San Francisco.[20] Company officers and mining brokers meanwhile had already become thoroughly practiced in the arts of manipulating stocks through mine management as well as through mining-exchange methods.

"In the palmy days of mining in Nevada and California," the *Mining and Scientific Press* later reminisced, "there was a certain class of mining superintendents employed at big salaries whose duties were exceedingly light. . . . They knew more about the stock market than they did about mines, and simply obeyed orders from headquarters where stocks were being manipulated. . . . The system lasted longer than one would have supposed possible."[21] This kind of superintendent had experienced subordinates to take care of the technical details, and his duties were simply to order an increase or decrease in productivity and to issue glowing or ominous reports accordingly. The productive mines always contained ores of varying grades, and the selection of ores could easily be adjusted as the needs of the market strategy dictated. If the ores discovered were rich enough to provide large profits in themselves, the superintendent would depress prices so that those on the inside could purchase shares cheaply in time to receive the anticipated dividends.

In such cases the miners were kept down in the shafts for days on end to prevent them from spreading word of the rich ore they were working. The superintendent would have the inferior ore transported to the mills and would levy a round of assessments which would discourage shareholders and depress the stock further, while bringing large amounts of added capital to the company and this then would be added to the dividends from the rich ore and would be distributed after the insiders had purchased the depreciated stock. News that the miners were being kept underground understandably tended to keep prices up. On the other hand it was a method which superintendents used to buoy up the market when the mines were, in fact, declining in yield.

The stockholders generally could do nothing about this situation, for they were substantially without legal rights. The company was not bound to give them any information it chose to withhold, and the superintendent was not bound to permit them to inspect the mines, until 1879, when Nevada passed a law providing for such entry.[22] Stockholders did on occasion attend company meetings, ask questions, and make demands but rarely to any effect. Furthermore, since the stocks commonly were held for purely speculative purposes, they changed hands so rapidly that often no continuing body of stockholders existed to assert its authority.

The stockbrokers might or might not be leagued with the

company operators. In any case, they maintained representatives on the lode, either miners or those who had contacts among the miners, to keep them constantly informed of changing developments.[23] Even without inside information, they were in a position to manipulate the market to some extent through such bull and bear operations as were commonly practiced by stockbrokers. They were further in the position to profit from the almost certain losses of their clients. The practice of "bucketing" customers' orders, though somewhat risky, had obvious advantages over investing directly in stocks. It consisted of pocketing the money of the customer in the expectation that when the customer would decide to sell, the market price would have declined.[24]

There was the added advantage to the bucketer that he could call upon his customer for assessments as these were levied and then pocket them for himself. It was also true that most mining-stock speculators bought on a 50 per cent margin. The bucketing broker was therefore in a position to charge a monthly interest on the other 50 per cent which he presumably had put up. Finally, brokers levied a standard one-per-cent service charge on all purchases and sales; so, if they chose to limit themselves to this charge, they, of all the groups involved, could have profited continuously at no risk whatever to themselves.

Obviously, blessed with an eager and gullible public, the superintendents, bankers, brokers, and other insiders should not have failed to make millions on the lost savings of tens of thousands of investors. The strange fact is that, at least in the early years, they did fail to do so. Many became millionaires from the Comstock Lode, but only in the seventies.[25] Despite the many advantages of the insiders during the sixties, the necessary unity was lacking within any group large enough to control the market effectively. Individual companies might be in absolute control so far as their own mines were concerned, but that was not enough. The main difficulty lay in the wholly illogical tendency of the stocks to rise and fall together, regardless of variations in the promise of the individual mines.

It was also true that a banker or broker could be as susceptible to Comstock fever as anybody else, especially when he was continually motivated by what usually proved to be a false sense of insidedness. The historian and successful businessman Hubert Howe Bancroft noted that "few after coming to California failed in business from excessive conscientiousness."[26] Nevertheless, when it came to dealing in what were known as "Comstocks," most of them, during the early years, failed anyway.

There remained one group, aside from the stockbrokers, who stood a good chance of making a killing in the early years. Ownership of the mines was not based on any Federal law nor on any understanding of the nature of the lode. Some claims were carelessly filed and many others were fraudulent; the result in Nevada during the ensuing six years was a barrage of litigation against the leading mines, at a cost in legal fees considerably greater than the total of all of the dividends paid by the mines during the same period.[27] Until 1866 it was the Comstock legal fraternity (and to a lesser degree the bench as well) which had been, of all the groups involved, the leading beneficiary of the bonanza. All of the leading lawyers of Virginia City might have retired to a life of ease on their earnings, had not all of them, with but two exceptions, lost their new fortunes in bad mining ventures.

III

Comstock law had its origins in California in 1849, when the gold miners joined together in mining districts and drew up their own social compacts, in accordance with a fundamental American tradition harking back to the Pilgrim Fathers. There had existed in California, at the time of the American conquest, a body of Spanish-Mexican law governing mining communities, based upon more than three hundred years of experience. According to Spanish mining law, all claims were to be clearly marked off, and the locator had rights to all of the ore which lay directly beneath that area. This, obviously, was a simple and workable system. The American miners held the Mexicans in low regard, however, and nothing was farther from their minds than to govern themselves according to Mexican law. Instead, they ruled that the locator had the right to his ore vein, including all its "dips and spurs," wherever they extended.[28]

It may be well imagined that a great deal of unpleasantness resulted from this law, when one man's dip ran into another man's spur. Nevertheless, the system worked after a fashion in California, and the law was enacted in one mining district after another. A separate set of rules and regulations was drawn up for quartz mining at a convention held in Nevada County, California, in 1852, but that same rule was retained which gave the locator rights to "all dips, angles and variations" in his ore vein.

The Nevada mining laws were essentially a reproduction of these rules and regulations. The chairman of the committee which had drawn up these quartz mining laws in California was William M. Stewart, who later earned a half million dollars as the leading lawyer litigating them on the Comstock and who still later was instrumental, as United States senator from Nevada, in incorporating much of the confusion of the local miners' regulations into federal law.[29] "No system could well be worse," commented the *Alta California* shortly after the federal law went into effect in 1866, "than that of local resolutions adopted by miners' meetings."[30]

The colorful tale of how this law was brought to the Comstock by James "Old Virginny" Finny and his cohorts—sad as the stories of clowns are sad—has long since been embellished into folklore. At the time of the discovery of the Comstock, Washoe, as the region was called, was a part of the Mormon domain, governed in theory from distant Salt Lake City. It was populated by the peaceful Paiute Indians in the area of Pyramid Lake, by a few farmers along the Truckee River, and by a hard scrabbling little mining community near the base of Sun Mountain. Virginny Finny was a member of this latter community. Working his way up Sun Mountain from the placer mines in Gold Canyon to the south, Finny led three companions to a likely location, which later became the town of Gold Hill. There, in a mole hole, he uncovered a rich find of gold dust. Accordingly, he and his friends each staked out fifty-foot claims. Several days later, five more men came upon the find and staked out additional claims of ten feet each.[31]

Keeping as quiet as they could, the men then met and organized the Gold Hill Mining District, where they confirmed their claims. The ore on their claims, although it contained gold, was primarily silver, which they knew nothing about and did not recognize. Even later, when it had been assayed, they remained oblivious to the bonanza which they owned, and thus most of them sold out for songs, the sales ranging down from $50,000 for a fifty-foot bonanza mine ledge to one dollar for a ten-foot ledge of the rich Yellow Jacket Mine.[32] Only two among the original locators held on to their claims and got rich. The ten-foot ledge of one won his widow a life of gracious ease. It was the good fortune of another, James "Sandy" Bowers, to marry a soothsayer, who was able to see the future in the end of an egg-shaped object. He retained his ten feet and she acquired an additional ten; together they realized an estimated one million dollars from their small and exceptionally rich holdings.[33]

All of the other miners came to more or less sad ends. Finny, who drank to excess, fell off a horse two years later and died. Henry Comstock, who was mentally unbalanced, shot himself to death. Another died in an insane asylum in California. Another eked out a living as a cook and was buried in paupers' ground. The Bowers built a gaudy mansion, took the Grand Tour of Europe, threw a champagne dinner for all of Virginia City, and found other means of spending their money as fast as it came in. As Bowers said in his champagne dinner speech, "I've been in this yer country amongst the fust that came here. I've had powerful good luck, and I've got money to throw at the birds."[34] He was still throwing it when he died, but his widow, known locally as the Washoe seeress, soon came to the end of the string and was driven to fortunetelling for a living.

All who have written about the Comstock have, understandably, loved to dwell upon these sad tales of simple souls before moving on to the account of how practical men with vision seized upon the lode and, under conditions of the most extreme adversity, brought its treasure forth to the world. It may therefore be not unworthy of comment that the bankers, brokers, lawyers, and mining engineers who assumed this responsibility in the early years did not show perceptibly greater restraint or judgment than had Finny and his comrades; nor, in the early years, did many of them realize greater profits.

Among those who came immediately after Finny to create the big mining companies, only one, George Hearst, kept his winnings and went on to amass the fortune which was the basis for the much larger fortune of his son, William Randolph Hearst. He had been "pretty near broke" at the age of 49, after a long period of failure in the California mines, but he had "had enough to buy a horse and the outfit" and he "started over the mountains from California with the boys," and amassed about $500,000, which he increased by many millions in mining ventures elsewhere. In later years, reflecting upon this turning point in his business career, he commented: "If you're ever inclined to think that there's no such thing as luck, just think of me."[35] But Hearst was the lucky exception among those who were directly connected with the Comstock mines in the early years.

There was the matter of governing this isolated mining community, and the miners gathered together in a state of nature, as John Locke would have had them do, to draw up a social compact under which to govern themselves. That was where the trouble started.

The Gold Hill miners joined together in solemn conclave to create social order out of chaos: "Whereas, the isolated position we occupy, far from all legal tribunals, and cut off from those fountains of justice which every American citizen should enjoy, renders it necessary that we organize in body politic for our mutual protection against the lawless, and for meting out justice between man and man; therefore, we, citizens of Gold Hill, do hereby agree to adopt the following rules and laws for our government." A justice of the peace, a constable, and a recorder would be elected for a period of six months. The recorder would "keep in a well-bound book a record of all claims," which were to be "properly defined by a stake at each end of the claim, with the number of members forming said company and the number of feet owned." Surface claims would be limited to two hundred feet and hill claims to fifty feet, and only one claim on a vein would be permitted. Murder would be punishable by death, wounding by such punishment as a jury determined, and the brandishing of deadly weapons, upon conviction, by fine or banishment.[36]

The Gold Hill rulings were the consequence of ignorance

of the law, ignorance of the nature of the Comstock Lode, and also of a crafty desire on the part of miners for loopholes, just in case. It appears that nobody took the laws very seriously. There were failures to record claims, a predating of claims, a general staking out of claims in excess of the stated limitations, and an extremely troublesome overlapping of claims. The disingenuousness of these founding fathers is made barefacedly plain in the first ten pages of the Gold Hill recorder's book, where erasures and additions were made, pages were torn, and parts of pages were removed altogether. "I hereby certify," wrote the recorder in his book on March 29, 1860, "that the above is true copy as near as I could decipher the *infernal* Chyrography of the Original. The above erasures and interlineations are the corrections of the parties concerned."[37]

Dozens of mining districts sprang up throughout the country, as rumors of new strikes sent miners scurrying through the desert. Nor was the problem of local government made much easier by the fact that in most districts little precious metal was discovered to tempt the miners. In *Roughing It*, Mark Twain describes one such barren district in the Humboldt River region, where the heady rumors of rich ore had drawn him along with the others. The "camp was filled up with people, and there was a constantly growing excitement about our Humboldt mines."

> We fell victims to the epidemic and strained every nerve to acquire more "feet." We prospected and took up new claims, put "notices" on them and gave them grandiloquent names. We traded some of our "feet" for "feet" in other people's claims. In a little while we owned largely in the "Gray Eagle," the "Columbiana," the "Branch Mint," the "Maria Jane," the "Universe," the "Root-Hog-or-Die," the "Samson and Delilah," the "Treasure Trove," the "Golconda," the "Sultana," the "Boomerang," the "Great Repub-

lic," the "Grand Mogul," and fifty other "mines" that had never been molested by a shovel or scratched with a pick. . . .

It was the strangest phase of life one can imagine. It was a beggars' revel. There was nothing doing in the district—no mining—no milling—no productive effort—no income. . . . Nothing but rocks. Every man's pockets were full of them; the floor of his cabin was littered with them; they were disposed in labeled rows on his shelves.[38]

The Star Mining District was one such district founded in the area of the Humboldt, one of a dozen or more in that unpromising region, and its recorder's book accordingly differs from that of the feverishly rich Gold Hill district. Its rules and regulations were similar to those of Gold Hill but somewhat more liberal; three-hundred-foot claims were permitted. Ten rules and regulations were drawn up at the original meeting, to which fifteen more were added four months later. Six months after that, in March 1862, a seven-man committee was appointed to overhaul the rules and regulations, and it drew up twenty-six articles, which were approved by the miners in April. In July a part of Star District seceded and formed St. Mary's District, ruled by a separate set of laws. Star District continued under its existing laws until a series of amendments were passed in February 1864 and another series in August.[39]

The general tendency of the successive amendments was to describe the recorder's duties in ever greater detail and to provide more carefully for the method of his election. Nothing whatever was said about "dips, angles and spurs," the provision that became so troublesome on the Comstock, perhaps because the dips and angles were not sufficiently extensive to trouble about. The revisions of 1864 were almost entirely about the handling of assessments.

How democratic the Star District was is not clear from the

recorder's book, but in its first years it appears to have been dominated completely by two men, one Judge Nicholson and his colleague—but perhaps only sidekick—O. B. O'Banion. And the result, as with most mining districts in the Humboldt region, seems to have been dishearteningly similar to that described by Mark Twain in *Roughing It.* On the Comstock Lode, however, the miners struck it rich, and all was "a mess of confusion," according to one observer. "Everybody's spurs were running into everybody else's angles. The Cedar Hill Company was spurring the Miller Company; the Virginia Ledge was spurring the Continuation; the Dow Company was spurring the Billy Chollar, etc. It was a free fight all around."[40]

Elsewhere in silver-mining districts, where rich yields were uncovered, troublesome overlappings also occurred, and they were accompanied by violence. Mine owners in Aurora, to name the most notorious example, hired gunmen to fight the matter out, and soon after, the town came to be run by a gang of professional killers. The Comstock had its celebrated killers, most notably the unspeakable Sam Brown, but the remarkable fact is that they were not employed in the mine disputes, even though these involved many millions of dollars.

The miners themselves in many cases were expected to double as muscle-men. Miners of the Keystone Company routed those of the Peerless Company and filled the rival shaft with rocks and dirt. Yellow Jacket miners tunneled into the Gentry Company's shaft and drove out the rivals, who then blocked up their own shaft above the tunnel and continued to operate. Yellow Jacket tunneled back again and set fires in the Gentry shaft, to which Gentry responded in kind, and the war continued for days "with all sorts of stinking smudges." Caledonian Mine men defeated the Baltic Company, and Gould & Curry miners were victorious over the Seneca men.

Hand-to-hand encounters continued to accompany law suits from 1861 throughout most of the territorial period, and the final fracas occurred in July 1864, when New Oregon miners smoked out the miners of the Gentle Annie Company. What remains most remarkable about these struggles is the fact that hired killers apparently were not used, as they were in other silver-mining areas, and there was no known loss of life.

IV

Comparative peace reigned in the mines in 1860, for that year was largely taken up with getting beneath the surface. By the end of the year, however, overlapping claims that covered about twice the extent of the Comstock Lode had been staked out. All of these companies, following the example of the Ophir, had incorporated, generally in San Francisco. They had elected trustees, issued stock, and levied assessments. Supported by California capital, they moved aggressively to disembowel the mountain. When that happened, settlement of the overlapping claims became the issue of the day.[41]

Legal matters were complicated by the fact that the miners were not in agreement as to whether any duly constituted judicial authority actually existed on the Comstock. Since the Washoe country was considered part of Utah Territory, the authorities at Salt Lake City appointed John Cradlebaugh as judge in Virginia City, but the miners did not like the Mormons and were disinclined to accept their appointment. Matters were made worse by President James Buchanan, when, acting without any clear authority, he removed Cradlebaugh and appointed another man in his place.

The Buchanan appointee displeased the community, for he arrived wearing a black silk hat, believed to be the only one in western Utah, and Cradlebaugh refused to vacate the position. The question of which appointment was legal went to the Utah Supreme Court, which upheld Cradlebaugh's authority. When his rival ignored the decision, big William Stewart, the leading lawyer for the major companies, laid hands on the elderly gentleman and forced him to sign his resignation. Stewart's concern was not to uphold Mormon authority; he wanted a single authorized judge in the area so that he could get on with his companies' cases. The court cases were nevertheless delayed for several months until Congress established Nevada Territory with its own system of territorial courts. In July 1861, President Lincoln appointed three territorial judges and the courts opened to consider more than a year's backlog of cases.

For the next three years there was an unceasing frenzy of litigation. The overlapping claims would of themselves have been sufficient to support a happy crowd of lawyers—there were 215 resident lawyers in Virginia City in 1863, in a year when the city's population dropped to less than ten thousand[42]—but an even more fruitful source of controversy arose out of the conflicting one-ledge-many-ledge theories. If, as turned out to be the case, the Comstock Lode was one immense fissure of ore instead of many separate, parallel ledges, then, according to the Gold Hill Mining District rules, it all belonged to the original locators. It was a number of years, however, before mining operations had progressed far enough to establish this geological fact. In the meantime, many claims had been staked out, and the majority of claimants were, for obvious reasons, opposed to this one-ledge theory.

The Ophir Company, purchaser of the claims of Finny and friends, would have owned the $375 million mountain according to the one-ledge theory, and in September 1860 Ophir had brought suit against an adjoining party of miners. The trial came to nothing when the jury refused to agree upon a verdict, possibly because there were three hundred armed men in the courtroom representing the two opposing sides. The case was followed by one about overlapping claims between the Savage Mining Company and the Bowers Company, which was decided in favor of the latter and upheld, despite the testimony of a juror that he had been bribed to so vote. That was a hint of things to come.

Once the territorial judges were installed, all of the major mines were entangled constantly in suits, most of them brought to court on the flimsiest of pretexts simply for blackmailing purposes. Down to 1867, the first district court, in which the Comstock was located, handled 245 suits involving the dozen richest companies. The Ophir, as the first of the bonanza mines, received the brunt of the litigation with 37 cases. Most notorious among those companies which had been organized solely for the purpose of swindling established mines was the Grosche Gold and Silver Mining Company.

The Grosche Company laid claim to the three richest mines on the Comstock, the Ophir, the Gould & Curry, and the Mexican, on the ground that the 3,750 feet of the mines had been originally located by two brothers named Grosh in 1857. The claim was obviously and outrageously absurd. There was no evidence to prove that the company was connected with the Groshes, whose name is mispelled, and that the Groshes had discovered the Comstock Lode. Even if they had, they had registered no claim, and even if they had registered one, it would have been invalid, for they had not worked the lode. Nevertheless, the suit cost the defendants thousands of dollars before it was dismissed.[43] Dozens of other companies were similarly formed on terms of the most specious legality, and they frequently received settlements out of court from the threatened mines.

Lawyers naturally poured into town by the dozens. "I

think I have a certain fortune ahead of me in this country," wrote one. "It is the wildest one for law that you ever heard of, indeed it is a lawyer's paradise. . . ." The law business picked up spontaneously every time a new ledge was found, he continued. "Then comes some old trumped up title to this newly discovered mine and into the law the whole thing plunges and lawyers are busy hunting up witnesses and this is invariably the case for if there is no outstanding title one will be trumped up and a suit commenced in order to depreciate the value of the claim, and then speculators buy in while it is low, perhaps the very men who started the suit through their agents—there is not a good claim that is not in law with only one exception and that is the Mexican mine. . . ."[44]

Undisputed king of the Comstock lawyers was the big, brawny, bearded Yale man, William Stewart, who had been chairman of the committee that framed the confusing quartz mining laws in California in the first place. By common agreement, the Virginia City bar was the most distinguished on the Pacific Coast—the most polished San Francisco lawyers having hurried over the Sierras to take up residence—and Stewart was not rated among the best of these in legal learning. Throughout the territorial period of Nevada, however, the law remained in that frontier state where cases were to be won through the bribing and browbeating of witnesses, juries, and justices, and as a frontier lawyer Stewart had no equal on the lode. Whether he committed all the acts of violence in courtrooms with which he has been credited may be doubted. Still, the gentle contemporary historian of the Nevada bench and bar conceded that "even Senator Stewart's best friends are inclined to consider his work a bit high-colored."[45]

As the acknowledged bully boy of the Comstock legal fraternity, Stewart handled the cases of most of the leading mines. His first step, according to his own account, was to reach a settlement among his San Francisco clients as to the end lines of their claims by having each company appoint a surveyor with authority to decide for the company.[46] He then busied himself with dozens of cases, most of them brought by fraudulent claimants purely for the purposes of blackmail. Some of the cases, however, involved legitimate issues which could be properly resolved only by a continuation of the mining activities which were the cause of the litigation.

Two suits especially, the Ophir *v.* Burning Moscow and the Chollar *v.* Potosi, absorbed the attention of the courts and continued on throughout the latter part of the territorial period. The Ophir, arguing the single-ledge thesis, brought suit against the Burning Moscow in December 1863, on the assumption that the Moscow was mining an extension of the Ophir ledge. The court refused to issue an injunction against the Moscow on the ground that it was "difficult to see how these two bodies of quartz, separated at one point by 50 or 55 feet of porphyry, as appears both from weight of evidence and from my personal examination, and at another point by 90 feet of the same material, can be one and the same ledge."

The court ruled that the proper time to determine the matter would be at a later date, when and if the veins joined together at a greater depth. The struggle between the two companies nevertheless continued through a series of cases, financed by heavy assessments on the stockholders and accompanied by sharp fluctuations in the value of the stocks. A final stalemate was reached in July 1865, with an evenly split jury. Thereafter Ophir stockholders quietly bought a controlling interest in the rival company and brought the disputes to an end.

The Choller *v.* Potosi case came to trial in January 1862 and continued through two trials until August 1864. Chollar sued on the ground that it had a surface claim to the area being mined by Potosi. Potosi replied that any such surface claim was immaterial; that Potosi had located a well-defined ledge of quartz, in accordance with the district laws, and that it was legally entitled to follow its ledge, regardless of anybody else's surface claim. The surface claims of the Chollar Company were upheld, and Potosi was constrained to abandon work on the ledge.

Potosi thereupon withdrew from the ledge, and, after mining a putatively separate ledge to the east, returned to the fight. The second suit, which revolved around whether the Potosi ledge was indeed separate from that of the Chollar, went on until March 1864, when the decision was rendered in favor of Potosi. By that time, both companies had been bled white by the expenses of the litigation, and in the following month they consolidated into the Chollar-Potosi Mining Company.

Rampant corruption was the rule in all of these cases. Support for any trumped-up claim could be, and was, obtained for a nominal price from any number of witnesses; twenty-eight were supplied by the Union Company, for example, and were refuted by fifty-seven for the Yellow Jacket Company. The juries were, of course, more valuable than the witnesses and the judges more valuable than the juries, and the amounts of the bribes appear to have increased accordingly. The territorial chief justice, noted one contemporary historian, "began to earn a reputation for being the shallowest, most egotistical and mercenary occupant of the Supreme Bench"; he demanded, it was charged, a standard bribe of $60,000 for a favorable decision.[47] No one admitted to giving him as much as that in bribes but Stewart admitted to passing him $5,000.[48]

It was the judge in whose district the Comstock lay who, initially, was the key member of the judiciary, for he tried all of its original cases. The other two judges later sat in judgment with him as the territorial supreme court, when the cases had been appealed, as they almost always were. Since the decisions of the Comstock's judge were uniformly in accordance with the one-ledge theory, they placed him on the side of the major companies and of their chief legal counsel, Stewart. His career as judge, however, came to a rewarding end in September 1863, when, in the midst of the Chollar-Potosi litigation, he resigned. According to the charges, which were subsequently upheld in a libel suit, he received $25,000 from Potosi, against which he had ruled, to vacate the bench. He was replaced by James A. North, whose successor was replaced by P. B. Locke, and Stewart's contest for the judges went into a new phase.

North was an able and industrious man, who appeared to be on the way to wealth and power in the new community, until he accepted the judgeship and placed himself in opposition to Stewart. Appointed surveyor general of the new territory, North had arrived in Virginia City in 1861 to make his fortune by entering the quartz-milling business. Eager to advance himself politically as well, he had accepted the position of district judge with high hopes and confidence. "My success as judge," he wrote a friend two months later, "has been much better than I dared hope. . . . I put on no airs; but took the reins with a firm hand and went to work with a will; and for seven weeks I put those lawyers through their paces as they had never been worked before."[49] At that time Stewart said of North that he was the "most honest, upright, and incorruptible judge that ever was."

North attended the first territorial Constitutional Convention in the fall of 1863 and was elected its president. He was pleasantly undecided in his own mind whether to accept the governorship when Nevada became a state or enter the United States Senate.[50] Then in December North rendered his decision in the Ophir *v.* Burning Moscow case against

Stewart and Stewart's client Ophir and went on to consider the Chollar-Potosi case. His political life in Nevada thereafter was a short and unhappy one.

According to North's own account of his downfall, the result of his independent judicial decisions was to be

> maligned and denounced by the most prominent lawyer in the Territory as a corrupt judge; and as having been bribed in a very important mining case. . . .
>
> But a few days passed before I learned that he was openly charging me with the grossest corruptions and with having been bribed by the opposite party to decide against the Ophir Company.
>
> I went to Virginia and made him publish a card pronouncing all those slanders without foundation, and stating that there was no just cause to suspect my judicial integrity or private character. I returned home supposing all was right. But he had deliberately determined to destroy me & by the free use of money got control of the County Convention; and got a resolution adopted instructing the delegates to the State Convention not to favor my nomination to any State office. . . . By bargaining with aspiring candidates he was able also to carry his point in defeating my nomination in the State Convention. . . .
>
> After the Convention he went to San Francisco and there reiterated the same stale slanders, and I soon heard what he was doing. By this time the people of Virginia City and Storey County had become thoroughly aroused with indignation at his conduct, and called on me to attend a public meeting at one of the Theaters to meet the charges. . . . There again he set his slanders in circulation. . . . The meeting wound up with three cheers for me & three groans for him. . . .[51]

A subsequent board of arbitration absolved North of bribery, but it went on to regret that he had accepted loans from "seemingly improper" persons while judge and to regret also that his quartz mill had been so well supplied by litigating companies.[52] At the same time it was generally conceded that, in comparison with his two colleagues on the bench, his standards of conduct had been high. His judgment was generally poor, however, as his correspondence indicates, and never more so than in his belief that he had won his fight with Stewart.

The Comstock litigation reached its climax in the spring of 1864, when North rendered his decision in the Chollar-Potosi case in favor of Potosi, and when the case was appealed to the three-man supreme court for Chollar by Stewart. Since North had already decided for Potosi and since the chief justice was generally conceded to be a Stewart man, the center of attention became the as yet uncommitted Judge Locke, who, in the opinion of Stewart, "was probably the most ignorant man who ever acted in any judicial capacity in any part of the world."[53] Stewart was successful in heading off a meeting at Lake Tahoe between Locke and a prominent Potosi stockholder. He and his partner then took Locke into their own custody and held him at a midnight supper party which lasted all night. Potosi interests countered with a party of their own for Locke, and then the Chollar supporters countered with a second party of *their* own. The result of all this was that, when the case came up, Locke concurred with the opinion filed by North, but he was then induced to file an addendum to his decision, which reopened the entire case from its 1861 beginnings. Later he was persuaded to revoke this addendum.[54]

Defeated in the courts, Stewart moved to destroy the territorial judiciary altogether, and in doing this he was aided by the public's discontent with the court's conduct. He controlled the Virginia City *Territorial Enterprise*, and through it he had been carrying on a campaign of denunciation against

North. Following defeat in the Potosi case, the *Enterprise* published a petition allegedly signed by 3,500 Comstock citizens calling for the three judges to resign. North was the first to bow to the storm, and the chief justice, after a conference with Stewart, followed suit. Locke hesitated at first and argued the impropriety of resigning without consulting his constituents. Stewart thereupon threw one final party for Locke, to which he invited all of the members of the bar. There he called for ink and paper and ordered the judge to "sit down and write your resignation," which the judge did.

The attempt to refill the territorial district courts with new appointments was defeated by Stewart. The court had hardly begun to consider the 304 cases on its docket, 217 of which were mining suits, but the decision was nevertheless made to await statehood and the election by the people of the forthcoming state's judges. According to the state's first attorney general, "Nevada became a state to escape the dead-fall of her Territorial courts."[55]

V

Five and a half years after Old Virginny Finny found gold in the mole hole, Sun Mountain and Carson Valley—with a vast, unpopulated desert thrown in—were admitted to the Union as the sovereign state of Nevada. The population of that new state was unknown, but it was estimated at between thirty and forty-five thousand. The Nevadans never thought there was anything odd about this swift development, but in later years, when civil war and reconstruction had spent themselves, and when Nevadans appeared to be on the way toward becoming almost entirely extinct, questions were increasingly raised as to why such a nearly non-existent state had been created. The answer is that three important elements simultaneously favored statehood: the Nevada mine operators, the Congress of the United States, and the President of the United States. These three elements joined together on the matter, and nothing else was needed.

From the point of view of Congress, Nevada Territory was performing a patriotic duty by supplying the Union with millions of dollars in support of the struggle with the Confederacy. Colorado was also doing well in this regard and was, with an equally sparse population, just as welcome to join the Union as a sovereign state, but intraterritorial conflicts prevented her from gaining statehood at that time. What appears to have made immediate statehood for both territories wise in the eyes of Congress in 1864 was the proposed thirteenth amendment to the Constitution, which abolished involuntary servitude. Ratification required the approval of three quarters of the states, and the government thought that Nevada and Colorado could both be counted upon to co-operate.

It has been argued that Lincoln's eagerness to admit these barren regions to statehood was motivated mainly by his concern for the success of the thirteenth amendment. The chief witness for this point of view is Charles Dana, who later remembered Lincoln's urging upon him the importance of Nevada's statehood for passage of the thirteenth amendment and the amendment's importance to the war effort. "It is a question of three votes or new armies," Dana remembered Lincoln as saying. It has also been argued that Lincoln was thinking principally of the approaching presidential election, which promised to be close enough to make every presidential elector important. At any rate, statehood for Nevada received enthusiastic support from Congress and was signed into being by Lincoln on October 31, 1864, one week before the presidential election. The only parties that had shown any considerable reluctance in the matter had been the shifting citizenry of Nevada itself.[56]

Territorial status had been eagerly awaited by the residents of the Washoe country to bring order to the strife-ridden Comstock, but little or nothing along that line had been accomplished. The crying need had been the appointment of territorial judges, and they had no sooner arrived than they were no longer wanted. In addition, territorial status had brought to the area a governor, James W. Nye of New York, and a secretary, Orion Clemens of Missouri, who, in turn, had brought his brother, Mark Twain, to act as his private secretary, until it was discovered that the federal government would not pay for Twain's post. For the total expenses of that government Congress had annually appropriated $20,000 in greenbacks, which were depreciated at times to 40 cents to the silver dollar. The annual salary of the judges was 1,500 of those greenbacks.[57]

The territorial government existed, but only barely. "There is something solemnly funny about the struggles of a new-born Territorial government to get a start in this world," Mark Twain later remembered.

> Ours had a trying time of it. The Organic Act and the "instructions" from the State Department commanded that a legislature should be elected at such-and-such a date. It was easy to get legislators, even at three dollars a day, although board was four dollars and fifty cents, for distinction has its charm in Nevada as well as elsewhere, and there were plenty of patriotic souls out of employment; but to get a legislative hall for them to meet in was another matter. Carson blandly declined to give a room rent-free or let one to the government on credit.[58]

A private citizen disembarrassed the government by lending it his stone building, and there the legislature met, divided the territory into nine counties, and drew up a civil and criminal code.

Mark Twain also reminisced about that early legislature:

> That was a fine collection of sovereigns, that first Nevada Legislature. They levied taxes to the amount of thirty or forty thousand dollars and ordered expenditures to the extent of about a million. . . .
>
> The Legislature sat sixty days and passed private toll-road franchises all the time. When they adjourned it was estimated that every citizen owned about three franchises, and it was believed that unless Congress gave the Territory another degree of longitude there would not be room enough to accommodate the toll-roads. The ends of them were hanging over the boundary line everywhere like a fringe.[59]

The most authoritative survey of early Nevada politics, Myron Angel's *Nevada,* pointed out that the first legislature met for only forty-nine days and that it actually granted but six toll-road franchises. It concluded, however, that, although Twain's facts were not to be relied upon, there was an over-all ring of truth to his account.

Urged on by President Lincoln in both his first and his second annual messages to Congress, the Nevada legislature of 1862 passed an act that authorized the calling of a state constitutional convention and that provided for the election of convention delegates in September 1863. It also provided that the draft of the constitution would be submitted to the people for their approval, and it authorized a referendum on the question of statehood. The result of the referendum was an overwhelming mandate, 6,600 to 1,502, and the delegates assembled in November 1863 to carry out the wishes of the voters.[60]

The legislature had erred badly, as it turned out, by deciding that all offices outlined in the proposed constitution should be filled before the constitution was ratified. A hot struggle within the convention for the positions followed, together with strong opposition to the proposed constitution on the part of the losers and their adherents. The losers within the Union party found ready support from the minority of

Southern secessionists, and all of them found a leader in William Stewart.

Stewart, who undoubtedly was determined to become one of Nevada's first United States senators, was faced with the fact that his own powerful Storey County delegation was favorable to another candidate for senator; and Judge North, as president of the convention, appeared to be in a good position to elevate himself to the other senatorship. Furthermore, in his capacity as the chief advocate of the owners of the leading mines, Stewart was bound to defend their interests in the convention. It was on the ground that the constitution was injurious to the mine owners that Stewart fought it in the convention and later did much to defeat it at the polls.

The target of Stewart's attack was the provision that "The legislature shall provide by law for a uniform and equal rate of assessment and taxation . . . including mines, and mining property. . . ." Stewart insisted that only the net proceeds of the mines were legitimately taxable, on the perhaps reasonable ground that it would "impose a burden upon the miners which would be heavier than they could bear. It would mean a tax on the shafts, drifts, and bedrock tunnels of the mines whether they were productive or not."[60] Stewart was ridiculed in the press for disguising the rich mining companies he represented in the garb of "poor miners." Mark Twain, in reporting the convention for the *Territorial Enterprise*, complained about having to "listen to that same old song over and over again" concerning "bedrock tunnels, blighted miners, and blasted hopes."[61] He had, Twain complained, "been reporting and reporting that infernal speech for the last thirty days . . . you can't play it off on this Convention any more. When I want it, I will repeat it myself—I know it by heart now."[61] The convention voted Stewart's tax proposals down. Stewart, for his part, thereupon moved aggressively and successfully against the constitution as a whole, and he brought his campaign for the "poor miners" to a resounding victory when the proposed constitution was defeated. Another reason for its defeat was the strong Democratic representation in the territory, which attacked the proposed constitution as a pro-Northern document.

No sooner was the constitution defeated than the decisions against Stewart's clients in the Ophir–Burning Moscow and Chollar-Potosi cases, with the enormous expenses they entailed, brought pressure from the mine owners for the more responsible government and judiciary that statehood promised. At the same time, the United States Senate Committee on Public Lands was arguing the advisability of expropriating the mines in order to help pay the costs of the Civil War. Amid these somewhat changed circumstances a second constitutional convention was authorized by Congress. The constitution drawn up was almost identical to the 1863 version, except that the manner of taxing the mines would be left to the legislature. The document was approved 6,530 to 2,262.

Like other state constitutions, that of Nevada provided for the election of its senators by the legislature. When the two branches of the new legislature met, Stewart was elected on the first ballot in a field of five candidates, and the former territorial governor James W. Nye was elected on a run-off ballot as his colleague, mainly, it appears, on the basis of Stewart's influence. Stewart seemed indeed the ruler of the Comstock, but, even though he was to serve, intermittently, for more than a generation in the United States Senate, the day of his uniquely great power in Nevada was at an end. The citizens of Nevada decided in favor of honest judges, and within a few years litigation as a form of swindle all but ceased. The lawyers returned to San Francisco, and—in what proved no better than an even exchange for Nevada—the biggest of the San Francisco banks came to Virginia City.

CHAPTER II

The Bank Crowd and the Bonanza Firm

William Chapman Ralston, the founder and cashier of the Bank of California, was the first gentleman of San Francisco throughout the heyday of the Comstock Lode, and rightly so. The city waxed fat under his ministrations, despite the many large and small fortunes lost on the Comstock, but Ralston was hardly a man to be measured merely by this achievement. There was a splendor about him that transcended plain money-making. He was associated with—and generally the initiator of—almost all of the main civic enterprises that gave San Francisco its glittering greatness in those years. His monument, completed after his death, was the Palace Hotel, which he had planned on a royally ostentatious scale, far beyond the requirements of his city.[1]

He was generous to a fault, whether in promoting dazzling civic projects or in entertaining openhandedly at his mansion, Belmont, or in giving munificently to innumerable charities.

And in all of his business dealings he was supported by a business community which was proud to call him leader. Then one fine summer day it was discovered that William Chapman Ralston had embezzled $4 million or $5 million from the bank—just how much was never made clear—and he resigned his position. Afterward he went down to the Bay by North Beach and swam out to his death. He had been by far the most brilliant operator of the Comstock, and he ended as its most distinguished victim.

It was hard to keep a good man down anywhere in the United States during the flush times of the gold rush era, and Ralston's rise was meteoric. Born in Ohio in 1825, he got an early start in the Mississippi steamboat business. Off to California at the news of the gold strikes, he stopped at Panama in 1850 to join forces with a shipping firm and went on to San Francisco three years later as its agent. There he at once attracted the favorable attention of the business community and became part of a prominent banking firm. During the next decade he was the leading spirit in banking circles, and he worked with a shifting series of partners. In 1864, with his ascendancy in the financial community universally acknowledged, he established the Bank of California, capitalized at $2 million, which he readily collected from local businessmen and soon afterward increased to $5,000,000. Under Ralston's direction the bank at once became the outstanding financial institution of far western America.

Ralston's choice as president of the Bank of California was Darius Ogden Mills, a successful Sacramento banker. Mills had the reputation of being the most solidly conservative banker in the state. (Leland Stanford said of him, "Mills was always wondering when he would get his money back.")[2] This reputation for solidity was the reason for Mills's appointment, and his responsibilities did not go beyond investing the Bank of California with its aura of respectability. He became a multimillionaire by presiding over an institution about whose operations he understood nothing of importance —at least if one can credit his later testimony in court. The bank was "Billy's" baby, and neither Mills nor the board of directors interfered with Ralston until the day the bank ran out of money and closed its doors in 1875.[3]

The great personal fortune that Ralston amassed during the intervening years was, in good measure, the by-product of his exertions on behalf of his city. He was instrumental in opening up direct steamer trade with Australia, China, and Japan, and thus developed the export trade in agricultural commodities which supplanted the ephemeral gold as the state's chief source of wealth. He also created industry in a city which had been corrupted by easy money flowing from the Mother Lode.

Among the dozens of industrial enterprises in which he had an interest were the Kimball Manufacturing Company for the making of carriages, the Mission Woolen Mills, the California Sugar Refinery, the Cornell Watch Factory, and the West Coast Furniture Factory, all of which he founded. He was responsible for the maritime development of Hunters Point, for the San Joaquin irrigating canal, and—much more ambitious than these—for the Spring Valley Water Company, which gave the city an adequate water supply at a cost of more than $15 million. In addition to the quixotic Palace Hotel, he was instrumental in building the Grand Hotel and the California Theater. To his admiring contemporaries he was the most important figure in the founding of the University of California. And basic to this panoramic achievement were Ralston's hugely rewarding operations on the Comstock Lode.

It is a matter for wonder that Ralston could have founded the San Francisco of his imagination on the shaky foundations of Nevada mining ventures with the confident acquiescence of the substantial element in the city; yet even after his prodigious peculations had been exposed, faith in him did not appear to flag among many of these men. Writing within a fortnight of Ralston's ruin, a business colleague made a statement which may be taken as representative:

> When Ralston first commenced to do business here I was struck by the talent he exhibited for banking. I never knew a man who so readily comprehended the principles of exchange, or one who was more quick to see advantages in certain methods of remittance . . . it was the general remark, not only of myself, but of the principal businessmen in the city, that he was a very cautious and prudent man. . . . [4]

That Ralston could have been viewed as "a very cautious and prudent man" by leading members of his business community at once lights up the most striking characteristic of San Francisco business in the eras of California gold and of Nevada silver.

In the early years of California, everybody was a gambler, the green grocer almost as much as the gold miner; for the price of dried apples fluctuated from five cents per pound to seventy-five cents, and even such a steady staple as whiskey ranged between forty cents and two dollars per gallon. In 1849, lumber sold at a horrendous four hundred dollars per thousand feet; in 1850 the price had dropped below the cost of shipping. In 1851 five firms cornered the flour market and made hundreds of thousands of dollars, only to hold on to their purchases too long and, in the face of increased shipments, go to ruin. In the early years, no absolute distinction could be made between playing the Comstocks and keeping the store.[5]

By the time Ralston appeared on the scene, much had been accomplished toward creating a civilized community in San Francisco. The tents and shanties had been replaced by substantial brick buildings, and a substantial citizenry had raised itself above the general ruck. Then, in 1856, these good people organized themselves into the vigilantes movement and assumed their responsibilities toward the city. Until that time there had been political rule by Australian ex-convicts and other vulgar people, and a bad record of one thousand murders against seven convictions. Thereafter a semblance of decency was imposed—but only a semblance—by the business leaders of the community.

This business community was recruited from a class of daring and rapacious poor boys—mainly from the States, but also from Europe—who had left their wives and families and had come to make their fortunes in a hurry. They disapproved of wanton murder and of the organized terrorism of the Australian "wharf rats," but otherwise their views were broad and liberal. Their leader, before Ralston, had been Henry Meiggs, who, arriving from New York, had gained prominence as a lumberman by 1850. Like Ralston, he associated himself wholeheartedly with the city and busied himself with urban development and self-improvement. When he bankrupted himself in his efforts to improve North Beach, it proved easy for him to forge city warrants—promissory notes from the city which drew no interest and which were therefore not checked on.

After forging an estimated $750,000 of these, in addition to committing other frauds, Meiggs gave up hope of recovery, bought a brig, and, with his family, sailed to South America, where he became enormously wealthy and was honored as a railroad developer. His later petition to return to California with his Latin-American fortune was approved by the state legislature but vetoed by the governor. He was generally regarded as a civic-minded founding father, who had discredited himself by defrauding unsuccessfully and had redeemed himself in another country.[6]

John Hittell's history of San Francisco deals extensively with Meiggs's career, and in the margin of the copy which belonged to the California historian-businessman H. H. Bancroft there appears in Bancroft's hand, the comment, "San Francisco has never been without her public-spirited gentlemanly and trusted scoundrels of the Meiggs and Ralston order."[7] This was the by-no-means un-American breed of businessmen which the gold and silver rushes of California and Nevada produced in quantity, and Ralston was indisputably the paragon among them.

In common with San Franciscans generally, Ralston plunged into Comstock ventures almost as soon as the "blue stuff" had been assayed as silver, and, as the leading San Franciscan, he took the leading role. When the Ophir Mining Company was incorporated, he became treasurer, and when the Gould & Curry and the Savage incorporated several months later, he was elected to the same position in those companies. Amid all of the commotion of early Comstock history, he and counsel William Stewart appear as the only two unifying and commanding persons, and, on the basis of Stewart's subsequent career, it appears probable that the counsel was taking orders from the treasurer while he was bullying the Comstock.[8]

Immediately after he organized his Bank of California, Ralston moved to bring Sun Mountain under his control by opening a branch bank in Virginia City and then proceeding to gather in the assets of the mountain. Stewart, went east to the United States Senate and Ralston sent a bantam rooster, wiry, five-foot-six, 125-pound William Sharon, to take Stewart's place as the cock of the Comstock. How Sharon got the job as Ralston's representative in Virginia remains a mystery. Ralston had already assigned a member of his group to the position, but another close associate and friend of Sharon's had, apparently, caused Ralston to change his mind.[9]

Sharon, who had lost a modest and recently acquired fortune in mining stocks, was being supported in his poverty by a $250 monthly remittance from Ralston, who appears to have known him only distantly. The evidence indicates that Ralston made the appointment reluctantly; yet he shortly went into partnership with Sharon and divided the mining profits equally with him. Sharon parlayed this—especially later amid the confusing circumstances surrounding Ralston's death—into a fortune of $25 million and became the second richest man in California.

It is probably impossible to find a really kind word that was ever said about Sharon and preserved in print, but a number of grudging tributes are on record. He was a first-rate poker player, and a close associate wrote that "his bewildering bluffs and high-class technique were long fragrant memories of the Comstock Lode."[10] This same high-class technique was noted also in his business ventures; in most cases, only after it was altogether too late for the other fellow. When he came to the lode, Sharon was seen as a small man, handsome, with a lofty, dome-like forehead, dressed in a simple black suit "pertaining rather of the clerical than of the orthodox business costume."[11] He was a man who kept his own counsel and did not mix well with others, but he was one, during his first years there, to whom a man could turn when he needed a loan on reasonable terms. During his first two years on the lode the needy operators all came to him, and he responded.

Sharon established the Virginia City branch of the Bank during the depression period on the Comstock, which began in 1863 and lasted, amid constant fluctuations, until 1871. Stocks were way down, and no new bonanzas were in sight. Millions of dollars of mining and milling equipment were on the point of losing value completely along with the nonproductive mines. Capital for continued operation was more and more difficult to come by, and its price was higher and higher. Instead of levying stockholder's assessments to meet operating expenses, companies would have to borrow from member banks of the Virginia City Bankers' Association, which had agreed to charge not less than five per cent per month on loans.

Refusing to have anything to do with the Bankers' Association, Sharon offered all comers who showed reasonable promise loans at the rate of two per cent per month. The first result of this was the destruction of the Association, followed shortly by the failure of several of its member banks. Of the remaining ones, the Bank of California absorbed the best two and in short order monopolized the banking facilities of the lode.

As security for its loans the Bank took in mining and milling equipment with a value far in excess of the loans. Conditions on the lode, however, clearly justified this; for, without paying ore, the mining and milling equipment was worthless, whatever its original cost. And, for six years after the establishment of the Virginia City branch of the Bank of California, the conditions in the mines continued to worsen. At first Sharon had appeared to be a very small greenhorn. He never appeared so again. He used his position as creditor in the mines to learn about them and to invest profitably. Much worse than that, he called in loans, and when they could not be repaid, he took over the equipment.

While Ralston in San Francisco was making himself treasurer of one after another of the Comstock mines, his agent, Sharon, was methodically gathering in their working equipment. Together the two men were completing Ralston's plan. Ralston retained his reputation, on the lode as elsewhere, as the friend of Western man; while Sharon soon came to be viewed as the scoundrel that he was. It appears, however, that he did nothing of importance except on the authority of the San Francisco philanthropist.[12] Ralston was in constant communication with his agent, and the following excerpt from one of his letters to Sharon is sufficient to expose the calculating side of Ralston, which appeared in the course of serious business.

> You have been entirely too severe on Requa, and I must express my surprise and regret at it. He is here, and is much excited. You must be more careful in the future. Remember he owns too much "Chollar" for us to make an enemy of him. Give him sugar and molasses at present, but when our time comes give him vinegar of the sharpest kind. He is our friend, and I think will assist us. But go slow in all your operations and do nothing without consulting me.[13]

Having gained control of the main milling facilities of the lode, the Bank Crowd—as they were coming to be known—organized the Union Mill and Mining Company in June 1867, to purchase and manage the mining equipment which the Bank had taken over. Owned principally by Ralston, Mills, and Sharon, the new company was independent of the Bank, and its earnings were therefore not dissipated among the stockholders of the Bank, who, even so, received a steady 12 per cent per annum on their investment. The stockholders in the mines were a good deal worse served; for, with assessments, they received less than nothing on their investments, and one reason for that was that the Union Mining and Milling Company charged such high rates for reducing ore that it siphoned off all of the possible profits. Ralston took great risks for his bank when he invested $3 million in the big Comstock gamble at a time when it appeared that the mines might be playing out. But his immediate private profits from the new milling company were certain.[14]

In the face of the bleak prospects of the lode, the Bank Crowd in 1869 pushed through the construction of the Virginia & Truckee Railroad, between the mines and the mills, twenty-one miles of some of the steepest, most twisting, and most expensive track ever laid in the country. In the process, however, the Crowd was successful in persuading the people they were about to fleece to pay the cost of the road. After obtaining a charter from the Nevada legislature, Sharon persuaded Storey and Ormsby counties to contribute a total of $500,000 to the construction of the road. The grant was hopefully made by those counties without any binding conditions, such as public control or limits on freight rates. Sharon then persuaded the mining companies to contribute an additional $700,000—a simpler task, since the Bank Crowd by then largely had them in its control. The cost of the railroad was $1,750,000. It became the outright possession of the same men who owned the Union Mill and Mining Company at a cost of about $550,000 to themselves.[15]

The Virginia & Truckee brought renewed prosperity to the lode at once. The price of cordwood—a highly important item—fell immediately from $15 to $11.50 per cord and later to $9. The rate of hauling ore from the lode to the mills in Carson Valley dropped from $3.50 per ton to $2.00. The result of this was the busy reworking of ore that could show a profit with cheaper transportation. This profit was slight, but the profit for the Bank Crowd from the Virginia & Truckee and the mills was impressive. Meanwhile, the Bank of California, having invested $3 million in Comstock ventures, was tottering on the brink of ruin, but its stockholders, collecting their one per cent per month, still had faith in Ralston and were blissfully unaware of his profitable private ventures.

The result of this Herculean effort might well have been the dissolution of the Bank of California and a severe curtailment of its directors' profits. Ralston, however, proved to be right once again: in 1871, new bonanzas were discovered on the lode. That stroke of fortune saved the bank, kept the stockholders satisfied, and buried the Bank Crowd in riches.

In 1875, at the height of its wealth on the Comstock, the Bank Crowd owned sixteen quartz mills, through the Union Mill and Mining Company, with an estimated value of $7 million, and the Virginia & Truckee Railroad, with an estimated value of $3 million. It also owned the Carson and Lake Tahoe Lumber Company, which was not included in this estimate, but which in those years earned $645,030 net for the Bank Crowd. The knowledgeable (but also prejudiced) investigator, Adolph Sutro, calculated that the annual income of the Bank Crowd from these undertakings was $4,150,000, or less than a million dollars short of the capitalization of their bank.[16]

These bank directors were the first men who really got rich on the Comstock, and they were also the first of the San Francisco nabob class. The *Alta California* had earlier noted the odd fact that, at a time when the mines of California were producing more ore than those of Nevada, San Francisco was "interested far more in the silver mines of Washoe than in the gold mines of California."[17] Correspondingly, it was Washoe silver and not California gold, that created the famous San Francisco fortunes. It was those Comstock bonanzas of the early seventies which secured the fortunes of these first Western millionaires, but it was also those same bonanzas which broke their control of the Comstock.

II

Throughout his business career, Ralston persisted in the belief that there was honor among thieves, a beguiling streak of guilelessness that ultimately did him in. It was not until the day of his death that he learned otherwise, but he was given a hint in 1870 with the discovery of the first of the new bonanzas.

At the time that the Bank Crowd had taken over the Kentuck mine, it had promised as little as any of their holdings. Its one indisputable asset was the superintendent, who was among the most capable and experienced on the lode. But the Bank Crowd never did see the mines in terms of technical operations, and this man was not, at the time, one of their group. Alvinza Hayward, though, was one of the Bank Crowd, and he had a friend, John Percival Jones, who needed a job. Jones, therefore, was given the position in 1867 instead of the experienced man, and became one of those "political" superintendents who so disgusted the editors of *Mining and Science Press*.[18]

Jones had been connected with various California mining ventures during his career, but he had been chiefly a politician and, following his brief and immensely rewarding career as mining superintendent, he continued as a politician—with a lucrative mining sideline—for more than a generation in the United States Senate. He had gone to California from Ohio in 1850, and for seventeen years he had made a modest living there in mining and politics. He had served as sheriff and state senator, and had been an unsuccessful candidate for lieutenant governor. After a period at the Kentuck mine, he was transferred to an equally inactive Bank Crowd mine, the Crown Point, and it was there that he made his fortune.

Shortly after his arrival at Crown Point, an ore vein was discovered which widened promisingly into bonanza proportions. Jones immediately reported this encouraging development to the Crowd, but he did not develop the vein as rapidly as the circumstances warranted. He even left the lode altogether for a while, giving as his reason the need to visit a sick child. The Bank Crowd jumped to the conclusion that Jones was trying to trick them, and, instead of buying, they sold short, to their later sorrow.[19]

Sharon, who was on the lode, was the first of the Bank

Crowd, except for Hayward, to know that a new bonanza had indeed been discovered, and he bought furiously in an attempt to retain control of the mine for the Crowd. By that time, however, Hayward and Jones were in firm control, and Sharon—the one betting man on the lode who reputedly knew when to stop—sold out to them for $1,200,000, the biggest transaction of its kind ever registered on the Comstock. In 1872 Hayward and Jones wrested control of the Savage mine from the Bank Crowd and developed its ore to the fullest extent. Then they bid up the price of its stock and then sold their shares at a handsome profit. They had been the chief beneficiaries of the boom that followed the Crown Point discoveries, and they were the chief beneficiaries of the bust that accompanied the Savage debacle.[20]

The Bank Crowd had at last broken ranks, but this sad situation was forgotten in the general jubilation over reports of the new discovery and the heady soaring of all the Bank Crowd mining stocks. The Crowd still controlled the neighboring Belcher mine, and it reaped the full benefits of the bonanza that soon developed there. It also stood to gain from the business which Hayward and Jones would be obliged to give to their auxiliary companies, but in this expectation they were disappointed. The new group, bypassing the Crowd's milling facilities, organized the Nevada Mill and Mining Company, developed their own sources for lumber, and invested in many promising mining properties. Their luck held and their earnings spiraled—Hayward admitted to being worth about $10 million[21]—but all such Comstock profits were made to look small during the next few years when James G. Fair and John W. Mackay uncovered the Big Bonanza.

• • •

III

John W. Mackay, the greatest of the Comstock miners, was, by everybody's account, the only one of his kind in the history of the lode. He was a sturdy, slow-thinking, slow-speaking, methodical Irishman from Dublin. He did not drink, smoke, or gamble; he did not even play the market in Comstocks. Upon arriving in Virginia City in 1859, he remarked that he hoped he would be able to make a fortune for himself of as much as $25,000. By the time he died, he had overshot that mark by $100 million, more or less, but never during his career did he go directly after money in the Comstock-San Francisco manner. He was driven all his life by the desire for self-improvement and accomplishment, and he owed his success in large measure to the fact that, of all the successful men on the lode, he was the one most nearly immune to the Comstock speculative fever.[22]

Mackay arrived on the lode after eight years of industry and failure in the California mines. Penniless, he hired himself out as a miner at the prevailing rate of four dollars a day. With the deepening of the shafts, he graduated to timberman at six dollars a day and then quit to establish himself as a contractor, taking part of his pay, as was the custom, in mining certificates. He early became convinced, apparently on a hunch, that the "outside" claims were worthless, and he decided that he would therefore restrict his activities to the main belt. His hunch, as it turned out, proved entirely correct.

In his career as a mine owner, Mackay was from the first associated with the few mines on the main belt that were not controlled by the Bank Crowd, and his ventures appear to have been successful on a modest scale from the beginning. His first big windfall came in 1862 with the seemingly worthless Kentuck, which he and a partner purchased with borrowed capital and worked into a mine that produced almost $5 million worth of bullion during the next three years. Then in 1869, in association with James G. Fair on the lode and with James Flood and William O'Brien in San Francisco, he won control of the Hale & Norcross mine from the Bank Crowd.

The four Irishmen who made up the Bonanza Firm were startlingly uncongenial. The diffident Victorian Mackay shared his responsibilities on the lode with the loudmouthed, lecherous, gluttonous, two-fisted drinker, Fair. Powerful and energetic, Fair spent more time underground than any other man on the lode, after which it was his custom to go bed, either with a woman or with a quart of brandy. He was an incomparable liar and claimed credit for Mackay's accomplishments, even when they took place in his own absence. "Fair is a very different sort of fellow [from Mackay]," a reporter noted. "He is full of bonhomie (the people hereabouts call it blarney), a good talker, good-looking, and particularly social. . . . Very sly is 'Slippery Jim,' as his admirers call him." The consensus on the Comstock was that Fair was probably half as good as he said he was, as a miner, which was very good indeed.[23]

O'Brien was "a bachelor of gentle manners, softspoken, and easy of approach, whose specialty is the real estate business of the Firm," according to another reporter. "Flood is a stout, middle-sized gentleman, with a round florid face that bears an almost boyish expression of frankness, mild blue eyes, dressed plain but of the best material, a calm and dignified manner . . ." Of these two men, it was Flood who was chiefly responsible for the San Francisco end of the business.

No great fortunes were ever won on the Comstock without the aid of a partner operating in the San Francisco stock exchange and banking district. Flood and O'Brien had started their careers as brokers by running the Auction Lunch Counter and gradually entering into the activities of their customers. Flood was soon to gain the reputation of being the most skillful operator on the exchange, sure in his judgments and unusually adroit in his methods. It became his practice to buy and sell stocks through a half dozen or more brokers, some ordered to buy and others simultaneously to sell, so that not even those working for him directly knew what he was doing.

Flood's first significant demonstration of this dexterity was in the Hale & Norcross purchase in 1869. A successful struggle for control by the Bank Crowd during the previous year had driven the price of stock to $8,000 per share before it plummeted to $41.50, at which point Flood had begun to buy. He delivered Sharon his first significant defeat; for Sharon was unaware that he had lost control of Hale & Norcross until the election of officers, when the Bank Crowd men were voted out. A rich new ore vein was discovered within weeks of the election, and the four Irishmen immediately strengthened their position on the lode by buying Sharon's interest in the Virginia & Gold Hill Water Company.[24]

These men were gaining wealth during the worst times that the Comstock had seen. The market hit an all-time low in 1870, when Consolidated Virginia, one of the mines on the main belt, dropped to $1 per share. This reduced its market value to about $11,500—for a mine which in the next decade produced about $100 million in bullion. In 1871 Mackay, Fair, Flood, and O'Brien were able to buy the Consolidated Virginia and the neighboring California mines for about $100,000.[25] Honeycombed with tunnels to the depth of five hundred feet, these mines had brought forth virtually no ore. After months of fruitless exploration, a thin vein was discovered in 1873 which broadened into the Big Bonanza, by all odds the richest single gold and silver mining strike in the world's history.

Consolidated Virginia and California were actually one single mine, kept divided for the purpose of making greater profits on the stock market. Altogether this bonanza yielded about $150 million in ore and paid $78,148,800 in dividends during a twenty-year period, though most of the production occurred between 1874 and 1879. Thus it accounted for almost half the output of the entire lode and provided four fifths of its dividends. The main beneficiaries were, of course, the four men who owned a majority of the mine's stock during its most productive days.[26]

Rich as these men were, their wealth was wildly overestimated by the most conservative and expert observers, who made calculations ranging from $200 million to $1 billion. Actually, by the close of their major mining operations in 1881, their earnings came to about $62 million: $10 million to O'Brien, $12 million to Flood, $15 million to Fair, and $25 million to Mackay.[27] In the wake of the Big Bonanza, Comstocks rose in total value from less than $5 million to more than $275 million and then, within a few years, dropped back to $30 million. It was during this brief period, when thousands of investors went to their ruin, that the big fortunes were made from the lode, largely by brokers and bankers in San Francisco.

The Bonanza Firm was quick to follow the lead of Jones and Hayward in freeing itself so far as possible from dependence upon the Bank Crowd, which persisted in attempting to charge monopoly prices for its services in the face of competitive conditions. The Bonanza Firm organized the Pacific Mill and Mining Company to reduce its own ore, and it set its rates below those of the Bank Crowd's Union Mill and Mining Company in order to attract customers. It also broke the monopoly of the Bank Crowd on fuel and timber by organizing its own Pacific Wood, Lumber & Flume Company,[28] In 1875 it challenged Ralston's authority in his own baliwick by establishing in San Francisco the Bank of Nevada, capitalized at $5 million and then—ostentatiously and apparently for no practical purpose—recapitalized at $10 million. It was during the month that the Bank of Nevada was preparing to open its doors that Ralston went so dramatically to his reward.

The circumstances surrounding the failure of the Bank of California remain almost as mysterious today as they were at the time. What is certainly true is that Ralston, given free rein by his fellow directors, had severely strained the bank's resources on far-ranging enterprises in the face of the nationwide depression of 1873. The accumulation of $5 million in gold by the Bonanza Firm for the opening of its own bank drained the Coast of specie at a crucial moment for Ralston. Then, in August 1875, when the credit of the bank was overstrained, Ralston issued 13,180 additional shares of stock, worth perhaps $2 million, without informing his colleagues. Rumors precipitated a run on the bank, and the leading financial institution of the Pacific Coast closed its doors. In the ensuing directors' meeting Mills asked Ralston to leave the room so they could confer. Ten minutes later, upon the request of the directors, he signed his resignation, and within a few hours he swam out into the Bay and drowned.[29]

The bank was swiftly reorganized by Mills and Sharon, and when it reopened in a month, it resumed its role as the leading bank of the West. Just how this was accomplished was never made clear; for there was no such thing as a professional accountant in San Francisco and no official examination was made of the bank records. Ralston had made a blanket deed of all his property to Sharon, and Sharon settled with the bank's and Ralston's creditors on various terms. Initially, creditors agreed to accept sixty cents on the dollar, but when other creditors received full payment, a suit was brought against Sharon, and a lawyer was brought in to go over Ralston's accounts. He concluded:

> As a result of that investigation, it was demonstrated that the assets received by Mr. Sharon under and by virtue of the blanket Deed, executed to him by Mr. Ralston, were amply sufficient to have paid every creditor of Mr. Ralston in full and would have left a very large surplus running into the millions.[30]

On the basis of that testimony the creditors received full payment.

Sharon bought Ralston's estate from the bank for $1.5 million and agreed to pay an additional $.5 million later if the value of the estate warranted it, but he never did. He also acquired Ralston's stock in the Spring Valley Water Company, which became profitable. He moved into Ralston's house at once, and sent Mrs. Ralston and her family to what had been the servants' quarters. Mrs. Ralston sued and, following a confusing trial, settled out of court for $250,000. Sharon was by then able to boast to a friend that he was the second richest man in California, Ralston's other chief protégé, D. O Mills, being the richest. On the evening of Ralston's death, Sharon had gone down to the morgue with a friend, and, viewing the corpse, had remarked to him that it was the "best thing he could have done."[31]

IV

Even though the gold and silver of the Far West drew men from all over the world, the leading figures in the struggle for the Comstock were all Celts and Anglo-Saxons, either from the States, mainly the Midwest, or from the British Isles, chiefly Ireland, with one exception: Adolph Sutro, a German Jew from the city of Aachen. All but Sutro played the game according to a generally accepted set of rules. The object was to accumulate as much money as possible, preferably at the expense of rivals. The rules allowed any devious and deceitful means conceivable to attain this goal, including the swindling of one's own partners. Alvinza Hayward was playing the game when he made his fortune at the expense of the Bank Crowd, which had trusted him and had given him a position. And in the eyes of Ralston's friends, his embezzlement of $4 million or so did not constitute an infraction of the rules. Those who were defeated in this game, however outrageously they had been taken, were expected to be good losers; otherwise they would be despised for their bad sportsmanship.

Mackay was something of an exception in his straightforward, workmanly approach to his job, as was Ralston, with his creative visions and his trust in friends. But only Sutro refused altogether to play by the rules, and was not accepted as a player. For fifteen years he fought alone against the united opposition of the Comstock kings for his own objectives. Then, worn down momentarily by the struggle, he gave up his fight, joined the game, and won a fortune, at the expense of those who had put their trust in him. Moving to San Francisco after this coup, he returned at once to his old paternalistic and philanthropic ways, and became the city's most honored and useful benefactor. During an active and honorable life he had fallen from grace but once, and that one time had proven sufficient to rescue a career tottering on the brink of failure.[32]

He arrived in California early in the gold rush period and, at the time of the rush to Washoe, was the owner of three cigar stores in San Francisco and a supplier of goods to the mines. A man of very little formal education, he was inquisitive about almost everything and as tirelessly energetic as a donkey engine; so when news of Washoe broke, he went there at once to see what was happening. His accounts, printed in the San Francisco *Bulletin,* are the best sources for some of the early history of the Comstock.

Going, typically, right to the heart of the problem, Sutro invented a method of quartz milling and built up a profitable trade with the Gould & Curry and other mines, which earned him large profits. Then, in 1863 during a depression, his mill burned down, and he stopped being one of the boys. He became an evangelist.

It was the idea of "crazy" Sutro, as he was called for a time, to cut a tunnel four miles into Mt. Davidson, to meet the Savage mine at the 1,600-foot level. The other main Comstock mines would then dig adits which would join them all to the Sutro Tunnel by way of the Savage. This would do many things for them. It would drain off the millions of gallons of water that plagued the mines. It would ventilate the horribly hot and smelly shafts. And it would provide a low-level access to ore, which would otherwise have to be hoisted up 1,600 feet, at considerable expense, to the surface of Mt. Davidson.

One would suppose that the miners would have welcomed Sutro's suggestion, and at first they did. The idea of anybody completing such a tunnel seemed a little fanciful, but the lode wished him luck, and so did the controlling San Franciscans. Accordingly, on February 7, 1865, Sutro received the unanimous consent of the Nevada legislature, and the Sutro Tunnel Company was formed, with Senator William M. Stewart as president and important men as directors. By the original terms, agreed to by the leading companies, each mine would give two dollars per ton for all ore brought from the mines, as payment for drainage and ventilation, and would pay an additional twenty-five cents per ton for all ore removed through the tunnel.

Because it was dealing with federal land, the enactment of the Nevada legislature was soon found to be invalid. Sutro, therefore, went to Washington, where he succeeded in winning passage of the Sutro Tunnel Act, which was signed by President Johnson on May 10, 1866. It was more authoritative than the Nevada act and provided more liberal terms: there was no time limit for the completion of this difficult project. With the legal problems cleared away, Sutro turned to the task of raising the $3 to $4 million capital needed for the enterprise. In the prospectus he wrote, he conceded that Virginia City and Gold Hill, with an assessed valuation of $6.8 million, would suffer; for the tunnel would make them nearly superfluous. But that loss would shortly be taken care of by an increase in profits which, according to his estimate, would be about $2.3 to $6 million per year, from a tunnel that would cost but $2 million.

At this point there may have been some Comstock landlords who protested, but the powers still supported Sutro. When he went to England to raise money, he carried a letter of introduction from William Chapman Ralston, highly recommending him and approving of all that he was undertaking. By 1867 Sutro had secured $600,000 in subscriptions, and he was virtually guranteed the necessary balance by such leading Eastern businessmen as August Belmont and Peter Cooper.

Then, in June 1867, the directors of the Crown Point mining company met and surprisingly voted against subscribing a proposed $75,000 to the Sutro Tunnel Company. This decision of Crown Point, which was still in the hands of the Bank Crowd, marked the abrupt reversal of policy toward Sutro and his tunnel, not only by Bank Crowd mines, but by all the important mines on the Comstock. Subscriptions were canceled on technical grounds, and Eastern capital consequently was not forthcoming. Sutro returned immediately to Europe, only to come back to San Francisco empty-handed in December. "Mr. A. Sutro of the great Sutro Tunnel scheme arrived yesterday from Europe on the *Russia*," Mark Twain reported in the *Alta California*. "He brought his tunnel back with him. He failed to sell it to the Europeans. They said it was a good tunnel, but they would look around a little before purchasing; if they could not find a tunnel to suit them nearer at home they would call again."

Off at once to Washington, Sutro fought for a government loan, against the opposition of the representatives of the leading mines. Sutro's brilliant defense of his case won a recommendation from the House of Representatives' Committee on Mines and Mining for a government loan of $5 million in exchange for a first mortgage on the property. This decision had been made against the wishes of the principal mine owners and superintendents, who had wired the committee, "We are opposed to the Sutro Tunnel project, and desire it defeated if possible." Several years later, when a special commission reported unfavorably to the congressional committee on the tunnel scheme, Sutro returned to Washington and once again demolished the arguments of the mine representatives. Once again the committee drew up a bill approving a loan, this time for $2 million. However, neither this loan bill nor the earlier one was passed by Congress.

Although Sutro had had good reason to suppose that victory was in sight, with his initial success before the Committee on Mines and Mining, he had not rested for a moment. When a fire in the mines killed forty-five men, he appeared on the lode as the champion of the miners against the inhumanity of the mine owners. Had the tunnel not been delayed by the Bank Crowd, he argued, it would have offered a means of escape for the trapped miners. Appealing to the miners in a mass meeting, Sutro raised a subscription of $50,000 from them, and thereafter he continued to enjoy close and friendly relations with their union. Significantly, he always commanded the unswerving loyalty of his workers, who were better treated than those in the mines, and at the same time antagonized his immediate subordinates, who were more peremptorily treated than their opposite numbers in the mines.

Construction of the tunnel commenced on a shoestring in 1869, when the Sutro Tunnel Company was formed in San Francisco, capitalized at a theoretical $12 million, of which Sutro received nearly half in exchange for his federal franchise and his past services. In 1871, supported by the congressional committee recommendation and by the miner's union subscription, Sutro secured a loan in England for $650,000. Thereafter the construction of the tunnel was financed largely by mortgage loans from leading British financiers. Sutro was meanwhile kept busy in Washington and elsewhere fighting legal actions of the mines to invalidate their early agreements to use the mine upon its completion. Against these odds, Sutro finished the tunnel in February 1879 and arrived at a new, although less favorable, agreement with the companies.

Why the mines fought the tunnel so bitterly for so many years has never been conclusively explained. Sutro was certain that the main reason was the determination of the Bank Crowd to destroy any threat to its monopolistic control of the Comstock. But the fact remained that the Crown Point group and the Bonanza Firm fought Sutro just as hard as the Bank Crowd did, although none of them could match Sutro in debate, despite his thick German accent.

The mines had their own sound economic reasons for opposing the tunnel. At the time they turned against Sutro, the water in the mines appeared to be drying up. Later, at the deeper levels, the mines were found to be wetter than ever, but, by then, pumping equipment was needed anyway to raise the water to the 1,600-foot level of the proposed tunnel. Even where pumping would have been unnecessary, expensive equipment had already been installed, which the tunnel would render worthless. The same objection—that existing equipment would become useless—presented itself in the case of the hoisting apparatus in the mines and in the case of the towns of Virginia City and Gold Hill, where, as Sutro boasted, "owls would roost" following completion of the tunnel. Taking these losses into consideration, it may have been true, as the mine owners argued, that the original terms agreed upon for use of the proposed tunnel were not to their advantage.

A more credible explanation for their opposition lies in the ambitious conception which Sutro appeared to hold of the role that he and his tunnel would play in the operation of the lode. The mine owners seemed to be convinced that the tunnel was not merely a money-making scheme in Sutro's mind, but, beyond that, the means by which he would assert comprehensive authority over the entire operation of the Comstock. The broad powers which Sutro won from Congress in 1866 were bestowed upon him at a time when the mining companies were legally no better than squatters on the public domain, unsupported in their possessions by any federal law. Such a federal law was presently forthcoming, under the urging of Senator Stewart (who dropped Sutro as soon as the mine companies turned against him), but it did not give them the advantages that Sutro had won for himself personally.

There was also a messianic streak in Sutro which was alien to their own ways of thinking. It had been all right for Stewart to stand forth as the demagogic leader of the "poor miner," because the mine owners had not taken him seriously. When Sutro rallied the miners in the name of justice, however, the owners began to fight him with a vengeance. Their hatred of Sutro stemmed from their conviction, on abundant evidence, that he was determined to take the lode over and govern it for the good of all.

No past defeat could ever have been half so bitter to Sutro as was his victory in 1879 with the completion of the tunnel. The bonanzas were all exhausted by then, the Consolidated Virginia and California having reached the limits of their rich ore the previous year. Nothing had come of Sutro's abiding expectation that he would himself strike a bonanza in the course of digging the tunnel. He knew as much about the mines as any man, and by all indications the mines were largely played out. The tunnel, which probably would have been worth a lot ten years earlier, was now all but worthless to its owners. At this time, Sutro, to assuage his bitterness, had been allowing himself the consolation of a Virginia City lady who later achieved notoriety as "the $90,000 diamond widow" because of the amount of jewelry she wore. A permanent separation from Mrs. Sutro soon followed.

A few weeks after breaking publicly with his wife, Sutro quietly got in touch with a New York broker who until then had not been prominently associated with mining securities. Converting his holdings in the Sutro Tunnel Company to small denominations, Sutro fed them into the market through his New York brokerage as fast as possible, dispersing them among small investors and gulled speculators. The selling started at $6.60 a share, and the last of his stocks went for $.06[33] a share, for a total profit of about $900,000. All of this was done without the knowledge of those who had financed the tunnel, principally McCalmont & Brothers of England, which finally settled for a loss of $775,000.

A man who had been instrumental in raising money for the tunnel had these bitter words to say before he died: "Mr. Sutro has accumulated a large fortune, a very large portion of which came out of me. . . ."[34] Sutro went on to invest this fortune profitably in San Francisco real estate and to make bountiful gifts to the people of the city. In 1894 the city returned his favors by electing him overwhelmingly as mayor on the Populist ticket, against the wishes of all the daily newspapers. These philanthropies, which are still much in evidence in San Francisco, were made possible by Sutro's one erratum—to use Benjamin Franklin's apt term—when, in the course of that profitable month or so, he adopted the code of the Comstock.

Sutro had been one of the last of the big operators to leave the lode. By the close of the seventies all of the main beneficiaries had settled comfortably in either San Francisco, New York, or Washington D.C. Taken as a whole, they demonstrated impressively that they had not won their millions from the lode by flukes, for they went on to multiply their millions in other ventures. Having picked the Comstock almost clean, they left Nevada to their superintendents and other employees. As a sovereign state it did not amount to much, but, such as it was, it was operated by these expatriates and other absentee controllers through their subordinates.

V

It was the contention of the frontier historian Frederick Jackson Turner that American democracy was created by the frontier conditions which the pioneers faced and which inspired in them the democratic qualities of individualism and equalitarianism. Not even Turner, however, was willing to argue that the conditions on a mining frontier such as the Comstock were conducive to this democracy.

> . . . when the arid lands and the mineral resources of the Far West were reached, no conquest was possible by the old individual pioneer methods. Here expensive irrigation works must be constructed, cooperative activity was demanded in utilization of the water supply, capital beyond the reach of the small farmer was required. In a word, the physiographic province itself decreed that the destiny of this new frontier should be social rather than individual.[35]

"Social" in this context can hardly be other than a euphemism for capitalistic authoritarianism. Democracy had had its fleeting day with the formation of the Gold Hill Mining District, and then, rather meekly, the Comstockers had allowed themselves to be placed in the service of the kings of the Comstock.

Grant Smith, a mining lawyer who grew up on the lode during the bonanza era, left a description of this ordered society.

> The Comstock had its aristocracy in the '70's, consisting of the leading professional men, bankers, brokers, and mine superintendents and their families. They lived at the best hotels or in fine residences and mixed comparatively little with people about town. They were spoken of as the "genteel" or "high-tone" people, both of which expressions were very common. (Those phrases were applied also to certain gamblers and, as well, to the larger houses of prostitution.) There appeared to be little or no resentment at the affected superiority of those people. They were accepted as a matter of course and perhaps with some pride in their success and attainments, for they were superior men and women as a rule. The men were democratic in their daily walks, frequenting their particular saloons along with the general public. The exclusiveness was confined to their wives and families, although in the churches and at public gatherings they too were friendly. On the whole, people generally were much more polite and considerate of one another than in a modern city.[36]

It was the assumption of this Comstock aristocracy that those who owned Nevada should rule it. H. M. Yerington, superintendent of the Virginia & Truckee Railroad, spoke for the establishment when he wrote of opposition to its authority as being such "a spirit of unrest & disquiet, it may properly be called communism."[37] The Bank Crowd and the Bonanza Firm remained at odds with each other over certain matters, but they usually stood together against those troublesome elements in Nevada society which were agitating for such communistic innovations as taxation of the mines and public regulation of the railroads.

At the same time, the duty of ruling Nevada was one which

the silver kings had no intention of assuming personally. To be the governor of such a pinchbeck province was well beneath the stations in life which they had attained. They delegated the task of maintaining order to subordinates such as V. & T. Superintendent Yerington. The position of governor was given to men of intermediate rank. The mining superintendent was exactly of this station, and three served as governor during this early period. The office of congressman was of even less consequence—the state never has had more than one of them at a time—but several of the early ones were selected from the Bank Crowd's payroll. As for the state legislature, not to speak of local officers, state central committees of the parties, and the like, so many political positions were available in this thinly populated state that almost anyone who was interested could have one. This situation was the source of continual trouble and expense to the establishment, but, in the long run, money almost always counted.

There was one area of political activity in Nevada, however, which was not designed to be left to underlings. In the United States Constitution there was the provision that each state, regardless of the size of its population, would be represented in the United States Senate by the same number of senators. Being a senator from Nevada was therefore more important than being governor of Nevada. The United States Senate was rising above politics in the late nineteenth century to become the "millionaires' club" of the nation's business geniuses, such as Leland Stanford and George Hearst. To become a member of this, the most exclusive of clubs, was an objective worthy of the wealthiest king of the Comstock.

There were, of course, not enough senatorships to go around. In the early years, there seemed to be in fact only one, for Senator Stewart was virtually unchallengeable. Entering the Senate as the leading representative of the large mining companies, Stewart had made himself their most redoubtable advocate in Washington. When the Central Pacific Railroad emerged as a power in Nevada, he became just as effective in its behalf.[38] With his position secured, only one senatorial post remained to be fought for, until Stewart temporarily retired from public life to act as a lawyer for the Central and Southern Pacific.

Except for J. P. Jones, none of the silver kings had been very much involved in politics previously. Grant Smith remembered him as "a genial man and a born politician . . . a large full-bodied man with a long chin beard and a benevolent countenance."[39] In California, Jones had served as justice of the peace, deputy sheriff, sheriff, and state senator, but was defeated for the post of lieutenant governor. His transfiguration into a silver king with the Crown Point bonanza did not serve to elevate him above politics, however, and in 1872 he staged a contest for the United States senatorship which set the style for such campaigns in the future.

Appearing for re-election in that year was Senator James Nye, the former territorial governor, who was a friendly and somewhat forlorn person. During his eight years in the Senate —he had started out with a two-year term—Nye had done nothing of note, and in the election of 1872 he was less "the grey eagle," as he was called, than a sitting duck. Sharon saw this as quickly as Jones and also entered the contest. Jones, however, was highly popular in the state; while Sharon was its most hated citizen. After a bitter and futile onslaught against Jones in the *Territorial Enterprise*, and in other newspapers controlled by the Bank Crowd, Sharon withdrew. The press at once became sympathetic to Jones, and the election—which probably had been in his bag anyway—went to him, at a cost, it was said, of half a million dollars.[40]

Being elected senator in Nevada in 1872 was much more chancy, complicated, and expensive than it became after the passage of the seventeenth amendment, which provided for the direct election of senators. What was required in Nevada until then was the election of a state legislature that could be counted upon to vote for the candidate when the matter would come up some months later. Jones was therefore faced with the tasks of seeing to the election of dozens of men pledged to support his candidacy and seeing that the new incumbents made good their promises. In spite of his popularity in the state, all of that took money. Jones never said how much money he spent on the project, but he never denied that it cost him well into the hundreds of thousands. There were fewer voters to be bought in Nevada than in any other state in the Union, but, for that reason, the price tended to be higher. Yerington noted the doleful fact that "coin counts with the Irish and Cornish miners and nothing else."[41]

The universally hated William Sharon had not put aside the idea of representing Nevada in the Senate, and in 1874 he returned to the fight. How he might have faired against Stewart was not to be known, for Stewart voluntarily withdrew from the race to his law library and to years of private service to those interests in Nevada which Sharon, among others, represented. It does not appear to have been even hinted that he withdrew upon orders from Sharon, but such a conclusion can be reached effortlessly. However much it had cost Jones to buy his election, it seems that the voters charged more when it came to the considerably more difficult task of voting for Sharon.[42] But he won handsomely and rested comfortably on his laurels—so comfortably, in fact, that he did not bother to go to Washington until one year after his election. After that session, he returned to California and remained away from the nation's capital for the next two and one half years.[43]

As had been the case with Stewart, Jones was looked upon as a man of professional political experience who was representing the mines, the mills, and the railroads in an authentically professional capacity. Sharon, though, was plainly a multi-millionaire dilettante whose senatorship was enshrined with no such moral sanctification. So, when Sharon's time was up, a contest ensued with the Bonanza Firm partner James G. Fair in what at once came to be known as "the battle of the money-bags."

To the extent that Nevada possessed a political tradition, it was Republican, which, of course, had been the basis for its admission to the Union in the first place. The rich men had all been on the side of the Republican Party, and they had been content to pay well for their victories. ". . . we carried the assemblymen, sheriff, county commissioners, treasurer," Yerington had written his employer D. O. Mills in 1876, ". . . *all friendly to us* (& God knows they ought to be). . . ."[44] Damned as the party of rebellion, the Democrats were additionally injured in Nevada by the exceptionally high cost of votes. They therefore determined to secure for themselves one of the rich men of the lode and buy themselves into power, and they found their man in the egotistical and politically illiterate Fair. At the time he was approached by the Democratic Party leaders, Fair could not have cared less. "I hardly knew which party I belonged to—I never did tell them which I belonged to," he later commented.[45] But after the needy Democrats worked on his ego by pointing out the grandness of the position and by reporting bad things that Sharon was saying about him, Fair went into the contest heart, soul, and wallet.

That great campaign of 1880 was never equaled for the prodigality of the "sack bearers," as the ubiquitous bribe-distributors were called. The two candidates were not only among the richest men the lode had produced; they were also among the most hated. The price of votes quickly rose to eighty dollars a head, which represented over three weeks' wages for the miners and a good deal more than that for most voters. Sharon had the resources to equal "Slippery Jim" Fair's outlay, but he allowed himself to be outbid, perhaps because he had already held the honor and thus valued it less. It was also true that Mackay, despite his Republican affiliations and his growing dislike for his partner, came to the support of Fair, out of friendship for Fair's wife and family (which Fair left behind him on moving to Washington). Mackay's support enabled Fair to give the miners in the Consolidated Virginia and the California the day off with full pay and to march them to the polls, with instructions to vote for him on penalty of losing their jobs. Under the voting system in use in Nevada, before the institution of the secret ballot, it was an easy matter to ascertain how each vote had gone.[46]

The result of the election was a Democratic legislature for the first time in Nevada's history, overwhelmingly pledged to Fair. Nevertheless, more sack-bearing proved necessary in the spring of 1881, when the legislature met to make its selection. Adolph Sutro yielded to none of the other Comstock millionaires in the fervency of his desire for senatorial honors. (He entered the three compaigns of 1872, 1876, and 1880 without even winning a legislative vote.) Busy in San Francisco at the time of the legislature campaign of 1880, he had sent a political agent to Nevada to organize his camapign, only—according to Sutro's account—to have had the man bought off by Fair. In the spring of 1881 Sutro himself took up quarters in Carson City and righteously rebribed the legislators to the extent of an estimated $250,000.[47] It was conceded that Sutro had managed to secure the necessary number of votes, but he could use them only upon one condition.

The legislators insisted that moral grounds be provided which would release them honorably from their obligations to Fair. This was to be supplied by the dramatic arrest of various representatives on the floor of the House on charges of purchasing votes for their own elections. The arrests were made according to plan, but no officials were to be found before whom a complaint could legally be sworn. Fair's managers had learned of the scheme and had taken all such officials into hiding. With that, Sutro's campaign collapsed, and Fair was elected to the Senate unopposed. Later asked by a newspaperman how much he thought it had cost Leland Stanford to win his seat in the Senate from California, Fair replied: "Well, I can judge of that only by my own experience. From what it cost me in Nevada, I should say it must have cost Stanford not less than a million."[48]

Sharon's days of personal glory were over in Nevada politics with his defeat in the hands of Fair, but, through his lieutenants, he continued to keep political matters in hand, and after him his nephew and namesake carried on the task even more effectively. In later years, the veteran Nevada newspaperman Sam Davis immortalized much of Nevada politics in verse, as was the custom in those days. In his "Lines to a Comstock Graveyard," quoted here, Storey" is the county containing the Comstock:

On yonder hillside, bleak and barren,
Lies many a friend of William Sharon,
Who in election's hurly-burly,
Voted often, voted early.

But since old Sharon went to glory
The younger Billy bosses Storey,
And at his beck those sons of witches
Rise, to vote without their britches.

To take a hand in the election
And hustle back without detection.
As we recall those mem'ries hoary,
Let's bless the graveyard vote of Storey.[49]

Fair spent more time in Washington than Sharon had, but he made no attempt to take any active part in the governing of the nation. He achieved fleeting notoriety in a news story for paying $250 for some nightshirts.[50] Otherwise all was silence. Nevertheless, he appears to have enjoyed himself well enough to want a second term. Unhappily for his prospects, he had been divorced by his wife, during his term in office, on grounds of "promiscuous adultery," which may not have injured him critically among the voters of Nevada but which turned Mackay against him. There was also the matter—which had been common talk on the lode for years—of Fair's having hired a prizefighter to give a beating to a personal enemy, who died from injuries received in the assault.[51]

What really appears to have defeated Fair in 1886 was the fact that he had served no very useful purpose so far as the mining and railroad interests were concerned. William Stewart returned from San Francisco six months before the election, to take up legal residence, in order to enter the contest, and it seems likely—as was generally assumed at the time—that he did so upon the orders of his employers, the Central Pacific and Southern Pacific railroads, which during the campaign gave him strong support.[52]

With Mackay, Jones, Sharon, Mills, and the Central Pacific Railroad working against him, Fair had become, as Yerington gleefully wrote, "like a cat in a strange garrett—no friends!"[53] Accordingly, the Democrats lost the legislature 47 to 13, and Stewart became the Republican legislature's choice when it met in 1887. Jones, still popular in the state and an effective champion of the Central Pacific in the Senate, had meanwhile won re-elections in 1879 and 1885 at little personal expense to himself and against no significant opposition. For a generation thereafter, Nevada would be represented in the Senate by loyal and effective spokesmen for what had by then supplanted mining as the dominant economic interest in the state, the Central Pacific Railroad.

CHAPTER III

Working on the Railroad

"I notice what you write about the Virginia & Truckee R.R. Co. extending their road to Paniment, &c.," the newly rich Collis P. Huntington of the Central Pacific Railroad wrote to his parvenu partner, Leland Stanford, in 1875. "I should hardly think such a thing possible; but, when men make money as fast as Jones and Sharon have, God knows what they will do."[1] God knew that Jones and Sharon would do whatever they thought they could get away with, but by 1875 that probably did not include any direct contest with the controllers of the C.P. By that time, after fifteen years of desperate struggle, and still slipping steadily deeper into debt to the federal government, the Big Four of the Central Pacific —Huntington, Stanford, Charles Crocker, and Mark Hopkins —were finally emerging as the dominant economic powers on the Pacific Coast. Thereafter, in the feudal system of the Gilded Age, the lords of the Comstock and of the San Francisco banking world were vassals to the lords of the Central Pacific.

In Nevada, in the years immediately following, the mines

turned swiftly from bonanza to borasca, and, except for the continued milling of low-grade ore, the economy had been stripped down to 450 miles of Central Pacific Railroad, with its railroad towns of Reno and Elko, and to an open-range livestock industry, which the coming of the railroad largely made possible. Inheriting this despicable province at a time when the anti-railroad granger movement was in full stride nationally, the Big Four found themselves in possession of a state which was fiercely embroiled in anti-railroad politics. That did not trouble the Big Four greatly. They appointed political agents to keep an eye on Nevada matters and left themselves free to get on with the world's work.[2]

These men were high and mighty indeed, and in large measure they owed their exalted positions to their business skill and daring and to the dogged work they had carried on for almost a decade before their road was completed. In even larger measure they owed their position to a fifth associate, Theodore D. Judah, whom they had joined after the project had been initiated and who had died just as he was on the point of arranging to buy out his erstwhile associates. To a remarkable extent the Central Pacific was the personal handiwork of Judah, a brilliant civil engineer and a man, much like Adolph Sutro, who was tirelessly energetic and stubbornly determined. Money talks in business history, however, and when Judah died suddenly before he had made his millions, he was soon forgotten; while Huntington, Stanford, Crocker, and Hopkins lived on to win fortunes and buy fame.

Trained at Rensselaer Polytechnic Institute, Judah was thoroughly experienced in railroad engineering by the time he arrived in California in 1854, specifically for the purpose of building the nation's first transcontinental railroad. The proposed construction of such a road, financed partly by federal land grants and subsidies, was one of the principal subjects for debate in Congress that year, and the Corps of Army Engineers was conducting a series of surveys to determine the best possible route. Made public in 1856, these surveys demonstrated that the route through the Deep South would be most favorable from a geographic point of view, bypassing, as it would, the great mountain chains of the Rockies and the Sierras.

Judah, himself, favored the route eastward from Sacramento through Nevada and Utah, and, while serving as chief engineer on the San Francisco & Sacramento Railroad, he made repeated trips to Washington to argue his case. To meet objections raised by the report of the Army Engineers, he conducted his own survey along a route which was 150 miles shorter than theirs and which required maximum grades of one hundred feet per mile through a pass 6,690 feet above sea level. How well he did his job is to be seen in the fact that his route has remained the most heavily used of the eight transcontinental systems.

Urged on by Judah, the California legislature called a railroad convention, which sent him to Washington as its representative. Bills were drawn up in committee, but they never came to a vote, and Judah returned to California in 1860 to organize a company without waiting for government support. At meetings in San Francisco he appealed for financial backing with a remarkable lack of success. At a time when Ralston and other San Francisco businessmen were plunging recklessly in Comstock investments, Judah was unable to win any active support for his project.

Considering the obvious importance to San Francisco of such a transcontinental railroad, as well as the general belief in its feasibility, this apparent lack of interest is somewhat difficult to account for. To begin with, however, there were economic interests opposed to the project, notably the steamship companies, with which Ralston was associated. A more serious obstacle was the incalculable vastness of the proposal.

Judah, himself, estimated it would cost $150 million for a road between the Missouri River and the Pacific Ocean. The financial resources of San Francisco were, of course, not remotely adequate for such an undertaking. There was every likelihood that the federal government would extend generous subsidies, but, even so, profits from the venture would be delayed until after completion of the road, which would take years to build. In the meantime the Comstock seemed to promise big quick winnings for the lucky; and San Francisco real estate presented a certain road to riches.

Returning empty-handed to Sacramento, Judah won his first victory with the businessmen of that city—men who, like those of San Francisco, had no real way of knowing what he was talking about. "While I was serving in the Legislature, this matter of building the railroad came up," Charles Crocker later remembered. "There was a meeting called at the St. George Hotel, in Sacramento, which I attended. . . . We none of us knew anything about railroad building, but at the same time were enterprising men, and anxious to have a road built, and have it come to Sacramento, having our property and interests there. . . ."[3] Accordingly, subscriptions were raised sufficient to complete surveys eastward to the Missouri River, and the Central Pacific Railroad Company was incorporated in San Francisco. With this tangible backing, Judah and Huntington traveled to Washington. Judah then became secretary of the Senate subcommittee and clerk of the House subcommittee which examined the project.

In the meantime Secession and Civil War had eliminated the southern routes from consideration, and the result of Judah's and Huntington's activities was the Railroad Act, signed by Lincoln July 1, 1862. This enactment, which was modified by subsequent amendments in 1864 and 1866, created the Union Pacific Railroad Company to share the project. Under the final terms the Central Pacific Company received a net grant of eight million acres of land, which proved of little direct value, for most of it extended through the wastelands of Nevada and Utah. Five million acres remained unsold by the mid-twentieth century, and during the period of the road's construction, only $107,000 was gained through land sales, although the unsold acres later made possible a $10 million land mortgage. In addition, direct subsidy bonds were granted, ranging from $16,000 to $48,000 per mile, depending on the difficulty of the terrain. The company gained a great initial advantage by persuading the government that the gently rolling plain twenty-two miles eastward from Sacramento was technically part of the Sierra Nevada range, and on that basis they received the maximum subsidy where the minimum was justified, for a temporary advantage to the company of $450,000. But there was an absolute limit placed upon subsidies for mountain mileage, which this helped to use up, so, eventually, the company realized only about $200,000 or less in additional subsidy bonds from this piece of chicanery.

Judah, although he was chief engineer for the railroad and an equal partner with his four associates, was an outsider in the company from the beginning. In the summer of 1863 he was presented the alternative by his associates of buying them out for $100,000 each or selling his share for $100,000. Judah chose the latter course and sailed for New York, apparently in order to gain financial backing from the Vanderbilt interests to buy out his former partners. In Panama, Judah came down with a fever, and he died several days after arriving in New York. The Big Four were thereafter left in undisturbed possession of an undertaking for which they were still lacking in experience and which they would have been happy to dispose of profitably at any time during the next decade.

Stanford, the most politically active of the four, held the position of president in the company and used his additional positions as governor of California and later as United States senator to forward the associates' interests. As vice president, Huntington operated mainly from New York and Washington; he was responsible for lobbying and for purchasing supplies for the company. Hopkins, the oldest of the four and the respected mediator among them, served as company treasurer, and Crocker was in charge of the actual construction of the road.

The company remained completely in the hands of these four men, partly because, unlike the operators of the Union Pacific, they were not obliged to deal with government-appointed directors, and partly because they could not persuade other businessmen to buy in. Despite the government subsidies, the financing of the road was uncertain almost to the last. "I looked at it as a business question," Lloyd Tevis, president of Wells Fargo Bank, later testified. "I thought it was liable to great embarrassment and I very much doubted their ability to carry out their contracts. . . . I am aware of the fact that the capital of those gentlemen was very limited—I refer to their individual means—because they were borrowing money in the market all the time, and of anybody that would loan it to them."[4] D. O. Mills similarly testified that "the sense of the community as well as my own, was against their being able to carry out the enterprise."[5]

Unlike the Union Pacific, the Central Pacific faced its most costly construction during the first years, and by the time the Nevada boundary had been reached, the company was about $5 million in debt. Thereafter, company bonds in addition to the government bonds were sufficient to defray the costs. Nevertheless, the four associates appear to have shared the doubts of the San Francisco business community as to their ability to complete the road, and they set out to make substantial profits for themselves, whether or not their company survived to become a paying proposition. This they achieved by creating their own construction companies and paying them generously out of the funds of the railroad company.

One of the main issues which had alienated Judah from the other four had been his plan to distribute contracts among smaller firms. After an initial contract to Crocker, Judah's scheme had been tried with little success. The rest of the road was then built by the Big Four, through Charles Crocker and Company and later the Contract and Finance Company. The exact operations of these companies were never revealed, because by the time Congress got around to investigating them in 1887, all of their books had been burned. The Central Pacific records were available, and these disclosed that it had paid out $46,989,320 for the construction of its road. A railroad engineering expert hired by the government testified that the legitimate costs of construction should not have exceeded $36 million.

The railroad was completed in 1869, and in the years that followed, the four associates did their best to sell out, with no luck whatever. Although the road had already shown a profit of more than $6 million by the time of its completion, it was saddled with an enormous debt and with rumors of exorbitant construction costs and a faulty roadbed. In 1873, the $48 million of Central Pacific stock had declined in value to $5 million or less, and the Big Four were obliged to remain in unwilling possession and to replace miles of inadequate rails.

Except for a growing burden of debt to the federal government, conditions steadily improved thereafter. The company paid its first dividend of three per cent in 1873, which rose to ten per cent in 1875.[6] Despite a temporary decline in dividends subsequently, during contests with the government, the road remained in a strong financial position from that time down to the Panic of '93, which it survived, mainly through the exertions of Huntington, the most able and industrious of the four and the most influential in Eastern financial circles. Under these circumstances the four men were able to sell large amounts of stock at large profits, without losing control of the company. Meanwhile they joined the C. P. to the Southern Pacific, and in 1884 the Southern Pacific Company of Kentucky was incorporated as a holding company; it operated two steamship lines as well. In 1890, Huntington ousted Stanford to take over the presidency of a corporation that eventually controlled a system of roads extending across the entire continent.

Poor, empty, used-up Nevada, meanwhile, was not entirely forgotten. It was expected to play a part in the grand program; a small part, it is true, but an important one. Even though it appeared to be returning to its original state of nature, its representation in the Senate naturally remained undiminished. Despite the bitter and entirely justified anti-railroad sentiment in Nevada, Huntington managed to win the state's senatatorial representation for himself and to employ its services for a generation in his struggles against the federal government.

II

Even though the bonanza days were gone forever, old Comstockers continued to work the leading mines and with surprisingly remunerative results. Senator Jones is credited with introducing new mining techniques by which old tailings and low-grade ores were reduced at a profit, and survivors of the Bank Crowd and the Bonanza Firm followed suit. Production of bullion maintained an annual average of about $3 million in the eighties and about half that much in the decade that followed.[7] During the eight years after 1882, the Jones and the Sharon interests reduced 750,000 tons of ore at a large profit to themselves and at the usual loss to the investors. No dividends were paid during the period; but assessments were periodically levied, and the profits went to the operators of the mills and to the V. & T. Railroad.[8]

The worse the quality of the ore, the better the V. & T. liked it. Production during the peak year of this borasca period was no more than one fourth of the bullion mined annually in the heyday of the Big Bonanza; yet Yerington was able to write Mills in April 1888: "Yesterday we shipped 128 cars of ore from the Comstock . . . making *1008 tons*, the biggest day in ore hauling known on the road."[9] That month V. & T. paid a dividend of 1.5 per cent, and it consistently paid monthly dividends of 0.75 per cent on into the twentieth century, even though the yield in 1900 dropped to $300,000.[10] Throughout this period, about thirty Comstock mines remained in active operation, with a full complement of presidents, vice presidents, treasurers, boards of directors, and superintendents, all of them maintained at the expense of those ever-ready San Francisco mining-stock investors.[11]

Except for the raising of livestock, agriculture added little to the wealth of the state. Only 126,000 acres were under cultivation in 1880.[12] By that time livestock-raising had begun to supplant gold and silver in economic importance to the state. Cattle had been brought to Nevada in the fifties, and in the seventies the cattleman replaced the homesteader, by purchasing the stream banks and acquiring a monopoly of the water rights. Elko, created by the Central Pacific in 1869, enjoyed a brief period of prosperity associated with the White Pines silver rush and then continued as the leading cattle center in the state.[13]

Cattle ranching in Nevada followed much the same course as it did elsewhere in the cattle kingdom. Vast areas were staked out for single ranches, the largest ranch extending for 1,800 square miles. The cattle were fattened with bunch grass, which was slow to renew itself and dependent upon unpredictable weather conditions. The bad winters of 1873 and 1874 resulted in severe losses, and the disastrous winter of 1889–90 caused damage estimated at $500,000 in Elko County alone, which ruined many cattlemen. Thereafter, ranchers in Nevada as elsewhere erected barbed-wire fences, stored hay, and generally retreated from the romance of the open range.[14]

The Nevada sheep and cattle industries became increasingly absentee owned. By the early twentieth century, three fourths of the privately owned land in the state was in the possession of less than one hundred individuals and corporations, who lived or were incorporated mainly outside the state —in San Francisco, New York, or even England. A study made in 1918 concluded that 15 per cent of the assessed valuation of the state was in mining, 24 per cent in cattle and sheep ranches, and 46 per cent in railroads and utilities; and that two thirds of these industries were absentee owned.[15]

Locally, the authority of the leading cattleman was apt to be all but unchallengeable. Nevertheless, they were at the mercy of the Central Pacific, which was able freely to adjust its rates and conditions to what the traffic would bear.[16] Farm areas throughout most of the nation had fallen into hard times by 1870, and the major blame for the depressed conditions was everywhere directed against the railroad monopolies. The Patrons of Husbandry, organized nationally several years earlier for purely social purposes, already had developed into the politically conscious granges, determined to capture the state governments for the farmers. Beginning in 1870, reform legislation was enacted in the state capitals of the Midwest, some of which created railroad commissions with the authority to set freight rates and otherwise regulate the railroads.

The Nevada cattle baron might have had little else in common with the Iowa corn grower, but in 1870 both shared a bitter animosity toward the newly created western railroad monopolies. Among the leading cattle ranchers of Nevada was L. R. Bradley, who had driven his herd to Nevada in 1860, had settled near Austin, and finally had established himself in Mound Valley to the north.[17] In 1870 the cattlemen demonstrated their political power for the first time by electing Bradley governor. The legislature of 1871 forthwith amended the Railroad Act of 1865 to give itself the power to "change the rates of fare and freight of all narrow gauge railroads constructed under the provisions of this act."[18]

That enactment did not affect the C. P., but in 1873 Bradley vetoed the Washoe Relief Bill, which would have benefited the C. P. financially. The C. P. responded at once by raising freight rates between Reno and San Francisco by twenty per cent.[19] Bradley was re-elected in 1874, and a bill was introduced into the Assembly during the next session "to regulate fares and rates in railroads in the state of Nevada." The bill came to nothing, and in 1878 Bradley was rather narrowly defeated for a third term by John H. Kinkead, who had been associated with various mining and milling ventures and with the V. & T. Railroad.[20] Thereafter, the ranchers, making no further attempt to gain direct control of the government, organized the Cattlemen's Association and went on to win tax reforms which were greatly advantageous to them. Cattle were declared to be taxable only when they were grazing on the home ranch. The cattlemen could therefore largely avoid taxation by grazing their cattle on distant ranges.[21]

The cattlemen were able at least to rest secure in the knowledge that they were profitable to the railroad and would therefore not be driven out of business by rate discrimination. The opposite assumption was true of most other economic enterprises in the state; for it remained the fixed policy of the railroad for forty years systematically to destroy any business whatever in Nevada which competed with San Francisco business. This apparently was not a policy initiated by the railroad itself, but rather one forced upon it by the San Francisco Board of Trade.[22]

Within Nevada the C. P. faced only such competition as was provided by mule trains. In good weather these mule trains could bring freight from Sacramento to Virginia City at the rate of $1.50 per cwt. Accordingly, the C. P. set its rates at $1.465 per cwt.[23] In San Francisco, the railroad faced the competition of the steamship lines, which gave the city merchants their decisive advantage. The San Francisco merchants wanted a rate schedule which would place the Nevada market, such as it was, in their hands, and that is what they were given.

Nevada suffered long-haul–short-haul rate discrimination with a vengeance. Freight from points east, destined for delivery in Nevada, was charged for as though it were being delivered to its destination by way of San Francisco. Thus the rate for ten tons of coal oil was $300 from New York to San Francisco and $536 from New York to Reno; machinery, $600 to San Francisco and $736 to Reno. The same prohibitive costs applied to freight originating in Nevada. The charge for the same ten tons of coal oil, which was $300 dollars when delivered to San Francisco from New York, was $500 when delivered from Elko to San Francisco.[24]

Rates were furthermore arbitrarily altered to meet any new competition which might arise in Nevada. Limestone, required for use in the ore mills, had been imported from California, until a quarry was discovered near the Comstock. When this quarry began to undersell California lime, the rate on California lime was dropped to the point where the Nevada quarry was forced out of business. Then the former rate was charged once more. Nevada was by this means denied the use of other of its natural assets, such as sulphur, salt, and soda. Geographically, Reno was the natural distribution point for a wide area, including a number of the mountain counties of northern California, but railroad policy cut it off from its natural opportunities.

III

It is not too much to say that the public image of the Central Pacific in Nevada was severely disfigured by its discriminatory policy. "Being a cattle thief dont disqualify a man for any thing political he may want in this state," complained Yerington to a fellow political boss. "Really, from instances I have known (and you too) it adds to a man's standing in the Community—being connected with a Railroad is what *lays a fellow out*."[25] With the issue of railroad repression always at hand, and with a voting population of only 20,000 or so, Nevada was easy political pickings for anti-railroad orators. During the seventies and eighties the standard procedure for winning a seat in the state legislature was to attack the Central Pacific, to demand higher railroad taxes, and to call for a state or national railroad commission to bring an end to railroad injustice. This procedure was referred to by the politicians and newspapermen as "working on the railroad."

The C. P. retained political agents in Nevada to deal with the legislatures as a matter of course, and so did the leading interests on the Comstock. During the seventies and eighties, Stephen J. Gage was the most active C. P. representative; and in the eighties and nineties, Charles "Black" Wallace, representing the C. P., became generally known as the most skillful political manipulator in the state.[26] Yerington, as superintendent of the V. & T. Railroad, principally represented D. O. Mills, who had retained control of the road. Senator Jones's brother Sam was superintendent of Jones's mines and also served as his political lieutenant. Senator Sharon placed his political and business affairs on the lode in the hands of his nephew, William E. Sharon, and later on the Sharon faction came to be spoken for by the senator's son-in-law, Senator Francis G. Newlands.[27]

The C. P. political agents, upon entering Nevada politics, easily adapted themselves to a series of practices which had already been worked out and thoroughly tested. Until the introduction of the secret ballot, the railroad workers were marched to the polls just as the miners continued to be. During close elections, additional miners were hired purely for voting purposes and put to make-work tasks such as rooting up the sagebrush on the hillsides. It was said that the C. P., on occasion, bought additional workers into the state for the same purpose.[28] Legislators had come to expect their free railroad passes from the V. & T., and the C. P. was, naturally, in a similar position to oblige.[29]

Bribery continued as a common practice, but by no means on the scale employed by Fair and Sharon. Fifteen thousand dollars in gold was judged sufficient to pass a highly unpopular measure which the Bonanza Firm wanted badly.[30] At the height of the anti-railroad excitement, in 1881, Yerington boasted to Mills that he had been able to defeat a series of railroad bills at no cost whatever. The pocketing of one bill was arranged by obtaining a job for the son of the author of the measure. Other nominally anti-railroad legislators had promised not to vote against the railroads even though they had campaigned to do so—sometimes making such promises "in *black* & *white*," as Yerington firmly noted—in exchange for support of the V. & T. or other interests.[31] At the close of that notably anti-railroad 1881 session, Yerington was able to write Mills: "The legislature having finally closed its labors I this a.m. wired the fact to you also stating that we had come through without a scratch, killing *every* anti R.R. bill against [us] and the C. P. . . . We now having two years of peace ahead of us."[32] So ended the granger movement, Nevada style, after more than a decade of hullaballoo. Nothing of importance had been accomplished in the legislature, although in 1874 the C. P. had lost its lawsuit in the federal courts, which tested the constitutionality of Nevada's state and county taxation of the railroad.

It would be far from the truth to say that the long and successful defense against granger legislation had been due to the harmonious co-operation of the vested interests in Nevada; for there had been little of that. Niggling differences had disturbed the harmony of the group. The V. & T. had thought that the C. P. might reasonably be expected to charge half-rates for the transportation of Chinese workers to Nevada, but Stanford had refused to do so. Poor co-operation between the two groups had resulted from this disagreeableness in the legislative session then in progress.[33]

Mackay went on grumbling about the V. & T. freight rates for more than a decade. He became "very gruffy" and threatened to fight for rate regulation in the legislature. Mackay and the rest of the Bonanza Firm were, meanwhile, in difficulties with the legislature over back taxes which they had refused to pay. "The Bonanza folks," Yerington wrote Mills in 1881, "are badly blocked in trying to get their Bullion tax & back penalty bill passed. They have mismanaged the whole business & now come to us to pull them through as they always do."[34] As the election of 1880 approached, Sharon, in his eagerness to defeat Fair, declared of the C. P. freight rates, according to a newspaper account, that "the evils complained of have existed a long time. The people had rights to be protected." This brought a furious letter of protest from Charles Crocker, declaring that "every allegation . . . is utterly false. . . ."[35]

Yerington continued to work in co-operation with the C. P., and he thought that he was getting along well with the C. P.'s Gage, but later he developed a strong dislike for the C. P.'s Black Wallace, and he felt frustratingly out of touch with what the C. P. was doing in the political line. The fact was that the Big Four were not able to take Nevada politics seriously in the way Yerington did, and Crocker explained to him why. "He said they would 'stand in' with us," Yerington wrote Mills, "but his disposition was to let Legislatures severely alone & if oppressive bills were passed to shut down their roads & keep them shut till the people became more fair and liberal."[36]

In that statement, Crocker was probably close to speaking the mind of the Big Four, at least on Nevada politics. They had never been associated with the Comstock, and thus were not interested in the neighborhood squabbles which made up so much of Nevada politics and were the stuff of life for Yerington. They could not take the Nevada legislature very seriously, because they did not see how it could harm them.

The Nevada legislature possessed potent political weapons to fight the C. P., but it apparently never knew how to use them. It cannot even be said that Nevada politicians knew they had such weapons; so, while they went noisily along, "working on the railroad," Huntington went out and took their senators away from them and kept them for his own use. With their help he eventually staved off the threat of disaster amid mounting debts to the federal government, which continued to dog the C. P. to the end of the century.

IV

The Railroad Acts of 1862 and 1864 had provided that the subsidy bonds to the C. P. be repaid in two ways. The company would return to the government five per cent of its net earnings and also one half of the compensation for services rendered the government by the railroad. This would continue until principal and interest had been repaid in full. At the time of its completion, the C. P. had been indebted to the government to the amount of $27,855,680, for which the annual interest, at six per cent, was $1,671,340.80. What soon became apparent—and to none sooner than to the associates—was that the system was working in reverse. The revenues to the government from the two sources year after year averaged less than $600,000; so, while the owners were larding the lean earth, their property was steadily sinking deeper into debt, at a rate of more than $1 million each year.[37]

Such a situation was especially noticeable during the decade of the granger movement, and in 1874, two bills were introduced into Congress to do something about it. One of these bills was reintroduced in a later session and became the Thurman Act, signed into law in April 1879. The simple purpose of the Thurman Act was so to alter the formula for the repayment of the debt that the C. P. would gradually return to the government the money it had borrowed, at the interest rate agreed upon. Under the new formula, it was estimated, the annual payments to the government would increase from an average of $530,000 to $1.9 million. Over the resourceful opposition of Huntington, the bill was passed by a handsome margin. (Governor Stanford gave it as his opinion that never before in the history of the country had any act been attempted which was so destructive to private right.)

For some reason, the Thurman Act did not work as anticipated, and the C. P.'s indebtedness to the government continued to increase by slightly more than $1 million annually. Renewed agitation against the C. P. followed upon the antirailroad Populist revolt at the opening of the nineties. In 1899, with the indebtedness of the C. P. standing at about $58 million, Congress pressed for a new solution, entailing a thoroughgoing reorganization and the creation of a new corporation. Under the new system, and in that new age of finance capitalism, liquidation of the debt rapidly took place. In 1909, the last of the refunded notes was paid. By that time none of the Big Four was any longer connected with the road. However, Huntington had remained the guiding force behind the C. P. until the end of the nineteenth century, and it had been primarily because of this "sinking fund" situation that he had assiduously cultivated leading Senators in general and those from California and Nevada in particular.

Huntington had a wonderful way of creating the feeling among his political friends that they were fortune's favorites. A Vermont Yankee who drove himself at his work fourteen hours a day, he was also an extremely gracious host, and in a good business cause he was the gentleman bountiful. So, for that matter, were his associates. Nevada had hardly become a state before these men had drawn Senators Nye and Stewart into their circle and had given them tokens of esteem, such as the 200 shares of (presumably Central Pacific) stock which Crocker presented to Stewart in 1866.[38] Huntington seems at first to have warmed especially to Nye, for he selected him, among all the Western senators, to sponsor a measure that would transfer Yerba Buena Island (then known as Goat Island), in the middle of San Francisco Bay, from the federal government to the C. P.

At the time of the Yerba Buena project, the C. P. was contemplating the construction of a town on the Truckee which would be named Reno. Huntington wrote Crocker:

> Senator Nye went over with me, and I talked Goat Island with him. He said that we ought to have it and that he would do all in his power to get it for us. . . . I told him that he ought to have an interest in the new city that must grow up on the Truckee, and he said he would take an interest with us.[39]

Stewart, however, was not long in making himself a great favorite of Huntington, who wrote Mark Hopkins in the spring of 1869, two weeks before the joining of the Central Pacific and the Union Pacific at Promontory Point:

I shall telegraph Crocker to-day to have sleeping car at Ogden for Senator Stewart and Judge Field. They were in the office yesterday and to-day. Stewart did not care much about it, but it will please Field very much.

Stewart is a *trump* and *no mistake.*[40]

One week after the driving of the symbolic spike, Huntington wrote Crocker:

Stewart leaves here this week for California, and you must see him and let him into some good things in and about San Francisco and Oakland. . . . He has always stood by us. He is peculiar, but thoroughly honest, and will bear no dictation, but I know he must live, and we must fix it so that he can make one or two hundred thousand dollars. It is to our interest and I think his right.[41]

Stewart served ten years in the Senate (his first term having been for four years) and then chose not to run again. Throughout those years he retained with absolute fidelity that public image which he had presented—amid the cat calls of Mark Twain and others—before the Nevada Constitutional Convention of 1863. He had continued to pose as, above all, the friend of the poor miner and the defender of that miner's drifts and shafts and tunnels. The one measure with which he had dramatically identified himself during those two terms had been the Mining Act of 1866, confirming the mine owners on the Comstock and elsewhere in the possession of their claims. And he had made his gesture then, as before, in the name of that same folk hero, the poor miner. When he returned again to the Senate in twelve years, his concern had broadened to comprehend all humanity, in the fight for free silver.

In the meantime he was off to California to help the Southern Pacific fight what Stanford called "the influences of the communistic sentiment," which were seeking to destroy, by regulating railroads, the principle that "every citizen is on an equality with every other citizen."[42] It was a fight in which Stewart would have to prove himself again; for Huntington was beginning to doubt him. "I fully appreciate your . . . need of Stewart's help," he wrote his chief West Coast political lieutenant, General David Colton. ". . . I fear when he gets there he will not be earnest in our interest as formerly. Stanford thinks I am mistaken and I hope I am."[43]

That was a time of gloomy forebodings for Huntington. William Sharon was due to join John P. Jones in the Senate (although as it turned out Sharon got there a year late), and, at that moment, Huntington had reason to hate and distrust those particular two men of all men on earth. For hardly more than two weeks had passed since he had heard the first rumor of a projected railroad that would parallel the C. P. from Nevada to the Pacific, to be built by Sharon and Jones.[44]

Jones had been a senator for two years, and he had been a problem to Huntington from the first, by reason of that great wealth which Jones had acquired with such indecent speed. A trip in a private railroad car would obviously not do, and a hundred thousand dollars or so of Oakland and San Francisco real estate, which might do very well for the less affluent Senator Stewart, would be even worse. Mark Hopkins had suggested to Huntington that the best way out of that quandary might well be to evict Jones from the Senate altogether. Jones had been elected when the scandals of the Grant administration were coming out into the open, and he had gained national notoriety for the lavishly generous "sack" he had provided. Hopkins thought that, given the national sentiment of moral outrage which prevailed at the moment, the Senate might very well be put in the position where it would feel it had to send Jones home. ". . . I believe Jones will be against us in Washington," Hopkins continued.

> But in order that he shall have no cause of hostility, newspapers in our interest have said nothing unfriendly regarding his *purchase* of his Senator's Commission. But they are treasuring up all the facts and circumstances so that in case it shall be proper to show him up, they will be prepared.[45]

Two years later it was clearly too late to put the Hopkins plan into action, and the Sharon-Jones rumors grew more ominous, as the dread Jay Gould made his appearance in them. "If I mistake not," Huntington wrote Colton, "Jones is a small gun compared with Gould."[46] In April, Stewart entered the plot and the proposed railroad crept eastward to Salt Lake City. In May, Huntington talked to Gould and "came to the conclusion that he was not likely to invest money in Jones' road. But doubtful things are uncertain."[47]

There is every likelihood that, in a later letter which has not been preserved, Huntington took the occasion to remark to Colton or to Hopkins, that it is always darkest before the dawn, and that every cloud has a silver lining; for never were these phrases so apropos. Whatever may originally have been contemplated, all that materialized was "Jones's Los Angeles Road" from that city to the Pacific. It was fairly innocuous from the point of view of the Southern Pacific and also useless to it. At the same time, it was a heaven-sent opportunity for Huntington graciously to bribe this formidably wealthy senator, and it came at the very moment when the Thurman Bill, dealing with the C. P.'s government debt, was being debated in Congress. Huntington made Jones an offer, much of it in Southern Pacific bonds, which Jones was quick to accept. The deal was concluded in the spring of 1877, and Huntington wrote Colton:

> "I think we can make more than the interest on the amount paid for Jones' road out of our other roads by not running Jones' road at all. . . . Jones is very good natured now, and

> we need his help in Congress very much, and I have no doubt we shall have it.[47]

Have it, they did! Jones remained as Nevada's senior senator for a full quarter of a century longer, and he was "a *trump*" to the last.

CHAPTER IV

Plutocratic Populism

During the last quarter of the nineteenth century the embattled American farmer stood—unavailingly for the most part—against the conquest of his nation by the armies of the industrial revolution. This revolution had improved the lot of many American farmers by opening up markets to them which enabled them to move out of the restrictive bounds of subsistence farming into a more affluent world of commercial farming. At the same time, it made them captive, as they had not previously been, to outside forces over which they had no control, such as the world price of wheat and the freight rate for hogs. America had been a nation of farmers, and its noblest aspirations had been guided by agrarian ideals. For a quarter of a century following the Civil War, farmers organized to win back their lost heritage, first in the granger movement of the 1870s and then in the Populist movement of the 1890s.

Spiritually Nevada was not closely akin to those movements, for Nevada had no farmers to speak of. There was, however, as much cause for grievance against the railroads in

Nevada in the 1870s as there was in Iowa, and a granger movement, Nevada style, had developed accordingly. In the nineties, Nevadans found an even better reason to join the discontented farmers. The Populists desired currency reform which would relieve them of the wretched consequences of deflation. One such projected currency reform was the unlimited issuance of silver dollars by the federal government at an arbitrarily pegged ratio of 16 to 1 with gold. It was hoped that this would place more currency in the hands of the farmer and would give him higher prices for his wheat and his hogs.

Whatever this reform might have accomplished for wheat and hogs—it is doubtful that it would have done much for them—it would certainly have done wonders for Nevada silver. Nevadans, therefore, turned Populist. They did so, of course, for a price. By the time it had reached its climax in 1896, the Populist movement had all but narrowed itself to a crusade for the free coinage of silver at the ratio of 16 to 1, owing in part to the fact that the mining operators were the most generous contributors to the party coffers. The issue of free silver, declared the disgusted Populist leader Henry Demarest Lloyd, was the cowbird which had pushed the legitimate Populist reforms out of the nest. For the sake of silver, Nevada entered the camp of radical reform in the late nineteenth century.

The last quarter of the nineteenth century witnessed a deflation of worldwide proportions, which worked to the advantage of creditors and to the disadvantage of debtors, the dollar to be repaid by the debtor having progressively achieved greater buying power than the dollar originally borrowed. A numerous class of debtors in the United States during that period was the American farmer, who owed money for land and for farm machinery and who, during a dismal period of falling prices, often could not find the money to repay his debts. It was natural for debtors of the age to associate the demonetization of silver with the cruel process of deflation.[1]

The farmer was oppressed by other conditions as well: high railroad rates, high grain-elevator storage rates, and a general loss of political influence in the nation as a whole. Faced with these conditions, after the prosperity of the Civil War period, American farmers organized politically in the granger movement during the seventies. They organized cooperatives to free themselves from dependence upon grain-elevator operators and other middlemen. They captured the state governments of the Middle West and organized state commissions to regulate the railroads, especially in the area of rates.

In the field of monetary policy they demanded a more flexible currency than that provided by the gold standard, and their main solution for deflation was the greenback. During the Civil War the Union government had issued more than $400 million in paper money, unsupported by backing in silver or gold specie, mainly as a cheap means of helping to finance the war. These greenbacks had quickly depreciated in value and had naturally driven gold and silver from the market by the operation of Gresham's law, that bad money drives out good.

The postwar period witnessed an excited struggle, first over the legality of the Legal Tender Acts, which had authorized issuance of the greenbacks, and next over the question of whether to retain or retire them. Hard money advocates, known as goldbugs, won with the Specie Resumption Act of 1875, by which the Treasury was ordered to accumulate a gold supply sufficient to back the greenbacks fully. Most greenbacks remained in circulation, but by the end of the seventies they had been, in effect, converted to gold certificates.

Out of this controversy emerged the Greenback Party, which called for the retention of paper money without backing in specie. Strong in the Midwest, the party polled more than a million votes in the congressional elections of 1878 and sent fourteen representatives to Congress. Then resumption of specie payments took place during the next year, and the party collapsed. By that time the granger railroad commissions had proved ineffective, the farmer co-operatives had mainly failed, and, amid somewhat improved economic conditions, the farmer was withdrawing from the politics of radical reform.

Nevada had been as hard hit by railroad discrimination as any part of the country, and the granger movement had dominated politics there. At the same time the allied greenback movement was naturally unacceptable in a state where livings were made chiefly through the mining of silver and gold. The defeat of the greenback cause, however, opened the way nationally for a new inflationary program, which became especially dear to the hearts of the Nevada mining interests.

Throughout the last quarter of the nineteenth century and into the twentieth the overriding aims of Nevada politics were the return to bimetallism and the checking of deflation by means of the unlimited coinage of silver at a ratio of 16 to 1 with gold. When American farmers later, in the Populist movement of the early nineties, returned to the politics of radical reform and managed inflation, they were therefore enthusiastically supported by the silver mining interests of the West, and the Populists responded in turn by adopting the cause of silver as a major part of their program.

During the early years of the Republic, America had attempted to maintain itself on the bimetallic standard. The system had proved unsatisfactory in America as elsewhere, because of the instability of the ratio between the value of the two metals. By 1853, new gold from California and Australia had depreciated the value of gold in relation to silver to the point where the silver dollar had risen in value to $1.04 in gold at the 16-to-1 ratio. Therefore, being worth more as metal than as money, it had vanished from circulation. Faced with this condition and with the increased supply of gold, Congress in 1853 passed a law effectively placing the nation on the gold standard. Silver coins continued to be minted, but the number of grains of silver in the dollar was reduced to the point where it was converted into a subsidiary metal. To the debasing of silver coins was added a legal limitation of five dollars in silver as the maximum amount required to be accepted for any transaction. The act was passed without any serious opposition and continued to function satisfactorily until, during the Civil War, greenbacks drove both gold and silver out of circulation.

In practice, from the time of this enactment, the silver dollar had been little used, and, accordingly, a subsequent act in 1873, although it continued to authorize the minting of silver dimes, quarters, and half dollars, discontinued the minting of silver dollars. This law was passed with little opposition after thorough discussion, as was the more significant act of 1853. It was this minor modification of the monetary system which later became known as "the crime of '73," and which was denounced as an international conspiracy by which the American people were systematically being robbed of the fruits of their toil. Millions of Americans became convinced that the nation had actually been on the bimetallic standard until the act of 1873, and that, as W. H. Harvey charged in his widely influential *Coin's Financial School*, "It was demonetized secretly, and since then a powerful money trust has used deception and misrepresentations that have led tens of thousands of honest minds astray."[2]

The act of 1873 was passed during the year of the discovery of the Big Bonanza on the Comstock and at a time when most of Europe was adopting the gold standard or a modified form of it. There followed a precipitous and unprecedented decline in the value of silver in relation to gold, from 15.57 to 1 in 1870 to 18.04 to 1 in 1880 to 31.57 to 1 in 1895.

Nevada now wanted to sell silver to the United States mint at the old ratio of 16 to 1, and so did Colorado. Together the voting population of those two states was small, but it was represented by four men in the United States Senate, and they argued with a correspondingly authoritative voice. Increasingly these four men were able to speak also for millions of American farmers, who were getting less money for their grain. Many farmers accepted the argument that deflationary conditions would be corrected through the unlimited coinage of silver at a fixed ratio of 16 to 1 with gold. In 1878, as a result, the Bland-Allison Act was passed, which provided for the purchase of from $2 million to $4 million of silver each month and for the minting of it. The purchases were to be made, however, at the going rate and not at an artificially pegged price.

This agreement between the frankly silverite Bland and the cagily conservative Allison stood as a working compromise for almost a decade. It provided a good market for the silver mines as well as an experiment in inflationary technique for the farmers, and, at the same time, it had no perceptible effect upon the deflationary cycle which so benefited the nation's creditors. As prices continued to go down, however, the farmers again became restive. Then, in 1889, the Omnibus Bill admitted to the Union the Dakotas, Washington, and Montana, followed the next year by Wyoming and Idaho. With twelve new senators, most of them standing in with the silverites, the silver issue took on a new dimension in the Senate.

The main problem for the silverites was the presidency. In

1888 Cleveland, a redoubtable goldbug, was running against Harrison. At the Republican convention of 1888, Senator Stewart won what he thought were assurances from Harrison that, if elected, he would not veto a bill calling for the free coinage of silver at a long-since-passed ratio of 16 to 1 with gold.[3] A correspondingly promising plank was written into the platform, and the silverites generally flocked to the Republican standard. At the first session of Congress under President Harrison, Senator Henry M. Teller of Colorado led a fight for free silver, supported principally by Senators Stewart and Jones, against the opposition of Harrison's administration.

The red-letter year for legislation was 1890, when the Sherman Anti-Trust Act, the Sherman Silver Purchase Act, and the McKinley Tariff were all passed. The Anti-Trust Act was a generally agreed-upon sop to public sentiment, which did not detain nor disorganize the Senate groupings. Not so the other two measures. Eastern Republican leaders equated gold with God and at the same time wanted high tariffs for high profits. The tariff meant comparatively little to Rocky Mountain Republicans, but for them silver was all important. The result was an agonizing compromise, which enacted both measures into law. Sherman craftily made his Silver Purchase Act as painless as possible by providing for the purchases in terms of ounces instead of dollars, in order to take advantage of the declining price of silver. According to the terms of the act, the government was required to buy 4.5 million ounces of silver per month and to issue silver certificates, redeemable in gold or silver.

Then the Panic of '93 came upon the United States, accompanied by a run on the nation's gold supply. President Cleveland thought that the bankers had a corner on wisdom, when it came to money, and he followed their advice and persuaded Congress to repeal the Sherman Silver Purchase

Act. The act, itself, in the meantime, had done nothing to halt the deflationary trend, and in 1892 in Omaha, the Peoples' (or Populist) party had been organized, mainly by trans-Mississippi and Southern farmers. It was dedicated to a radical program of reform, which included prominently the free coinage of silver at a ratio of 16 to 1 with gold. There were still no farmers in Nevada to speak of, but there was a lot of low-grade ore that could be mined, if the price of silver were high enough to pay the milling costs. Thus Nevada, which, except for James G. Fair's victory as a Democrat after his sack-carrying campaign of 1880, had always been staunchly Republican in politics, threw itself abruptly into the agrarian crusade.

II

John P. Jones was an affable and rather indolent man. His whirlwind success in the mines and his subsequent achievements in later mining ventures were due to ability and good fortune rather than to hard work. Jones was also able and indolent as a senator.[4] He took little part in senatorial debates or committee work, but in the cause of silver, which was important to his state and even more important to himself, he assumed a leading role from the outset. His major speeches in behalf of the free coinage of silver—clear, informed, and reasonable—were accounted the best expositions of the subject to be found anywhere. He was later ably assisted in the silver fight by William M. Stewart, returned to the Senate in 1887—apparently at the behest of Stewart's employer, Collis P. Huntington.

In the early years of this silver fight, Jones was poorly assisted by the junior senators from Nevada. Senator Sharon through much of his tour of duty, remained at Belmont with his mistress, and, despite the fact that the free-silver issue was as important to him as it was to Jones, he did nothing of importance about it during his six years in office. Unlike Sharon, Senator Fair was married at the time of his election. He went at once to Washington, leaving his wife and family behind him, and he faithfully kept up his residence in Washington throughout his term, even after his wife had left him in one of the most celebrated and scandalous divorce cases of the time. Fair seems to have taken his job with a degree of seriousness; he made himself available to visiting Nevadans, answered his correspondence, and did what he could for people who asked favors of him. But in Senate proceedings he took no initiative whatever, even though he personally would have benefited as much as either Jones or Sharon from the free coinage of silver at a ratio of 16 to 1.[5]

The voters of Nevada may not have been much disturbed by the incompetence of Sharon and Fair, for they had been well paid for their votes, and it was only toward the close of Fair's term that the cause of free silver began to be a hopeful one. The Central Pacific, however, was coming increasingly under attack, following the failure of the Thurman Act of 1879 to reduce the C. P.'s debt to the government. Furthermore, a railroad regulation measure was pending in Congress, the bill which became the Interstate Commerce Act of 1887. Neither Sharon nor Fair were worth anything to Huntington in his fight against federal control and for the outright cancellation of the C. P. debt, and in 1886 he and his colleagues did something about it. Fair wanted another term, just as Sharon had before him, but he was no match for the political machine of the Southern Pacific and the Central Pacific. William Stewart left his San Francisco law offices in that year to establish his residence on Nevada, and he won the senatorial seat from Fair.

Stewart could hardly be said to have been a strong candidate in 1886, from the point of view of statewide popularity. There was no way to disguise the fact that he had been making his living during the previous twelve years as counsel for the hated Central Pacific crowd. While engaged in that employment, he had been living in San Francisco, returning to Nevada only in time to make himself legally qualified to run for the Senate from that state. He had always been a belligerent man who had made enemies, even though, by 1886, his beard was turning snowy white, giving him a deceptively Santa Claus-like appearance. He had, however, the backing of the Southern Pacific, which counted John W. Mackay on its board of directors, and, in opposing Fair, Stewart had the good fortune to oppose a man who was at least as disliked as he was, himself. Fair's divorce had precipitated the final break between Fair and Mackay, and Fair was no longer in command of the votes of the miners working the bonanza mines. The "carpetbagger," as Stewart was called by his enemies, therefore won easily.

There was no thought that Stewart would give up his job as counsel for the Southern Pacific, simply because he had taken on the added responsibility of representing Nevada in the United States Senate. He worked diligently at what he conceived to be his senatorial duties, and still had time for the railroad's cases and for those of other clients.[6] Stewart had taken William F. Herrin into his law firm in San Francisco and had accepted him as a partner.[7] Herrin went on to become the general counsel for the Southern Pacific and, for many years, the director of what was popularly known as the S. P. Political Bureau, which operated mainly in California and Nevada. During his first years back in the Senate, Stewart devoted himself, in his correspondence, most of all to Herrin and other leading figures in the S. P. Political Bureau: Black Wallace, Sam Davis, A. C. Cleveland, and, of course, Stanford and Huntington.

Stewart had hardly returned to office before the Interstate

Commerce Act had been passed, which, among other things, sought to curtail the railroad pass privileges which had been standard fringe benefits for politicians. Stewart wrote Yerington in 1888:

> Since the passage of the Inter-State Commerce Law my traveling expenses on the railroads have been very heavy. It occurred to me that the Virginia & Truckee Railroad Company might make me an officer or employee of that Company so that I could come under the exception provided by section 22 of the Inter-State Commerce Act. Why could I not be your attorney? I am a pretty good lawyer and you couldn't get a cheaper one under these circumstances. Let me know if you can figure it out so that what little salary I get won't be all used up in traveling expenses.[8]

Whether or not Yerington accepted Stewart's offer, Stewart continued to receive free passes from the V. & T. Railroad, even though Yerington disliked Stewart bitterly.

As far as the Southern Pacific was concerned, Section 22 of the Interstate Commerce Act held no terrors for Stewart, because he continued to be a member of that firm during his second senatorial career. His proprietary feeling toward that road—and, indeed, toward American railroads in general—may be seen in his letter of instruction to an S. P. official in 1905:

> Your kind letter offering to ship my belongings to Nevada from New York via Galveston was received some time ago. I do not believe that I could pack my furniture and other things in such a manner as to prevent injury from so much handling. The Pennsylvania Company will furnish me a large car here and will transport it to Chicago free of charge. I have a promise of like transportation over the Chicago & Northwestern to Omaha. If the Union and Southern Pacific Companies will do likewise from Omaha to Tonopah, I will be greatly accommodated.[9]

This proprietary air did not by any means rise to encompass the top controllers of the railroads. Stewart's correspondence with Huntington, during his later senatorial career, is muffled in mystery, so little sense can be made of it by the outsider. Yet, the obsequious tone is constant. One example of it follows:

> Your esteemed favor of the 29th ult. with express package, came duly to hand. I have no words which can express my obligation to you for your great kindness. I hope I may be able to show you how I appreciate what you have done for me.[10]

During the campaign of 1886, "Friend Huntington" had gone to Nevada personally to help out with Stewart's election, and in Stewart he had had a loyal subordinate in the Senate, to whom he could issue orders, in a way that he could not do to the agreeable but independent Senator Jones.

Throughout his career, Stewart was just as busily engaged in mining ventures as Jones, but without the latter's success. Had he held on to the great fees he earned as a lawyer throughout his life, he would have become wealthy. Instead, he lost several rather sizable fortunes and was obliged to live modestly, in relation to the company he kept. When he became senator for the second time, he was operating mines hopefully in Bodie and Panamint, California, and in Mexico.[11] Thus, although he would have done well to have left silver mining alone, he had, from a selfish point of view, as much reason to take up the silver issue as Jones had.

The issue then became the great crying cause of Stewart's career. For fourteen years, until he lost hope in the face of the great gold discoveries around the world at the close of the century, he was a tireless and tiresome advocate of silver. His speeches in the Senate, notably his "Money, the Answer to All Things," were a credit to him in Nevada, where the advantages of free silver were well understood. But they put him in conflict with his patron, Collis P. Huntington, and this was a source of keen distress to him. "Your letters," he wrote Huntington in 1893, "give me great pain. . . . I cannot understand why you should want the purchasing clause of the so-called Sherman act repealed. I have given the subject more study and reflection than I ever devoted to any other question.[12] And he continued for five pages, explaining the rights of man as well as the needs of Nevada to Huntington in terms of silver. He was convinced that "the absolute cessation of silver mining, which in my firm belief must necessarily result from the proposed legislation for many years to come, would paralyze and practically ruin the mining states and territories." And finally, with good neighborly thoughtfulness, he added: "It would have a similar effect on the mining states of Mexico."

Stewart as a politician had always carefully cultivated his public image as the defender of the poor miner. Upon his return to the Senate he expanded this image of himself to that of the protector of the common people everywhere against the encroachments of the money power. Although he by no means forsook his old friends at the Southern Pacific Railroad, he extended his political friendships to include such agrarian radicals as General Coxey, Ignatius Donnelly, and William Jennings Bryan. Throughout the decade of the nineties, the great bulk of his heavy correspondence consisted of endless repetitions of his main arguments on behalf of bimetallism, no matter what information or what favor his correspondent had requested. Characteristically, Stewart wrote a brief reply, followed by the same lengthy sermon on silver. This discourse, repeated from time to time on the floor of the Senate, was the alpha and omega of Stewart's statesmanship during his second term in Washington. It was also, at the level of political principle, the alpha and omega of Nevada politics during the same period. The goldbug Huntington, in order to retain political control over Nevada, was obliged to permit not only Stewart and Jones but also the Southern Pacific political agents in the state to rally to the cause of free silver and agrarian radicalism.

III

The Silver Party, which dominated Nevada in the nineties, was doctrinaire, parochial, and childishly self-interested. Government purchase of silver at a ratio of 16 to 1 with gold would benefit the mines; therefore it was urged upon the nation as the salvation of society. Whether it would in fact have eased the hardships of deflation will, of course, never be known, because the experiment was not tried. Whether Nevada as a whole would have benefited much from it is equally open to question, even though Nevadans were persuaded that it would. For Nevada's senators and for other mine owners, however, it indisputably meant more money in the bank, and these men were driven by this ideal.

It is no doubt true that the Populists were as narrowly self-interested as the silverites with whom they united; for they, too, chiefly wanted more money for their commodities. The older, more settled regions of the Midwest, which a generation earlier had gone granger, remained mainly Republican during the Populist revolt. Diversified farming, local markets, and a degree of control over railroad rates had relieved them of some of their earlier grievances and had reoriented their ways of thinking. Populism was rampant mainly among the one-crop farmers in the cotton country, and in the corn and wheat belts. This radicalism was to be explained by the fact that corn sold for less than fifteen cents a bushel and cotton for less than five cents a pound. Thus a government program to raise the price of basic commodities might have appeared to them as the best fundamental reform to save the nation.[13]

The Populists, however, inherited a reform program that was the result of a long history of intermittent rural discontent and that was developed during a period when the farmer could still think of himself as representive of the nation as a whole. Because the Populists inherited the granger programs, they attracted such diverse urban reformers as Terence Powderly, Frances Willard, and Henry Demarest Lloyd. They were still ambitious to speak, not simply for their own narrow interests, but for the nation as a whole, and they made this abundantly evident in their Omaha platform of 1892.

This platform was instinct with revolutionary fervor: ". . . we meet in the midst of a nation brought to the verge of moral, political, and material ruin. Corruption dominates the ballot, the legislatures, the Congress, and touches even the ermine of the bench. . . . The fruits of the toil of millions are boldly stolen to build up colossal fortunes for a few. . . . From the same prolific womb of governmental injustice we breed the two great classes—tramps and millionaires." These ills required radical remedies.

As for politics, the people should be returned to power through the secret ballot, the direct election of senators, and the procedures of initiative and referendum. Labor should receive legal protection in its unequal struggle with the plutocracy, and the private armies of Pinkerton police, employed by management against labor, should be abolished. As for the railroads: "The time has come when the railroad corporations will either own the people or the people must own the railroads. . . ." The government should take over the management of the railroads, and "all persons engaged in the government service shall be placed under a civil service regulation of the most rigid character, so as to prevent the increase of the power of the national administration by the use of such additional government employees."

Finally, there was the issue of monetary reform, which

brought the Populists into harmony with the Nevada silverites:

> We demand a national currency, safe, sound and flexible, issued by the general government only, a full legal tender for all debts, public and private, and that, without the use of banking corporations. . . .
>
> (a) We demand free and unlimited coinage of silver and gold at the present legal ratio of sixteen to one.
>
> (b) We demand that the amount of circulating medium be speedily increased to not less than fifty dollars per capita.

Only one specifically pro-farm plank, dealing with a government subtreasury program for storing the farmers' grain and lending money on it, was included in the platform. The focus of attention was rather on the rights of the workingman; for one of the chief purposes of the document was to cement a farm-labor alliance which would sweep the nation for Populism.

Unhappily, the worker and the farmer could not be friends. Rural America was predominantly Anglo-Saxon, Protestant, and prohibitionist. Industrial America was predominantly recent-immigrant, Catholic, and wet and therefore generally abhorrent to the Populists. The Populist leaders consequently failed in their efforts to create a farm-labor alliance. It enjoyed greater success in its minor objective of capturing the silver states with its free-silver plank.

The Populists were by no means silverites in the manner of Senators Jones and Stewart. They disbelieved in both the gold standard and the gold and silver standard. They believed—as, indeed did many industrialists in new and developing industries—that money was legitimately based not on precious metals but upon the needs of society, and that it was the responsibility of the government to expand the flow of currency as the needs of society increased. The proper method of achieving this end was the issuance of greenbacks by the government as the economy expanded, without any concern for backing in gold and silver.[14] Still, as between the gold standard and the bimetallic standard, the silverites were working the right side of the street, and the Populists welcomed their support accordingly.

In January 1885, following the election of the goldbug Cleveland, the Nevada legislature called a convention, which formed the Nevada Silver Association to work for the free coinage of silver at a ratio 16 to 1 with gold. In November 1889, a national silver convention met in St. Louis, and Nevada sent a large delegation, including Senator Stewart. Out of this convention emerged a permanent national organization, which became the American Bimetallic League, charged with the task of securing federal free-coinage legislation. By 1892 the League had secured a majority of votes in the Senate for its measure but had yet to gain a majority in the House. In 1893, the year of the repeal of the purchasing clause of the Sherman Silver Purchase Act, silver conventions were held in Washington, Chicago, and St. Louis. The Chicago session included among its members William Jennings Bryan, Terence Powderly, and Ignatius Donnelly.[15]

In 1892 Nevada cast its three electoral votes for the Populist candidate, and in the following years the Populists returned the favor by concentrating increasingly on the free-silver issue. They did so, in part, because silver had proved their most popular issue in the campaign of 1892. Throughout American history, reformers have tended to have a weakness for the single-idea panacea. The Populist program, taken as a whole, was a complicated one, and many of its proposals, such as nationalization of the railroads, were looked upon as impossible to fulfill. And even if they were carried out, they offered no quick solutions to the nation's ills. On the other hand, silver could be coined immediately at a ratio of 16 to 1 by congressional enactment, and, if the arguments of the silverites proved true, direct relief from deflation would result.

The free-silver plank was backed both by the Bimetallic League and by a highly financed special-interest group, as was no other plank in the platform. For the most part, the Populist party was obliged to depend upon impoverished farmers for its finances. So long as the party supported free silver, however, it was able to tap the wealth of the mining interests, and thus economic pressure insensibly forced the party and its leaders to adopt as their prime issue a cause which originally had not been theirs at all.

In Nevada a Silver Party was organized in opposition to the Populist Party, and many Populists feared the threat of a national Silver Party. Leading Populists advocated the removal of planks from the platform which the silverites might find objectionable, and Governor "Bloody Bridles" Waite of Colorado tried to call a national convention to do so.[16] Thus bribed and threatened by the silverites, the Populists entered the campaign of 1896 with their program intact but with free silver as their one crying issue. They joined the Democratic Party in nominating as their candidate William Jennings Bryan, a politician who was identified with the cause of free silver rather than with Populism.

Some party leaders such as Henry Demarest Lloyd left in disgust, and Populism and free silver went hand in hand to defeat. The election of McKinley was followed by an age of farm prosperity and by prodigious new gold discoveries, which the Populist Party did not survive. The silverites fought on to victory in the twentieth century, by taking advantage of their disproportionate strength in the United States Senate. As a party issue, however, free silver died with the death of the Populists.

In Nevada the Silver Party, organized in 1892, enlisted the support of most of the leading political figures in the state, including Senators Jones and Stewart, William Sharon and the Southern Pacific's Black Wallace. Until that time, these men had been Republicans as a matter of course. Against the goldbug Democratic President Cleveland, the Nevadans had no reason to defect to that party; so, after the apostasy of the Republican President Harrison, they created a party of their own. Republican, Democratic, and Populist parties continued their separate existences, but many Republicans and most Democrats were lost to the new creation. Added to this was the disorder of Fusion—a joining of the Silver and Democratic parties—which acted as an independent political force while those parties retained their separate identities. Thanks to old diehards such as Yerington the Republicans were still the main opposition party, but the Silver Party, with or without Fusion, dominated the state into the twentieth century.[17]

IV

Nevada went Populist in the presidential election of 1892, Democratic-Populist in 1896, and Democratic in 1900, all while under railroad management. The Southern Pacific Political Bureau was probably never more powerful in the state than in the nineties. It was acknowledged as the only real political machine in the state and one which commanded the loyalties of all the "smaller politicians and county statesmen."[18] S. P.'s Black Wallace dominated the politics of the state during the decade, and he was a commanding figure in the founding of the Silver Party, at a time when his employer, Huntington, probably opposed the whole of the Populist platform, including, certainly, its plank on the nationalization of the railroads. Huntington also opposed the silver plank, and he obviously, therefore, opposed the Silver Party, which his political agent was helping to create. Such considerations were as nothing, however, when balanced against the difficult position the Central Pacific was in, during the nineties, with its ever-increasing debt to the government, amid rising prejudice against the railroads. Huntington was a practical man. Nevada got its Silver Party, and Huntington got its Silver senators.

The threat to Huntington's control of the state's Senate seats came, as it had before, not from the poor people, but from a rich person. Francis G. Newlands was a brilliant and dashing lawyer who had arrived in San Francisco from the East, full of large ambitions. Like Senator Stewart before him, he had left Yale College before he finished his studies (to become a lawyer, he merely had to pass a bar examination), but unlike Stewart he was later awarded an honorary degree by Yale. In San Francisco he was placed in charge of the properties of William Sharon, and in 1874 he married Sharon's daughter.

Newlands thus came early into great wealth, and in 1888, in a move which was generally recognized as political in intent, he built an imposing home on the Truckee River and transferred his legal residence to Reno. Newlands was an excellent speaker and a lavish entertainer. He was happy to pay well for what he wanted, and, in his cousin-in-law Will Sharon of the Comstock, he had the aid of a skillful political lieutenant. He and his fortune were independent of the railroad, and when he found it worthwhile, he could use the old railroad issue to good effect.[19]

Newlands remained a unique figure in Nevada politics, until the later rise of Senator Patrick McCarran; for he aspired to be not only a senator but also a statesman. He proposed to use the narrow and crooked field of Nevada politics as a rotten borough in the best English tradition. Just as, in the eighteenth century, Old Sarum had sent the William Pitts, father and son, into Parliament and into history, so Nevada would send Francis G. Newlands into Congress and into history.

From the outset, Newlands faced a situation which had not confronted any of his predecessors; for in 1891 Nevada adopted the secret ballot.[20] The day was therefore over when miners on the Sharon properties could be marched to the polls from work to vote against the opposing vote of the similarly mustered railroad workers. The result was a radical change in sack-handling, which proved a great economy for senatorial aspirants. The money would no longer be doled out to the voters, but only to the candidates for the legislature, who, in return, would pledge their votes to the donor.

A man of Newlands's wealth, however, could not get off that cheaply. He required a state-wide political organization of his own, and this could not be purchased, but only rented. He was expected to pay all of his own campaign expenses and then to contribute to the campaigns of other party candidates. In 1908, when he was running for a second term in the Senate, he agreed to pay, in addition to his expenses, $8,000 to the state central committee for operational expenses and an additional $5,000 for election day expenses. His total bill came to $39,502.04, in a campaign where he was assumed to be an easy winner.[21] He had fought four congressional and two senatorial campaigns previously, most of them under less favorable circumstances, and therefore, it may be inferred, at a greater personal cost.

Newlands lived to see an end to old-time rotten borough politics in Nevada, and he continued in office long enough to triumph under the new democratic dispensation. By the time of his campaign for re-election in 1914, the seventeenth amendment to the Constitution had been adopted, providing for the direct election of United States senators by the people. He was still expected to foot a large part of the bill for the Democratic Party in the state, but, with a long and distinguished congressional and senatorial record behind him, he refused to do so. He told Sharon that he had earned re-election and would go down to defeat rather than feed those hungry political wolves any longer. He won by 38 votes.[22]

Newlands entered Nevada politics during the confusing period of the organization of the Silver Party, which drew heavily from the Republicans and practically took over the Democrats. A few old-timers such as Yerington and A. C. Cleveland remained doggedly Republican, and out of power, but Wallace, Sharon, Newlands, Stewart, and Jones all went over. The result for the next decade was a one-party system of government in which all politics of any consequence took place in the conventions of the Silver Party and the Fusion Party. In those conventions, two factions established themselves, beginning in 1892, and for ten years they fought the bitterest political fight that the state had ever seen.[23]

The principals in the fight within the Silver Party were Stewart and his manager Black Wallace on the one side and Newlands and his manager Will Sharon on the other. In the filling of the Southern Pacific machine's war chest, Wallace could no doubt count on liberal contributions from the railroad in case of absolute need, but it appears that, so far as possible, he was expected to live off the country. In 1890, when Wallace was still in the Republican Party, Yerington wrote a fellow Republican that Wallace had "frightened me with his enormous demands. . . . To work the state on the basis that he figures for your county alone would burst the Bank of Cal."[24] The Newlands forces, for their part, levied contributions on all candidates on the principle of: from each according to his ability to each according to his need, which in both cases was mainly Newlands.

Newlands received the Silver Party nomination for the state's one seat in the House of Representatives, and the Republicans, fearful of the money he might spend in the campaign, followed at once by nominating him as their candidate as well. The Silver Party managers, however, told him that he could not accept the Republican nomination, and he accordingly declined it, then went on to win overwhelmingly against his Republican opponent.[25] In that contest, he was supported, at least nominally, by the Stewart-Wallace forces, but such co-operation as may have existed between them does not appear to have survived Stewart's campaign for re-election to the Senate in 1893, when it was rumored that Newlands harbored senatorial ambitions of his own. According to Yerington, Stewart was violently stirring up troublesome political issues, presumably because of "his fear of Newlands under present condition of things, being the choice of the Legislature, and winning the Senatorial fight." He added that "this man Stewart is a bulldozing, foul-mouthed, ungrateful rascal, and I do hope he will be thoroughly beaten."[26]

In 1896 Senator Jones was up for re-election, and Newlands's supporters were again hopeful that the time for his candidacy had arrived. He had the support of D. O. Mills, who, although long since removed to New York, retained control of the V. & T. Railroad and, through Yerington, remained in constant touch with Nevada politics. The Southern Pacific machine declared for Jones, however, and Newlands was obliged to defer his hopes for three more years.[27] The Silver Party meanwhile had elected all of its nominees on the state ticket two years previously and had secured an almost unanimous following in both houses of the state legislature. Yerington wrote bitterly to Mackay that "altho. supposed to be dead the Repub party in Nevada made a gallant fight against that awful fraud known as the Silver Party composed very largely of dyed in the wool Democrats."[28] The cup of poison was finally filled for Yerington when Jones and Stewart, after campaigning for Bryan in 1896, and again in 1900, were both times given the Republican patronage in the state by McKinley.[29]

Newlands was determined to fight Stewart in 1899, against

the advice of one of his chief political lieutenants, George S. Nixon of Winnemucca. "I believe it would be policy," Nixon wrote in 1898, "to serve as Congressman until four years from now and in the campaign of 1900 declare your candidacy for Jones place (if he is still alive) and fight that year for hold over Senators on the quiet. I can unquestionably take Wallace into camp on such a situation as he would promise almost anything to prevent a break, politically, between you and Stewart." But in 1899 Nixon thought Newlands had little chance against Stewart.

> Wallace has been all over the State recently and to my certain knowledge has "fixed" about all the papers and many of the principle wire pullers in different sections. This is not hearsay but comes from actual knowledge. There has also been a slight current started for some one else for Congress other than yourself, this of course, no doubt to influence you. . . .[30]

Will Sharon, on the other hand, saw hopes for Newlands which were not apparent to Nixon; they were based upon the hatred of many Nevadans for Stewart, especially the loyal old Republicans. A. C. Cleveland, by then the state's leading loyal Republican, promised Sharon he would support Newlands against Stewart and so presumably would Yerington, who wrote Mills in 1898:

> I note your remarks about Senator Stewart and heartily agree with you, for he appears to be crazy, so offensively dictatorial that he has quarreled with many of our best citizens and appears to have but very few real friends in Nevada. . . .[31]

In 1898 Newlands secured this promising alliance by running successfully for re-election to Congress on the Republican as well as the Silver ticket. Stewart retaliated against Yerington and the V. & T. Railroad by threatening personally to put it under political harassment, "all of which is bosh," Yerington commented to Mills, "but shows the little meanness of this incredible U. S. Senator and wonderful Silver Champion."[32]

In December 1898, Newlands announced his senatorial candidacy, and Stewart arrived in Nevada, accompanied by what Newlands described as "a crowd of desperadoes," one of whom announced that he intended to kill Will Sharon.[33] With the aid of a good deal of terrorism, Stewart won the first encounter, when Sharon, who was chairman of the Silver Party state central committee, and Newlands were both read out of the Silver Party, after bitter debate. Newlands was still strongly supported in the House, but the Stewart forces had successfully purchased control of the Senate and held a number of written pledges to vote for Stewart, received in exchange for payment of campaign expenses. The Senate accordingly elected Stewart by a majority of two.

In the House, the Stewart forces had succeeded in getting only 15 out of 30 votes, and there appeared to be no way for them to gain the additional votes needed. Matters were made worse by the failure of one of the pledged members of the House to appear. When that happened, according to an account by a Wallace associate, the Stewart forces moved with typical straightforwardness. The missing legislator was hunted down and brought to the House at the point of a six shooter. One of the anti-Stewart legislators was kidnapped and kept prisoner for two days and then, reportedly, mollified by a gift of $1,800. Stewart therefore won, 15 to 14, returned to the Senate, immediately renounced the Silver Party, and returned to the Republican fold, apparently oblivious to the abuse which was heaped upon him as a consequence.[34]

• • •

V

The senatorial campaign of 1899 proved to be the swan song of the Southern Pacific Political Bureau in Nevada. That year saw the completion of the arrangements whereby the Central Pacific eventually paid off its enormous debt to the federal government. Huntington was the only remaining member of the Big Four, and in 1901 he severed his connection with the Southern Pacific and the Central Pacific. The roads were taken over by Edward H. Harriman and absorbed into a much larger national system. The death of Black Wallace in 1901 marked the end of the political bureau in the state, but the change in railroad management was the fundamental cause. Huntington had wanted Nevada only for its two United States senators; Harriman does not appear to have felt the need even for these.

Following the election of 1899, Wallace was found to be working busily in behalf of both the Southern Pacific Railroad and its Nevada political machine. The C. P. reorganization act was still before Congress, and Wallace was working on a Nevada bill which would aid in the consolidation of the C. P. and the S. P., so as to facilitate the desired settlement from Congress. Accordingly he urged Yerington to say some untruths which would aid in passing the Nevada measure, observing, according to Yerington, that "I have often lied for you, which I denied. . . ." But, "Feeling that anything I could do for the interest of Mr. Huntington would meet with your approval, I have consented. . . ."[35]

Wallace was away almost at once to Winnemucca to consult with Newland's supporter, George Nixon. "He said, 'I have nothing against Newlands now that Stewart is elected and there is no reason why he cannot succeed Jones if he wants to.' "[36] Even the bulldozer Stewart saw fit to make his peace with Yerington, who wrote Mills in 1900: "On the day of Senator Stewart's arrival here he came in to see me, said we had been warm friends for 30 years, and he now wanted to bury the hatchet . . . and we shook hands on it."

All appeared to be going well for Newlands in his campaign for Jones's senatorial seat in 1903, his only important question appearing to be whether to run again for the House of Representatives in 1900 or stay out of the fight and concentrate on the election of hold-over legislators in Nevada, pledged to vote for him as senator when the time came. Then in the spring of 1900, Sharon received bad news from the S. P.'s general counsel, Herrin.

> He expressed himself in the most friendly way towards you, but back of this I could see he felt Huntington was not friendly to you and gave me one or two reasons for his not being. . . . I could also see they have no present intention of deposing Wallace or in any way curtailing his power in this state and my opinion is Wallace's instructions from Huntington are to fight you to the end. . . . You are beset with difficulties everywhere.[37]

Newlands, amid the confusion which accompanied the gradual dissolution of the Silver Party, took his stand with the Democratic Party nationally and put himself into the fight for another term in Congress. Wallace thereupon appeared at the Silver convention in Reno, and a leading party worker for Newlands reported:

> He eagerly seized each delegate and commenced on them and is making it a personal fight and appealing to them to defeat you. . . . He states that Stewart Jones and yourself are all frauds and turn you down. He says to the Silver men, you have been taken into camp by the Democrats. A handfull of Democrats have absorbed you. Now come back to the Republican party where you belong. . . .
>
> John P. Jones will be here next week. It is his intention to

> come out as a Democrat and run a Democrat in every county for the State Senate as a Jones man. Result, Either a Jones man or a Republican will be elected. In the mean time Jones will employ every energy to defeat you.[38]

Newlands, meanwhile, spent heavily and won by a large margin; thereafter everything went his way.

Most importantly, Senator Jones, after thirty rather relaxed years in the Senate, and with a beard that could grow no longer, decided to retire from politics and move to Southern California. Yerington was overjoyed at the rumor that Harriman had "given orders that the S. P. Co. stand in with the Repubs *for all its worth*,"[39] but it does not appear to have materialized. Wallace was dead, and the Silver and Democratic parties appeared to be filled with the spirit of Fusion. The Republicans were hopeless in producing a candidate to match Newlands. He was, of course, as he noted, "compelled to advance most all the money used in the Democratic campaign," in addition to $2,000 here and $5,000 there to needy Nevada candidates in the year following, but after fifteen years he had reached his home in the Senate cloakroom at last.[40]

Yerington was beside himself with despair, he wrote Mills. "The Press dispatches will have told you ere this that Nevada has gone Democratic-Silver-Fusion even worse than two years ago. They have elected every State Officer with a large legislative majority, so that Newlands is safe for the U.S. Senate."[41] Yerington could take satisfaction only in a small, but significant, defensive move. Concentrating on the recently created Board of Equalization, he claimed he had, at a relatively small cost, succeeded in winning the election of two of the three commissioners, who had the authority to set the tax rates in the state, at a time when tax increases on railroads were being much discussed.

So overwhelming was the Fusion victory, despite the exertions for the Republicans by the great Mark Hanna himself, that the Fusion group was guaranteed control of the state senate in 1905, when Stewart's term would be over. Stewart, therefore, was forced into retirement, the last remnant of the old railroad power.[42] With the death of Black Wallace, the election of Newlands, and the retirement of Stewart, the railroad era in Nevada politics came to an end.

The influence, however, lingered on. Stewart's successor was George S. Nixon, a close associate of Newlands in the fight against Wallace and the S. P. Political Bureau. By the time of Nixon's election, according to Newlands, the S. P. had long since disbanded its Nevada apparatus, under pressure from the Fusionists. "The Southern Pacific Co.," he wrote, "took us at our word, withdrew their political managers and lobbyists, and the result has been that under the last six years of Democratic administration we have had the cleanest government that has ever existed in Nevada, legislative lobbying being entirely done away with."[43] Newlands added, however, and not entirely without incongruity, that Nixon "is State Agent for the Southern Pacific Co. and represents them in all matters of taxation and in a quiet way in matters of legislation." The S. P. evidently did not cease being politically active altogether in Nevada with the transfer of ownership from Huntington to Harriman.

VI

Money had always made the mare go in Nevada politics, partly because of the large number of needy local newspapers which had to be appeased during political campaigns and, in some cases, sustained permanently by the political parties. It was not possible to support one or two large papers with statewide circulations, for no such newspapers existed. By 1881 ninety-one newspapers had been established in Nevada, of which twenty-eight were currently in circulation, nineteen of them dailies with a total circulation of 16,385, or an average of slightly more than 850. At the average subscription price of $10, the income aside from advertising would have been $8,500 annually, out of which the compositor was paid $50 per week and the reporters $50 per week or more.[44] These figures explain the high mortality rate of Nevada newspapers, but they do not explain the successful exceptions.

There were many stories of the great financial success of some of these newspapers, but these stories can easily be disbelieved. The Comstock editor Wells Drury, who should have been in a good position to know, remembered that the famous *Territorial Enterprise*, during the flush days of the Comstock, had earned a clear profit of $1,000 a day;[45] yet the owner sold out during that period for $50,000 to persons who valued it for its political rather than its financial value.[46] In 1882 Yerington, who acted as the representative of the Bank Crowd and the Bonanza Firm publishers, estimated the total value of the *Enterprise* to be less than $7,000, at a time when it was still considered the most successful and influential paper in the state.[47]

Everybody is familiar with the stereotype in Western lore of the fearless crusading printer-editor, who arrives in town with his type and other simple equipment and defies the corrupt cattle baron. Sad to say, no editor in the journalistic history of early Nevada appears to have fit this description. Most were fearless to a degree; for their writings opened them to the threat of duels and canings. All of them were crusaders; for that was the style of the day, but they crusaded for profit. If one Nevada newspaperman could be singled out as the prototype of the Western newspaper hero, it would probably be Rollin M. Daggett—even though he was five feet eight, weighed 200 pounds, and waddled.

Daggett was the most eloquent and scholarly critic of the Central Pacific Railroad among Nevada newspapermen, and he entered politics on this issue, winning one term in Congress. He was, according to Wells Drury, "The Cyrano de Bergerac of Comstock journalism."[48] Yet he does not appear ever to have taken himself seriously as a crusader. To another colleague he laid down this principle concerning his crusading: "When you become wiser—I should hate to wait for the time—you will learn that there come times in men's lives when it is duty to assume a virtue, though they have it not." That colleague, who admired Daggett greatly, later remembered that "his character from a Christian standpoint, was a good deal shopworn in spots."[49]

Where Daggett crusaded for pleasure, other editors crusaded for pay. Denis McCarthy, a colleague of Daggett's on the *Enterprise*, later established his own rival paper, the Virginia City *Chronicle*, which lashed out at the railroad interests fairly often. In 1881, after a series of denunciations of the V. & T. Railroad, McCarthy was offered $100 per month for six months by Yerington "to keep his hands off us. Told him . . . the only result of his war on us would be to urge on a lot of harpies & blackmailers to rob us if they could. . . ." He added:

> He said this was all true but his action agst us sold his papers largely and he believed it would also help the Democratic party two years later. . . . He said he must refuse any monthly stipend—wanted to sell his paper, or half of it, finally said his offer was to take $12500—for ½ of the paper, he to manage it but we to dictate its course so far as our interests were concerned. . . .[50]

Yerington suggested to Mills that "we can save money by closing with McCarty (sic), and with him out of our way think a very small sum will see us safely thro the session." With the "warm approval" of S. J. Gage of the Southern

Pacific, Yerington made some kind of settlement with McCarthy, involving a profit to the editor of $5,000. Yerington was able to write Mills two weeks later:

> I enclose McCarty's editorial on our statement. You see he is living right up to his agreement made with me. I assure you its helping us wonderfully.[51]

"Working on the railroad" appears to have been a relatively profitable practice for Nevada newspapers; as the railroad monopoly, easily disturbed by the little papers and their editorials, was happy to pay. When the Central Pacific government debt was under discussion in Congress in 1876, Huntington pointed out to Hopkins that "it would help us very much if the press of Cal., Nevada and Utah would come out and advocate the Government taking the lands back [in exchange for the debt]. . . . I think you better pay $50,000 to the press than not to have such aid."[52]

Western newspapers saw as much profit in blackmailing rich individuals as in blackmailing rich corporations. "The San Francisco newspapers of the '70's," commented the *Alta California* in 1877, "were brilliantly edited, but, with the exception of the *Alta*, were specializing in self-righteous attacks upon individuals, politicians and corporatons. Enterprising men lived in terror. Blackmail was rampant."[53] The *Alta*'s exception of itself from the rule appears to have been no more than the truth; for the *Alta* had been consistently the most reliable newspaper on the Coast.

At the time the *Alta* made its comment, the San Francisco *Chronicle* was launched upon a full-scale attack against the Bonanza Firm, for the purpose, according to members of the Firm, of being bought off with blackmail money. According to James Flood, Charles de Young, editor of the *Chronicle*, had lost thousands of dollars in a bear attack on Consolidated Virginia stock in the summer of 1876. Until that point, the

Chronicle, the leading newspaper on the Coast, had been fulsome in its praise of the Bonanza Crowd and their operations. Thereafter, it hounded the Crowd for years with unremitting violence:

THE BONANZA KINGS
THEIR SPLENDOR THRONED ON HUMAN MISERY
ROLLING IN WEALTH WRUNG FROM RUINED THOUSANDS
CALIFORNIA AND NEVADA IMPOVERISHED TO ENRICH FOUR MEN
PLAIN HISTORY OF SWINDLING PERPETRATED ON A GIGANTIC SCALE
COLOSSAL MONEY POWER THAT MENACES PACIFIC COAST PROPERTY[54]

The Bonanza Crowd, the least guilty of unfair practices of any important group connected with the Comstock, continued to suffer these abuses rather than to pay de Young the amount he had allegedly demanded, which was sufficient to cover his losses.

Blackmail might be richly rewarding on occasion, but in Nevada, political patronage remained the bread and butter of journalism. With the population dispersed about the state in widely separated hamlets, each served by its own local press, the problem of currying state-wide press support was a constant, exasperating, and expensive one for the main political parties and the wealthy candidates. In 1912 there were thirty-six newspapers in the state, including two in Reno, two in Carson, and presumably two in every other sizeable community, each generally paired off Democratic and Republican. Among these, fifteen were officially listed as Democratic and sixteen as Republican, and probably all expected to be paid for their allegiance or to go out of business.[55]

There was, of course, constant haggling between editor and patron, with results generally satisfactory to neither. For either major political party to keep fifteen to twenty newspapers going was a dreadful burden, and the amounts reluctantly doled out were correspondingly meager for the editors. During the political dry season, newspapers tended to go out of business, to await the rains of a new political campaign. Thus Yerington wrote Mills of one such seasonal editor, that he "now wishes to start up his paper again, and he will do all that is possible for your interests." He continued:

> Seeing that his is the only Republican paper of any standing out East it does seem to me that he should be assisted. He wants to borrow $1500. He expects the Repub Central Committee to pay him from 12 to $1500 this fall for services. . . . He also says Mr. Sharon said he would advance half of the $1500.[56]

During campaign time, skilled reinforcements were sometimes brought in from the Coast to give new life to dormant papers. During Fair's campaign for the Senate on the Democratic ticket in 1886, Yerington wrote Mills: "Yesterday a.m. that fellow McEwen, that used to be on the Va Chronicle with McCarthy & fought us as hard, came up from San Fran to take charge of the 'Chronicle,' and as a test of his writing you have in the inclosed slip taken from last evenings paper."[57] Against Fair's money, Yerington could obviously do nothing here, but wherever the opportunity knocked in the newspaper world, he opened the door.

For the Comstock Lode, the days of glory were over by 1881, and the golden days of Comstock journalism—of Mark Twain, Dan De Quille, Rollin M. Daggett, Joe Goodman, and Sam P. Davis—could not long continue after that. This era came officially to a close with the discontinuation of the *Territorial Enterprise* in 1893. The literary quality of Nevada journalism declined as a consequence, but, politically and economically, no change whatever took place. As the twentieth century opened with the discoveries of bonanzas in Tonopah and Goldfield, the old need was felt by new economic and political groupings. "It is almost essential," United States Senator Key Pittman of Tonopah wrote one of his brothers in 1916, "that I have a daily press in Tonopah during the campaign. . . . Booth's paper, of course, is already subsidized by Sam Platt and the National Republican Committee. Garside seems to be on the fence. I think he is looking for support from some source. . . .[58] It was the literary age only that was over in Nevada journalism. The bought press continued as before, one for each party, in each Nevada town, its rhetoric now almost as barren as the hills of Tonopah, from which the new powers emerged.

CHAPTER V

The Rise of Nevadaism

I

Politically, nineteenth-century Nevada had permitted itself to be used as an agency of the Southern Pacific Railroad, and as the plaything of San Francisco nabobs. Economically, Nevada had provided a rich treasure house which San Franciscans had robbed to build mansions on Nob Hill. Not content with that, those San Franciscans who controlled the Central Pacific Railroad had systematically smothered economic development in the state through rate discrimination. They had not needed to sow the soil with salt; for nature had anticipated them there. They had, however, so regulated the freight rates on salt, as well as on soda, lime, and sulphur, that Nevadans had been unable to profit from the meager resources which had been left to them.

By the close of the nineteenth century, there came of age a generation of native Nevadans, sired and reared in the "Battle-Born State," as it came increasingly to be called in proud reference to its patriotic Civil War origins. These native sons were determined to free themselves from carpetbag rule and to assert their sovereignty. As yet they were too few to think of limiting political office to themselves, and it was not until 1932, with the election of Pat McCarran, that Nevada could boast a United States senator who had been born on Nevada soil. Nevertheless, those, like Francis G. Newlands and Key Pittman, who had established residence in Nevada for political purposes, were obliged to become real Nevadans, or lose office. There were to be no more Stewarts and Joneses, not to speak of Sharons and Fairs. This was a reaction which was experienced in most Western states having small populations.

Nevada at the turn of the century was a subject for discussion in periodicals as the rotten borough of the nation, which should never have been admitted to the Union. There was even discussion as to whether a state, once in the Union, could constitutionally be put out of it when it became depopulated. The effect of this discussion upon native Nevadans can readily be imagined. They became fiercely assertive concerning their state sovereignty, the more so, since the paucity of their population gave them a personal experience of sovereignty which was lacking in the populous states.

Nevada politics in the twentieth century down to World War II had a town-meeting air about it. Had not the expanse of the state prohibited it, all of the voters could have assembled conveniently on the beautiful lawn of the state-university campus at Reno and there argued out their affairs and selected their public officers. Once the Southern Pacific Political Bureau dismantled itself, Nevada politics became smalltownish and gossipy. Key Pittman boasted that he knew almost every one of his constituents personally, and he could not have doubted that his constituents in turn knew all about him.

Nevadans were attracted to politics by the unusual opportunities for political participation. There were the same county and state central committees for the political parties that existed in other states and the same public offices, but the number of political participants was few. Nevadans, consequently, lived their political lives in a way that was not to be conceived of in the large states. This helped give them a sense of citizenship that was unexcelled in the nation.

The hero and the spokesman and, for many Nevadans, the apotheosis of this twentieth-century Nevada spirit was Senator Pat McCarran, standing forth in the name of Americanism against Communist subversion from within and invasion by aliens from without. In Nevada's hagiology, McCarran stands with John W. Mackay and no third person; for he personified citizenship as the concept had been enlarged by Nevada's peculiar circumstances.

As the twentieth century opened, the rich gold and silver strikes at Goldfield and Tonopah gave Nevadans a chance at last to achieve a measure of economic independence from San Francisco, and they took full advantage of it. After having been grievously gulled by mining-stock promoters for more than a generation, San Franciscans left the new mining companies comparatively alone. Eastern interests entered the area, avidly, but they did not win the lion's share of the profits. Nevadans got there first and they were the ones who made the most money. Far fewer millions were taken from Tonopah and Goldfield and lesser producers in the region such as Bullfrog than had been culled from the incomparable Comstock. The Tonopah and Goldfield earnings, however, remained in the state, to build up a monolithic economic power of which all Nevadans could be proud; for it was controlled by the Nevadans George Wingfield and George S. Nixon.[1]

Tonopah did much to emancipate Nevada politically as well. Withdrawal of the Southern Pacific from Nevada politics, taking place at the time of the new discoveries, created a vacuum into which anything might have rushed. Aside from the railroad, the only economic interest in the state of any considerable importance was the livestock industry, which was largely absentee-owned. The best guess is that, except for the new bonanzas, Nevada's political destinies would have been determined by Nevada cattle corporations, united by common interests, whether they were in San Francisco or New York. This possibility was obviated by Jim Butler's discovery of gold and silver in west-central Nevada. A rich home-owned industry, Tonopah mining, came into being and provided an economic basis for home rule. During the next half century, nearly every nationally important political figure in the state was a man from Tonopah.

II

Tonopah, more desolate than the Comstock and more than sixty miles from the nearest railroad, was come upon by Mr. and Mrs. Jim Butler. According to Butler's account of the discovery, he picked up a rock to throw at a mule and found it to be a piece of ore-bearing quartz. The outcropping from which it had originated was found nearby. Returning to the nearest point of settlement, Butler offered a representative of some New York investigators, Tasker L. Oddie, half interest, if Oddie would make an assay of the minerals. Oddie, in his turn, gave half of his interest to Walter Gayhart for an assay, which proved the samples to be very rich in both gold and silver. Accordingly, in August 1900, the Butlers located the Desert Queen mine for themselves and the Burro mine for Oddie. Butler, Oddie, and a third associate realized $800 on their first load of ore, and they knew that they were on the top of a bonanza.[2]

News of the find brought a rush of miners, but it stirred remarkably little interest among those Comstockers who had the money as well as the experience to make the best of the new mines. Yerington wrote to Mills, who apparently wanted nothing to do with the new mines, that, "San Francisco and Virginia City operators have no faith in its stocks and take very little interest in them." He found that hard to understand, in view of the millions in sight, but he conceded that that was the way it was.[3]

The field was thus left to poor men, who staked out dozens of claims, without having the means to develop them. The result was a leasing system, in which companies equipped to undertake quartz-mining operations rented claims for periods of three months or six months and worked them as fast as possible. All of this was done, originally, without written agreements and without anything like the tangle of litigation which had accompanied the Comstock development. The happy lessors drew a royalty of from 22 to 30 per cent on the gross production.[4]

Comstockers and San Franciscans wrongly judged the richness of the new mining region and rightly judged the character of most of the new mining companies, and for those reasons many stayed out. As in the case of the Comstock frenzy, innumerable companies were formed purely for speculative purposes, with no intention of uncovering precious ore. The standard procedure was explained by a broker, who had had a good deal of experience in the business, "not always to my benefit, morally or financially!"

> The trouble with most of the recent flotation is that the capitalization is too large, and the promotion stock is altogether out of proportion to the Treasury stock. A Company is organized usually for a Million in a million shares of $1. par value each, of which anywhere from 500,000 to 750,000 shares is "promotional stock" ostensibly paid for the claims and expenses of organization, but which represents an actual cost to the "promoters" of a cent or two, to in some instances a very small fraction of a cent per share. Then if a Broker tries to handle a portion of the Treasury stock, say

> 50,000 shares, and by hard work manages to make a market for some of it—any moment he is liable to be swamped and his market knocked into a cocked hat by blocks of promotion stock coming on the market from parties who cannot resist the temptation to "take their profits."[5]

One other comparatively scrupulous businessman wrote to the head of the Western Mining Company, which had, as yet, not acquired any mining property, that it would cost the company about $80 to incorporate, but "I don't want to incorporate this Company and spend this money if there is no such company in existence."[6] By 1910 there had been two hundred companies established to operate mines in Goldfield alone, representing an investment of about $30 million. About $40 million worth of ore had been taken out, but not, in most cases, to the profit of the investors.[7]

Eastern financiers who plunged profitably into Tonopah and Goldfield ventures included Charles M. Schwab, Bernard Baruch, Frederick Augustus Heinze, John W. Brock, W. A. Clark, and the Guggenheims.[8] Among these, the Guggenheims fared best in Nevada mining, but in copper at Ely rather than in gold and silver at Tonopah.[9] Eastern interests were at the same time taking possession of the Comstock mines.[10] Brock, of Philadelphia, with Oddie as manager, organized the Tonopah-Goldfield Railroad. Completed in 1904, that road was immediately profitable, as the V. & T. had been before it, paying dividends of 27 per cent in its first year.[11]

Some of these Easterners, such as the Guggenheims, with their copper mines, retained large economic holdings in Nevada long after the gold and silver mines were largely worked out. Others, like Baruch, continued their interest in Nevada politics. For most, however, it appears to have been a temporary money-making—or losing—venture, which never much involved them in Nevada's political affairs. Furthermore, the bankers' panic of 1907 was the occasion for a sharp decline in interest in Nevada mining on the part of California and New York investors.[12] In the long run, those who benefited most from the new mines were those Nevadans who established a new economic and political order on that basis.

The big winner in Tonopah-Goldfield, and the richest and politically perhaps most powerful man in the state for a generation thereafter, was George Wingfield of Winnemucca. Arriving nearly penniless in Tonopah in 1902, Wingfield worked as a dealer in the Tonopah Club. The $2,200 he won at faro gave him the capital to organize the gambling concession of the club, in partnership with another man. Gambling profits of $200,000 annually for the next few years gave Wingfield the capital he used to acquire the richest properties in Goldfield.[13] Having made his stake at the Tonopah Club, Wingfield persuaded the Winnemucca banker, George S. Nixon, to join him, and together they gathered in the largest share of the profits from the mines, which, throughout the region, produced about $250 million in gold and silver.[14]

Nixon had already established himself as the boss of Winnemucca when Wingfield called him to the richer fields of Tonopah-Goldfield. The extent to which he controlled the town was indicated in a letter from the district attorney of Winnemucca, Clarence D. Van Duzer, to Francis Newlands in 1899:

> Mr. Nixon is a cashier in a bank, a stock man, runs a saloon and hotel, has gone into the merchandise business, is an insurance agent, and sells stock, cattle wool etc. on a commission and monkeys with mines. . . .
>
> Nixon is strong and powerful with his friends and a large element who support him because they fear him. He is all powerful in the County and I find myself continually where my duty calls on me to act as I have been taught to act, openly and honestly, in opposition to him. . . .
>
> Nixon is foreman of the Grand Jury now in session. Victor Bouton stole fifty head of cattle and sold them to Thies.

> Thies knew they were stolen cattle yet he bought them and I have proof that Bouton rode Thies horses while doing the stealing. I have six indictments against Bouton. There is strong feeling in this County on the cattle stealing owing to the publicity of it. Yet when it comes to indicting Mr. Thies who is a director of the First National Bank we meet the opposition of Mr. Nixon who naturally desires to protect his friend.[15]

In partnership with the able Nixon, Wingfield, after an initial failure, began to buy the Goldfield properties which were the basis of his great fortune. The main purchases were made in 1906, beginning with $1 million of stock in the Red Top and Jumbo mines, followed by acquisition of the controlling interest in the Mohawk mine. In November 1906, the various holdings were united into the Goldfield Consolidated Mines Company, with the assistance of Bernard Baruch.[16] The company completed its hundred-stamp mill in 1908. For the next decade it remained as the most important gold-producing area of the state, and, with the exception of the Big Bonanza, by far the richest gold and silver-mining property in the history of Nevada. The Goldfield Consolidated Mines Company reached the peak of its production in 1910 with $11,214,278 worth of ore. By the close of 1914, it had grossed $63,568,088 worth, and by the time it closed its mills in 1919, it had paid out $29,177,789 in dividends.[17]

These mining ventures were apparently directed primarily by Wingfield, and Nixon, more experienced in banking than mining, sold his mining holdings to his associate for $3 million. Wingfield went on to acquire virtually all of the important gold and silver mines in the state.[18] Nixon, concentrating on the expansion of his banking interests, took control of banks in Tonopah, Carson City, Reno, and Winnemucca, as well as extensive real estate holdings. At the time of his death in 1912, he was worth an estimated $35 million.[19]

Nixon, long involved in Nevada politics, had a strong desire for a seat in the United States Senate. One of the original founders of the Silver Party in 1892, he had been one of Newlands's closest political associates in the nineties, and they remained allied politically, even after the Silver Party fell apart, although Newlands became a Democrat and Nixon a Republican. With the assistance of Newlands, Nixon made his first bid for the Senate in 1896 against the unbeatable John P. Jones and managed to win only three votes in the legislature.[20] In 1903, when Jones retired, Nixon allowed his much more wealthy friend Newlands to have his turn at the Senate. Then, in 1905, with the retirement of Stewart, the by then very rich Nixon offered his services and his silver to his fellow citizens and won his seat. After serving with that lack of distinction which was traditional among Nevada Senators, he was re-elected in 1910, only to die in 1912.

Upon Nixon's death, Wingfield became the main controller of banking in the state, as well as the owner of hotels, including the Riverside in Reno, cattle ranches, and other properties.[21] Until bankruptcy overtook him during the Great Depression, Wingfield remained the economic, and perhaps the political, overlord of Nevada. He served for years as Republican national committeeman, and after his resignation the position was held by one of his lawyers, Noble Getchell.[22] In addition, another of his lawyers served as Democratic national committeeman.[23] Wingfield, however, was a man without political ambitions in the usual sense: in 1912, when he was appointed to serve out Nixon's term as United States senator, he refused the honor.

Whether Wingfield used the power he possessed systematically and extensively is a baffling question. The most scholarly authority on twentieth-century Nevada history has written that "The real capital of Nevada was Room 201 in the Reno National Bank Building, Wingfield's main office and headquarters for his henchmen, the lawyers George B. Thatcher and William Woodburn."[24] This may have been so, but no good evidence has been produced to prove it, and the evidence that is available indicates that it was not the case.

The findings imply that because Wingfield ruled the state economically he was constantly drawn into a world of politics, about which he cared little. Shortly before he received the appointment to the Senate and refused it in 1912, Pittman wrote to a political associate: "I think that George Wingfield has in his mind running for Governor. I do not believe that he is weak enough to be induced to run for the U. S. Senate. . . . While George is not equipped to hold a position as U. S. Senator, there is no doubt that he has considerable executive ability, and would at least make a fine governor."[25]

Pittman was no doubt whistling in the wind; for against Wingfield, he would probably have had a very poor chance of winning the Senate seat. But his condescending attitude toward Wingfield, and toward Wingfield's qualifications for the Senate, is significant. With all of his power and his evident executive ability, Wingfield made no concerted attempt to overawe his fellow Nevadans or to control them politically. George B. Thatcher, a lawyer of his and a leading politician in the state, wrote a friend that Wingfield had never so much as offered suggestions to him regarding his political activities.[26] Both Governor (and later Senator) Tasker L. Oddie and Senator Pittman were closely associated with Wingfield; yet there is nothing in their correspondence to suggest that he ever directed them in any way.

During Wingfield's economic supremacy, a system of "bipartisan politics" operated in Nevada, in which the two main parties traded off political positions, rather than oppose each other in elections. In that period the Senate seats were paired off, one Democratic and one Republican.[27] This typically Nevadan form of bipartisanship has been attributed to Wingfield, but the Democratic Senator Newlands did not see it in that light when he was running for re-election in 1914. According to Newlands, Wingfield's chain of banks had "become a strong political machine undisguisedly using its credits in the interest of the Republican Party," and, in that election, against Newlands.[28]

What appears to have been the case is that Wingfield, trying to mind his own business, was involved in politics in spite of himself, by virtue of his great economic power. He was constantly drawn into politics by those personal friendships and animosities which so often overrode political considerations in a state where everybody knew everybody else and had strong opinions about each of them. It was Pittman's contention that in the senatorial election of 1910,

> George Wingfield was brought into the fight because we insisted upon nominating Sprague for Congress. . . . Before the primary commenced, Wingfield served notice upon Dickerson and myself that if we supported Sprague for the nomination and nominated him he would fight the whole Democratic ticket. . . . I think that we might have sailed through had it not been for Wingfield's fight.[29]

Later, Wingfield, presumably the state's Republican leader, was to become a strong supporter of the Democrat Pittman, for he was uninhibited by party loyalties, which in Nevada did not prevail over personal animosities and friendships on the one hand and over the unifying ideology of Nevadaism on the other.

III

There can be no question that Wingfield's partner, George S. Nixon, with his millions and his moxie, was a fit contender in the hurly-burly of Nevada politics. Nevertheless, in the campaign of 1910 he ran scared against an opponent who, although less rich, was as tough a man as Nevada politics had seen since big Bill Stewart.

Key Pittman, who, after losing narrowly to Nixon in 1910, was to serve Nevada in the United States Senate from 1913 to his death in 1940, was the one really wild man to emerge from Nevada into national and international politics. Raised on a Louisiana plantation and well-educated, Pittman practiced law fretfully until news of the Klondike sent him rushing to Alaska. There, after harrowing and unrewarding times as a sourdough, he gained a reputation and some compensation as a legal adviser. Returning to the States in 1902, he heard of the gold and silver strikes at Tonopah and Goldfield, and he went there at once.[30]

Pittman arrived in Tonopah with the reputation of being an effective mining lawyer. The area did not provide him with the rich legal opportunities that the Comstock had offered William M. Stewart, but, given those he had, Pittman quickly became the Stewart of Tonopah, sought out as counselor by all of the leading mine companies. He also became an officer in many companies associated with the Tonopah-Goldfield region, and, unlike Stewart, he profited well from his mining speculations. By 1904 he was a fairly wealthy man, a stockholder in many mining companies and a director on the boards of more than a hundred mining, banking, and utility companies.

A skillful and tireless lawyer, Pittman was also a hopeless drunkard with homocidal tendencies. Concerning this weakness, he wrote his wife:

> I was and have been for years a periodical drunkard. . . . For months my mind worked ceaselessly, with feverish energy—. . . . Then came the reaction. . . . All of the savage in me asserted itself in me—I longed for, and nothing satisfied me but, the most intense excitement—I longed to murder kill and howle with delight at the sound of death dealing

> instruments and the sight of human blood. . . . It was a mental disease strong and terrible.[31]

Pittman owned a silver six-shooter, which he usually carried with him. In later years, when he was chairman of the Senate Foreign Relations Committee, he would go on sustained drinking sprees in Washington, and when he was refused service by bars and restaurants, he would whip out his pistol and threaten to shoot up the place. His wife, Mimosa, would be summoned to administer coffee to him; she was the only person who had influence over him. During his later years, it appears that he was rarely entirely sober.[32]

At the time of his coming to Nevada, Pittman's creative energy overcame his drunkenness, and he was moved by dreams of political power, in a state where carpetbag politics still offered opportunities to new arrivals as well as to old settlers. "I am thinking of making our home in Nevada," he wrote his wife shortly after his arrival, "and growing up with the country. I see many opportunities here both in law, mines and politics. I feel very confident that I will be employed in most of the large suits and the boys are even now talking of running me for the legislature."[33]

Several months later he won appointment to the state central committee of the Silver Party, and he wrote a fellow member: "I am a new comer and may seem presumptuous but I assure you that I take the greatest interest in the Silver Cause, and firmly believe that it is a subject of more interest to the people of the State of Nevada and every poor man in the United States than any other question of Public Policy."[34]

To another committeeman he wrote: "Although I am a tenderfoot in your midst, I intend to make Nevada my home, and naturally feel as every other good citizen a great interest in the politics of our State. . . . I think we should take immediate steps to organize a County Central Committee, similar to that recently organized by the Democratic Party. . . ."[35] The county committee was thereupon organized with Pittman as its chairman. In 1904, with his eyes fixed steadily on the United States Senate seat, Pittman quit the disintegrating Silver Party and became a Democrat.

That same year Pittman's former associate in the Silver Party, George Nixon, was running for the Senate on the Republican ticket, and Pittman was as yet in no position to take on such an opponent. In 1908 Pittman's fellow Democrat, Senator Newlands, was a candidate for that office, and Pittman waited. In 1910 Senator Nixon came up for re-election, and Pittman made his play. What followed was the roughest election which Nevada had seen since the Newlands-Stewart fracas of 1898.

The Nevada Democratic Party has had a considerable advantage over the Republican throughout the twentieth century, in terms of the stated affiliation of the voters, but this has not been much reflected in the senatorial contests, for the people have cast their ballots, not so much for the party as for the man and the money. As Pittman, himself, expressed it, "By reason of our small vote and the transient character of some of our people, money is very influential in elections."[36] By 1910 Pittman had accumulated a good deal of money, but his wealth did not compare to Nixon's and he lost the election.

Pittman won the Democratic nomination for Senator at the poker table, according to his account. On the night of the famous Johnson-Jeffries fight, staged in Reno by Tex Rickard, Pittman won $5,000 against other members of the Democratic State Central Committee. Already clearly eligible for the nomination, he pushed his easy money across the table and offered it for what he wanted and closed the deal.[37] Thereafter the campaign against the rich and influential Nixon provided greater difficulties.

Pittman campaigned primarily on the argument that he represented the poor men of the state against the so-called money power. In a letter, he declared:

> I defended 500 miners for trespassing on the rich beach sands [in Alaska] and cleared them. I was one of the attorneys that prosecuted the gang of robbers in Alaska described by Rex Beach in "The Spoilers." . . . I am a poor man but have a lucrative law practice. . . . I have never before sought an election to any office.[38]

Running on a platform of progressive reform, he wrote: "I am satisfied that this year will witness a fight to a finish in this state . . . against the money and corrupt influences of Nixon and the Southern Pacific Railroad. . . ." Pittman asserted that Nixon personally spent more than $250,000 on the election and that the Southern Pacific, with which Nixon had long been associated, gave an equal amount. So far as the voters were concerned, Pittman wrote, "It was simply $5 before and $10 after election if Nixon won."[39] It may be doubted whether the S. P. involved itself in the election to the extent of contributing large amounts of money; for there is no good evidence to indicate that it participated actively in Nevada politics following its acquisition by the Harriman interests. It is also doubtful whether Nixon was obliged to spend the amount alleged by Pittman, since, at the rate per vote which Pittman quoted, Nixon could have bought his election for a fraction of the amount cited by him.

Nixon clearly had the advantage in money, however, and he also had Wingfield's backing. Pittman complained that "the Consolidated is constantly discharging men so as to disqualify them from voting at the coming primaries. I think there will be very few miners voting in Goldfield; they will be driven out of Goldfield and will not reside in other precincts long enough to vote."[40] If Wingfield and Nixon actually employed this drastic tactic, the results did not justify it;

for the miners, now protected by the secret ballot, failed to rally to the support of the poor man's candidate. "The railroad men and the miners both went back on me," Pittman wrote after the election, ". . . the great body of men either did not understand or, if they did understand, were too dishonest to follow the dictates of their consciences."[41] Pittman lost, in 1910, by about 600 votes.

Two years later, Nixon's death and Wingfield's refusal to fill out the term finally offered Pittman the opportunity to become a senator. In 1912 the Progressive movement, with which Nevadans were well acquainted, reached a crest. Pittman ran against William A. Massey, who had been temporarily appointed to the post following Wingfield's refusal, and campaigned on a platform advocating the Progressive principles of Woodrow Wilson, the Democratic presidential candidate. Two years earlier—Progressive even then—he had challenged Nixon to accept the results of the popular vote, even though constitutionally, the legislature was still empowered to select the senator. That had proved the wrong course for him to take; for the Democrats won control of the legislature, and Nixon won the majority of the votes. In 1912, Massey, in his turn, challenged Pittman to accept the suffrages of the people, and on that basis Massey went down to defeat by a narrow margin.[42]

It had been a hard fight for Pittman, but once he was in the Senate, he made himself into an invincible candidate.[43] His continued success during five subsequent campaigns was due mainly to the fact that, as United States senator, he was an unremitting advocate of Nevada and of Nevadans, introducing in a single session thirty-five bills that would aid his state and his people.[44] A self-willed man who, as he grew older, became a confirmed drunkard and more and more irascible, he went his own way in political campaigns against the advice of his political lieutenants, and he always won handily.

In 1928, in the face of Alfred E. Smith's obvious unpopularity in Nevada, Pittman tied his own campaign to the cause of Smith's election and paid newspapers for political advertisements consisting of pictures of himself and Smith. Smith was overwhelmingly defeated in the state, and Pittman won by a landslide. Mortally ill during his final campaign in 1940, Pittman remained dead drunk during the last weeks of his political fight and entered Washoe Hospital four days before the election. Once again he won handsomely against his perennial Republican opponent, the native-born Sam Platt, but he died a few days later.[45]

Although the Republican Wingfield had fought the Democrat Pittman during the latter's first campaign against Wingfield's partner, Nixon, Pittman appears in time to have been admitted to the Wingfield machine, if there was such a thing. "Wingfield dropped into the office this morning," William Woodburn wrote Pittman in 1922, "and told me that he felt that you were as good as elected, and that any report to the contrary, he proposed not doing a single thing against you; that hundreds of Republicans had told him they were going to support you, and that he said nothing which would make them change their minds."[46] Wingfield's lieutenant, Woodburn had been, and continued to be, one of Pittman's most active supporters.

Woodburn, who must, himself, have nursed hopes of a senatorial seat over a period of several generations, was a key figure in Nevada politics during the first half of the twentieth century. He was a native son, and the son of a Nevada congressman. While studying for the bar in 1906, he was on close terms with Senator Newlands,[47] and thereafter, so far as the great men of Nevada business and politics were concerned, he always pleased. "The appointment of Woodburn for U. S. District Attorney," Sam Davis wrote Pittman in 1915, "gave the best of satisfaction with almost everybody."[48] Woodburn remained Wingfield's right bower, and he brought

Wingfield into Pittman's camp. When Pittman was running for re-election in 1922, Wingfield resigned from the position of Republican National Committeeman, at Woodburn's insistence, rather than embarrass Pittman.[49]

Pittman, for his part, reciprocated, although it was a long time before he was able to do so. Following his election in 1912, when he had espoused Wilsonian Progressivism, Pittman had been amply rewarded by federal patronage.[50] Then, following the dry Republican spell of the twenties, Pittman had strongly supported Franklin D. Roosevelt, but the expected patronage had not been forthcoming. The main federal dispenser of patronage for Nevada was the Secretary of the Interior, Harold L. Ickes, an ostentatiously honest man. He wrote Pittman: "I am the dictator of patronage and I shall continue to be so long as I am head of this Department."[51] Despairing of Ickes, Pittman appealed to the more politic President, and Roosevelt told him to "dig up the names of one or two really first-class men." Faced with this first good opportunity for patronage, Pittman advanced the names of two Wingfield associates, Frank H. Norcross and William Woodburn, who were each given judicial positions.

By the time of Roosevelt's election, Pittman had been in the Senate for twenty years, and he was therefore in possession of the great powers which senators accumulate in the course of long tenure in office. In 1916, he had succeeded in winning an appointment to the Foreign Relations Committee, not because he was interested in foreign affairs, but because he believed that membership on some major Senate committee would redound to his political advantage at home in Nevada.[52] He continued to be re-elected to the upper house for a sufficient number of times to become chairman of the Foreign Relations Committee, when the Roosevelt landslide in 1932 brought the Democrats into control of the Senate.

From the rise of Hitler, through the Spanish Revolution,

the conquest of Ethiopia, the invasion of China, the Anschluss of Austria, the decision at Munich, the invasion of Poland, and the Nazi conquest of Western Europe, Key Pittman held the post in American government which, in foreign affairs, is third in importance to those of the President and the Secretary of State. Diplomacy had never impinged much upon his thinking, and he had generally taken an active part in committee work only where the interests of Nevada were concerned, as in the case of international regulations concerning silver. The duties involved in the chairmanship of this essentially non-Nevadan committee unnerved him. His drinking sprees became more frequent and of longer duration, and he had a liquor cabinet installed in the committee chamber.[53]

Upon Pittman's death, his beautiful and long-suffering wife, Mimosa, was asked to write a summary evaluation of his career. The erasures and crossings-out on the document she produced attest to the earnestness with which she approached the assignment. Her final version read: "Key loved our State and its people."[54] It had been Senator Pittman's destiny to become the first international spokesman for Nevadaism.

IV

A signal triumph of Nevadaism came with the advent of Tasker L. Oddie to the United States Senate; for Oddie had been one of the first men in Tonopah and he was actually a poor man when he ran for the Senate. During the early years of Tonopah, he had accumulated a sizable fortune, but it had been wiped out in the panic of 1907, leaving him with a good many small debts, which became the bane of his existence.[55] In 1910, without funds, Oddie ran for governor and won, aided by small contributions sufficient to pay for his food and for gasoline.[56]

Oddie ran against a Democratic incumbent who had made a good reputation for himself. As an Oddie supporter, wrote him: "You are running in a democratic State and in a democratic year against a man who has proved himself a good governor and is mighty close to the hearts of a lot of voters. . . . If the party carries anything in the State it will be largely due to the fact that your name heads the ticket."[57] Oddie won, probably on the basis of his name, which was intimately associated with the new prosperity of the state, derived from the Tonopah-Goldfield gold and silver strikes.

Oddie's tour of duty in the state house is testimony either to his incorruptibility or to the insignificance of the governorship, for he left office as poor as he had been when he entered it, and while in office he was subjected without letup to dunnings from various creditors. "Our means for collections are most effectual and somewhat annoying," wrote one collection agency, "and we trust you will save us the necessity of crowding you. . . ." Another wrote: "You have frequently written us that you were going to do something when you got on your feet, and that was six years ago. Surely it is not possible that in six years you have not made a fortune. . . ."[58] It was possible, even for the governor of a state. "I note what you say about 50¢ pieces," Governor Oddie wrote a friend. "They are scarcer than hen's teeth with me just now and look bigger than the Pacific Ocean, but I am looking forward to getting hold of a good mine some day soon which will bring in barrels of them. I have a hunch that I will soon have one, but do not know where it will be or when it will materialize."[59]

There is no indication in the Oddie correspondence that he ever thought to use his political position to rescue himself from his economic misfortune. Oddie and the prodigiously wealthy Wingfield had been fairly closely associated during the early days of Tonopah and Goldfield, and they corresponded occasionally during Oddie's career as governor. Nowhere in this correspondence does it appear that Oddie thought of wringing something from his wealthy friend in exchange for a political favor, and nowhere does it appear that Oddie felt obliged to do Wingfield's bidding. Oddie made some of the appointments that Wingfield urged, but he declined to make others, and in the friendly exchange between the two men there is no evidence that the rich Wingfield felt himself in a position to command Oddie.

In 1920 Oddie ran successfully for the United States Senate, and in 1926 he was re-elected. Apparently he never found that rich mine for which he had been continuously searching, but homey Nevada of the early twentieth century took this honest Tonopah boy to its heart and gave him a position which would pay a good living wage.

V

Probably little was expected of Oddie in the Senate, and his career was an uneventful one, but that could not be said of his successor, Pat McCarran. McCarran had worked longer and harder for the office than had any other senator from Nevada, and he was determined to make more of it than any of his predecessors. Through his statesmanship Nevada became a formative influence upon the nation and later the world. To this end he worked tirelessly to consolidate his position in the state, and with the death of Pittman in 1940, he became its unrivaled spokesman.

The statesmanship of McCarran has to be understood within the context of his early career in Nevada, where for many years he was not liked and was not given the senatorial position he thought himself entitled to. McCarran, a native Nevadan, was born on a ranch near Reno in 1876. He received his law degree from the University of Nevada and entered the state legislature in 1903. He was district attorney of Nye County—which is to say Tonopah—from 1906 to 1908. He was thereafter elevated to the state supreme court, of which he became chief justice in 1917.[60] But all of that time, his primary objective was the United States Senate.

McCarran was obliged to sit it out for a whole generation, so far as his Senate seat was concerned, because the other men from Tonopah did not like him. He was active on behalf of his own future Democratic candidacy as early as 1904, and he attempted to gain control of the state senate. But, according to Pittman, "McCarran has no strength because his reputation as a double-crosser is too well established throughout the State."[61]

In 1916, when he was forty years old, McCarran came out in the Democratic primaries against Key Pittman and forced a rupture in the dominant Democratic Party which lasted until after Pittman's death. Pittman declared that he would fight McCarran "now as well as for every nomination that he ever seeks."[62] Pittman beat McCarran with no trouble, vigorously supported by what was known as the Wingfield machine. Before the primaries, George Bartlett, a lawyer employed by Wingfield, wrote W. H. Metson: "Believe me, Billy, I have never been more earnest in the accomplishment of anything than I am in the election of Pittman to the Senate."[63]

McCarran bided his time a while longer, and after losing the nomination once more in 1926, he won it finally in 1932 and ran against Oddie. Normally he would not have had a fighting chance, but voters that year were largely Democratic throughout the nation, and Nevadans responded accordingly. McCarran beat Oddie, and—at the age of fifty-seven—he at long last entered the Senate chambers. There he suffered under the continued hostility of Pittman, who wrote Woodburn in 1933: "If they give me a factional fight in my own party . . . I am going to attempt to wipe the whole damn bunch out when I get in here, wipe them out politically."[64]

The collapse of the Wingfield fortunes may have made McCarran's rise to power possible. In 1929 Wingfield held the controlling interest in twelve banks, located at Reno, Carson City, Sparks, Fallon, Virginia City, Tonopah, and Elko. He owned the Reno Securities Company, which in turn owned the Golden Hotel and the Riverside, the two main hotels in Reno, as well as other real estate holdings. He was also extensively involved in ranching and, of course, in mining. Then, with the depression, his banks all closed in 1932 and remained closed, his assets were sold, and he was left, according to his own statement, in possession of a Packard car, membership in the Cohisa Duck Club, and nothing else. Wingfield later managed to recover to some extent economically, but his days of power were over.[65]

Pittman's power was not at an end, however, and he and his fellow Democrat McCarran fought it out until Pittman's death in 1940. In the final days of Pittman's campaign for re-election in 1934, an anonymous article was circulated in which Pittman was accused of being a nabob in the pay of the Wall Street interests. He thought it written by McCarran.[66] In 1940, during Pittman's own campaign for re-election, Pittman was "certain that McCarran's crowd had been doing everything they could to boost Governor Carville for the Senate nomination . . . ,"[67] but by the eve of the primaries, Pittman concluded that McCarran had given up. "McCarran has commenced to realize that there is nothing to be gained by keeping up a fight against me, and that party harmony may be quite necessary in the Democratic Party two years from now and four years from now."[68] One reason that the two men had been able to afford the luxury of such party-destroying factionalism was that the registered Democrats were beginning to outnumber the Republicans in the state almost two to one.

Death did not end the Pittman-McCarran struggle, for in 1944, when McCarran came up for re-election, Pittman's brother, and longtime chief political aide, Vail Pittman, entered the primaries, in what McCarran later described as "really a bitter one, and the nastiest I have ever seen in this section of the country. . . . I was confronted by one of the most vicious smear campaigns that I have ever seen in America—but I was successful, and all is well that ends well."[69] He was successful, however, by a rather narrow margin of about 1,500 votes. Vail Pittman went on the next year to settle for the governorship of the state, and McCarran's control over the state thereafter steadily strengthened.

In Nevada, lawyers were probably even more important to the political machinery of the state in the thirties and forties than they were elsewhere in a country that gives the legal profession a predominating political position. In part, the great influence of Nevada lawyers rested upon the unusual legal opportunities that Nevada afforded in divorce cases. In part, however, it was the result of a concerted program begun by Pittman and emulated later by McCarran. To develop some forms of patronage during the New Deal, in the face of the obduracy of Ickes and other New Dealers, Pittman had brought deserving Nevada boys to Washington and found them government jobs to help them work their way through law school.[70] This practice was continued by McCarran and resulted in the recruitment in both parties of loyal followers in the Nevada legal profession.

Out-of-state economic interests had ceased to dominate Nevada politically. McCarran therefore, with Wingfield down and Pittman out, had the state to himself, and he gained prestige among Nevadans such as would never have been anticipated on the basis of his early career. He brought Basque shepherds to his state, to the benefit of a leading industry, and, at the same time, he kept out of the nation ethnic groups which Nevada considered undesirable. To the gratification of

Nevadans, he tackled the Communist menace head on. His had been a discouragingly long wait for the call of the people, but once McCarran won the mandate, he made himself the epitome of Nevadaism.

VI

McCarran's influence and power attained their greatest extent and strength in the years immediately following World War II, although the ideology of Nevadaism was rapidly declining in his home state during that same period. The population of Nevada had grown imperceptibly for generations, and in 1940 it stood at only 110,000. During the next two decades, however, Nevada's population increased proportionately more rapidly than that of any other state in the Union, and in 1960 it stood at 280,000. The increase was accounted for in part by the influx of military personnel and in much larger part by the mushrooming of Nevada's major postwar industry, gambling, and the tourism associated with it.

From the discovery of the Comstock Lode to the beinning of World War II, the center of population of Nevada had shifted only about twelve miles, north from Virginia City to Reno, except for a temporary period during the Tonopah-Goldfield bonanzas. Reno, throughout the party struggles of Pittman and McCarran, was the political center of the state, and it still is today. Since the building of Boulder Dam in 1931, however, Las Vegas has grown rapidly and has long since outdistanced the northern metropolitan area of Carson City, Reno, and Sparks in population. It is largely populated by non-Nevadans, and for that reason it has never been admitted to full participation in Nevada politics. It was chiefly the unwanted burgeoning of Las Vegas which vitiated Nevadaism at the very time when, with McCarran, it was launched nationally upon its crusade to save America.

The decline of Nevadaism was dramatically demonstrated in 1952 by Tom Mechling, a young newspaperman who came to the state and took up residence for the purpose of battling the McCarran machine. He ran his campaign on his savings of $12,000, much of which had been earned by his wife, while working in Washington D. C. as a stenographer for Senator McCarran. He campaigned in the Democratic primaries in the customary way, by shaking hands with every living citizen in the state, and he beat Alan Bible, the McCarran candidate for the junior senatorial seat, by 475 votes.[71]

In the general election he faced George Malone, a true Nevadan, who had been captain of the University of Nevada football team and who would have made small work of Mechling a decade earlier. Mechling, according to his own account, was approached by representatives of McCarran during the campaign and offered his support on the condition that he place himself entirely under the senator's political control. When Mechling refused the bargain, McCarran threw his support to Mechling's Republican opponent, "Molly" Malone. According to Mechling's account, his telephone was tapped, his mail was opened, his speeches were ignored or misreported by the newspapers of the state, and a taped recording was edited in such a way as to distort his words slanderously.[72]

In the election that followed, again as reported by Mechling, the graveyard vote was brought out in force, and Malone won by a majority of 2,722 votes. Las Vegas, however, gave Mechling a plurality of more than 6,000 votes against the combined opposition of the Republican Party and the McCarran machine.[73] In 1954 McCarran's cherubic protégé, Alan Bible, came back to win the seat vacated by McCarran's death, but the old Nevadans who voted for him did not suppose that he would take up the standard of Nevadaism which his dedicated predecessor had held high until death.

After having narrowly staved off defeat from the left in the person of the New Deal "carpetbagger" Tom Mechling, the Nevadaists faced a threat from the right in 1958 from the industrialist carpetbagger Erret L. Cord. Famous principally for his Cord automobile, Cord had settled in Nevada, where he could enjoy one of the world's best climates and pay no state income tax. He had no political practice and apparently no political inclination before he went to Nevada, but he was unable to resist the opportunities that the great rotten borough presented. It was charged that he tried to buy the Democratic Party and that he poured $75,000 into the gubernatorial campaign. This blatantly carpetbagging effort so aroused the old Nevadans that, in a normally Democratic state, Cord's candidate was beaten 20,168 to 13,345 by the Republican opponent.[74] Plainly, Nevadaism is not dead. It is weak, however, and it has yet to show that it can assert itself against the new conquering lords of the state, the nationally organized gambling operators.

CHAPTER VI

Nevada and the Nation

Nevada remains the most egregious result of the original sin, the so-called "Great Compromise,'" which made possible the formation of the Union in the Constitutional Convention of 1787. Meeting in Philadelphia during a typically bad Philadelphia summer, the Convention had nearly reached the end of its rope in the contest between the populous states, such as Virginia and Massachusetts, and the unpopulous ones, such as Delaware and New Jersey. There was general agreement that the lower house should be chosen according to the principle of proportional representation, although William Patterson of New Jersey, leader of the small-state forces, opposed it.[1]

The discussion about the character of the upper house nearly broke up the meeting. Benjamin Franklin wrote: ". . . till this point . . . came before us, our debates were carried on with great coolness and temper."[2] The week that followed was rancorous. Worst of all was the cantankerous delegate from Maryland, Luther Martin, who held forth for two days on the rights of the small states and expressed himself so vehemently and so badly that James Madison, that most competent reporter, found it difficult to record what had been said. Madison is accepted as the father of the Constitution, but he was very far from fathering the Senate, with its equal representation of the states. In the course of the debates, Madison spoke of such an arrangement as being "inadmissible, being evidently unjust," for it violated the principle of proportional representation.[3]

Against a good deal of opposition, a committee was formed made up mostly of small-state advocates—probably through a cloakroom maneuver—which recommended that members of the House of Representatives be elected by the proportional representation system and that senators be elected by the legislatures of the states, two to each state. That was the Great Compromise. It seemed so unreasonable to Madison that he intimated he was willing to accept whatever consequences might follow its rejection. The more stoutly centralist Gouverneur Morris, who was a congenital saber-rattler, declared of things generally that "if persuasion does not unite it, the sword will."[4]

Nevertheless, in the middle of that very hot July, the Great Compromise was accepted by a narrow margin. Voting for it were Connecticut, New Jersey, Delaware, Maryland, and North Carolina. Voting against it were Pennsylvania, Virginia, South Carolina, and Georgia. The vote of Massachusetts was divided; and no vote was cast by New York; by then all members of that delegation had left in disgust. Thus the compromise that made possible the creation of the new nation was narrowly passed.

When it came to defending the compromise in the classic *Federalist* papers, during the ratification fight in New York, the task devolved upon Madison; for his chief co-author, Hamilton, had made that compromise the occasion for his indignant departure from the convention. How awkward the task was for Madison, normally a most clearheaded and lucid arguer, may at once be seen in his convoluted discussion:

> The equality of representation in the senate is another point, which, being evidently the result of compromise between the opposite pretensions of the large and the small states, does not call for much discussion. If indeed it be right that among a people thoroughly incorporated into one nation, every district ought to have a *proportional* share in the government; and that among independent and sovereign states bound together by a simple league, the parties however unequal in size, ought to have an *equal* share in the common councils, it does not appear to be without some reason, that in a compound republic partaking both of the national and federal character, the government ought to be founded on a mixture of the principles of proportional and equal representation. But it is superfluous to try by the standards of theory, a part of the constitution which is allowed on all hands to be the result not of theory, but "of a spirit of amity, and that mutual deference and concession which the peculiarity of our political situation rendered indispensable." . . . The advice of prudence must be, to embrace the lesser evil . . . instead of indulging a fruitless anticipation of the possible mischiefs.[5]

Thomas Jefferson and John Adams were the two men most conspicuous by their absence from the Constitutional Convention. Jefferson was serving the government of the Articles of Confederation as minister to France, and Adams, as minister to England. Each, of course, had his opinion about the Great Compromise. Jefferson was apparently quite unbothered by the violation of the principle of proportional representation. He found the Senate, as it was constituted, to be a "captivating" solution to a difficult problem.[6]

John Adams, on the other hand, took a more orthodox view. Adams argued that if it "is a council, whose character is *wisdom*, there is perfect propriety in the States, large and small, sending the same number of Senators each; but this is a monstrosity when they are, as now, endowed with *power*, which in representatives ought to be proportioned to the power of the represented." It was his recommendation that the power of the Senate be removed and that it operate only in an advisory capacity.[7]

Whatever the merits of Adams's reform, it was not feasible once the Constitution was ratified. With the exception of Rhode Island, which had refused to send delegates, the small states ratified the Constitution as quickly as they could. Delaware was ready to ratify as soon as the Convention had concluded its business, and it was the first state to do so, earning for itself the proud title of the first state in the Union.[8]

The founding fathers contemplated no more for the small states in the Senate than equality with the large states, but the Senate itself, as it worked out its own rules, in practice conferred greater powers upon small-state senators than upon those from the large states. Small-state senators had the advantage of representing relatively few major economic interests. They were therefore in a position to trade votes advantageously, in order to pass the relatively few measures which the interests they represented wanted badly. Furthermore, when their party was in power, they generally commanded more federal patronage, proportionate to the number of their constituents, than did the senators from the large states.

The consequence was that small-state senators were so well equipped for the mending of political fences at home that, once in office, they could reasonably look forward to remaining there for the rest of their lives. In Nevada, no senatorial incumbent has been defeated for re-election since 1889, with the exceptions of the Republican Oddie in the Democratic landslide of 1932 and the Republican Malone in the Democratic year of 1958. Nevada's senators, therefore, have been in the best possible position to reap the unearned benefits that are to be derived from the senatorial seniority system. Once on the committee of his choice, a Nevada senator has only to wait out deaths and defeats to become its chairman, as did McCarran with the Senate Judiciary Committee or Pittman with the Foreign Relations Committee. Much has been written about the power that the seniority system has given in the Senate to the one-party states of the South. It has hardly, however, worked less to the advantage of the relatively unpopulated Western states: the Dakotas, Idaho, Montana, Wyoming, Colorado, Utah, Arizona, New Mexico, and Nevada.

II

In 1864 the Battle-Born State sent Territorial Governor Nye and counselor William M. Stewart forth to Washington, D. C., to guard its equal condition among the sovereign states of the nation. Governor Nye had not had a strong following in Nevada, and, although he served Huntington and the Central Pacific loyally in the upper house, he fell by the wayside in 1872, without having done a great deal either for himself or for his state. It was left to Stewart to make the force of the new state felt on Capitol Hill, and he lost no time doing it. For the mining interests that he represented, there was no time to lose.

The annual report of the Secretary of the Interior appearing on December 5, 1864, declared:

> The attention of Congress has frequently been called to the importance of securing an income to the national treasury from the products of the mines and placers. . . . Congress has taken no legislative action. . . . Sound policy dictates the propriety of levying a revenue tax upon those who are en-

> gaged in gathering individual wealth from this national property. The Bureau of Internal Revenue, recently established in the Department of the Treasury, furnishes a ready and suitable instrumentality for collecting it.[9]

The report recommended a leasing system for the mines and a tax of one per cent upon its products. The Treasury Department, for its part, recommended selling the mining land for thirty dollars per acre, perhaps because it had less faith than the Department of the Interior that its fledgling Bureau of Internal Revenue would ever be able to collect that much.

The mining interests were in a poor legal position to meet these threats; for they were working lands that belonged, not to them but to the federal government. And they were doing so during a great civil war, when many people were calling for sacrifices in the interest of preserving the Union. Only one day after the senators from Nevada were seated, Representative George P. Julian of Indiana, chairman of the House Committee on Public Lands, introduced a bill to subdivide and sell the public lands, including those with minerals. In the Senate, meanwhile, in accordance with the senators' concern for the interests of the states, a Committee on Mines and Mining was created, with Stewart as a member.

Stewart, and the interests he represented, would have been happy to pay about thirty dollars per acre for their Comstock mines, but the placer miners in California found these terms unacceptable. What was frightening Stewart's people, at the time, was the horrendous litigation on the Comstock, with the threat of eviction from premises containing untold millions worth of silver and gold for lack of land title. It was in the defense of these "poor miners" that Stewart concentrated the full force of his energies.

His first good opportunity to secure the mining companies' legal titles came with the Courts Bill, providing for a District and Circuit Court of the United States for the District of

Nevada, which, at the time, was a crying necessity. To the Courts Bill, Stewart offered this amendment: "That in actions respecting mining claims, the customs and regulations of the miners shall be regarded as law, and enforced by the courts of the United States, provided this shall not be so construed as to effect in any wise the right or ownership of the United States to the same."[10]

It might be expected that California, also a mining state, would have agreed with Nevada on the matter of mining legislation, but California was not greatly concerned with quartz mining, and it had not suffered from litigation as Nevada had. Both of the senators from California attacked Stewart's amendment, one of them pointing out the undeniable truth that the district mining laws were "as multifarious, as numerous, as different and as many as there are localities and communities." The California senators simply wanted possessory title, which suited the needs of California mining, and they were given it in the bill.

In 1865, Representative Julian reintroduced his public lands bill, and Senator John Sherman of Ohio followed in the upper house with a similar one. Senators Stewart and Nye were quick to follow in May with a bill, which added rich lands to the state and included an amendment providing "that all possessory rights acquired by citizens of the United States to mining claims, discovered, located and originally recorded in compliance with the rules and regulations adopted by miners in the Pah-Ranagat and other mining districts in the territory . . . shall remain as valid and subsisting mining claims. . . ."[11]

It appeared for a time that Julian would succeed in fending off Stewart when he wrested the companion House measure from the House Committee on Mines and buried it in his Public Lands Committee. The Committee on Mines, however, produced a bill dealing with ditches, and when that bill reached the Senate, Stewart's mining bill was attached to it.

Passed in the Senate, the bill went to the Speaker's table in the House, where it required a majority vote to refer it to the floor. Julian was powerless to organize a majority against a measure which was of no direct concern to most members. The bill passed without amendment as "An Act granting the right of way to ditch and canal owners through the public lands, and for other purposes," and was thereafter referred to as the Mining Law of 1866.

The Mining Law of 1866 provided that mineral lands were open to occupation, "and subject, also, to the local customs or rules of miners in the several mining districts, so far as the same may not be in conflict with the laws of the United States." Upon payment of a patent fee, the locator gained possessory rights to the claim, "together with the right to follow said vein or lode with its dips, angles, and variations to any depth, although it may enter the land adjoining, which land adjoining shall be sold subject to this condition."

The law was amended in 1870 and again in 1872, placing additional valuable metals under its provisions and providing a separate set of laws for placer mines. Henceforth, placer mines would require a square surface location, and the locator would be entitled only to the ore found within that location. Following the adoption of this sensible, centuries-old Spanish mining law, placer mining in the United States remained largely free of litigation over disputed locations.

Quartz mining continued to be plagued by the legal confusions which inevitably arose out of the quaint old provision concerning "dips, angles, and variations." Stewart, by virtue of the states' rights weapon of senatorial courtesy, subsequently defeated efforts to amend the law. It was the later opinion of *Mining and Scientific Press* that the law had "corrupted and debauched lawyers, judges, jurors and legislators, has sent thousands to suicides' graves, has wreaked ruin on thousands of others, and has deterred millions of willing dollars from mining investment."[12] This list of disastrous consequences, rising in crescendo through corruption and suicide to actual loss of potential investments, is marred by hyperbole. Yet it remains the statement of the leading journal of the industry.

Following the triumph of his mining law, Stewart confined his senatorial activities largely to helping out the Southern Pacific Company in a quiet way, and, with his colleague Jones, to fighting for the cause of free silver. He himself, looking back over his long political career, saw as his crowning achievement the fashioning of an enduring national statute, which—however it may have otherwise affected the nation—placed the leading Comstock mines on the right side of the law.

III

Francis G. Newlands, when he took up residence in Reno in 1888 to enter national politics, was cordially welcomed as a generous political gift-bearer in the tradition of his father-in-law, Senator Sharon. A lavish and gracious host in his home on the Truckee, he met, and perhaps exceeded, those expectations; then, going at once to the main point of Nevada politics, he assisted in the organization of the Silver Party.[13] In 1893 he entered the House of Representatives as Nevada's lone congressman, purely on the silver platform, apparently impelled there solely to save humanity by achieving the free coinage of silver at a ratio of 16 to 1 with gold. Newlands continued loyally in the silver crusade until all hope was gone by the turn of the century, and he then returned to the Democratic Party.

He was far from limiting himself to the silver question, however. While constantly sowing the state with the money necessary to reap a future Senate seat, Newlands entered energetically into the activities of the House of Representatives. By the time he reached the Senate in 1903 he was nationally famous for the excellent Newlands Reclamation Act of 1902, and he was well on his way toward forming a consistent and comprehensive plan for a reconstitution of the federal government itself to meet the requirements of social justice in industrial America. Despite a politically essential concern for free silver, Newlands was a national statesman from the time he entered the House, and as such, he remains a unique phenomenon in Nevada politics: the man who bought his way into Congress in order to serve the nation.

A brilliant, independent, and reasonable man, Newlands envisioned an American democracy operating through politically disinterested agencies of experts, held in check by Congress, but, within that democratic limitation, able to initiate policies on their own authority. Newlands's political theory was similar to that later developed by Herbert Croly in *The Promise of American Life*, which appeared in 1912, and which was at once vigorously and vaguely endorsed by Theodore Roosevelt in his unsuccessful campaign for the presidency that year. Croly's concept of a "New Nationalism," as he called it, repudiated the Jeffersonian idea of a people who were equal under the law. A nation he argued, was made up, not of an abstract "people," but of a complex of conflicting interests, the advantage of one being gained at the expense of another. The duty of government, Croly argued, was not to insure the spurious equality of a nonexistent "people," but rather to arbitrate between the conflicting interests for the good of the whole.

Newlands proceeded from that premise long before Croly put it into theory, and it was perhaps not remarkable that he should have; for congressmen had not needed to hear from Croly to know that Congress was concerned with the interests rather than with the people. What distinguished Newlands from most of his colleagues was his national outlook with respect to these interests. Busily working on a variety of committees, he identified himself with basic national problems which hardly affected his Nevada constituency at all. His attitude was made possible by the fact that he could purchase party loyalty in his constituency, whereas other congressmen could remain in office only by making many deals and shaking a great many hands.[14]

Newlands accepted the idea that the national government was truly responsible for the general welfare, despite the claims of the states to sovereignty. At the same time, he avoided the dubious mysticism of Croly's identification of democracy with virtue, and, unlike Croly, he presented his ideas in the form of practical, immediate legislation, rather than as a distant Utopia. The reforms he advocated were, on the whole, rather too radical for Progressive America and, in the course of the Progressive Movement, dozens of his bills were accordingly buried in committee. He nevertheless exerted some influence upon all major national legislation during the Progressive era.

Newlands's first significant legislative victory, and the only one for which he is remembered, was the Newlands Reclamation Act of 1902, passed during his last year as a congressman. This act, which provided for federally financed irrigation projects in the arid regions of the West, obviously was politically agreeable to Nevadans, who were, indeed, the first to benefit from it. The Truckee-Carson Project, initiated a year after the act was passed, had placed more than forty thousand acres of extremely rich land under irrigation by the time of Newlands's last election in 1914 and had created the towns of Fallon and Fernley, with a combined population of about three thousand, representing, for Nevada, a sizable voting block.[15]

In this light, the project may appear to have been politically self-interested, but such was certainly not the case. Newlands's first purpose was to encourage the development of single-family farming in Nevada and elsewhere, and he consequently offended the Nevada ranchers by restricting claims to eighty-acre homesteads, later increased to one hundred and sixty acres under pressure from other congressmen. Newlands was among the early advocates—and by far the most effective advocate in Congress—of the cause of national, rather than state, development of the public lands. Nevada, possessing more than one quarter of the entire public domain, might have expected its representative to have taken a different view.

In Progressive America, the two great political champions of conservation were the Republican President, Theodore Roosevelt, and the Democratic congressman, and later senator, Francis Newlands. Roosevelt supported the Newlands Act in his first message to Congress, and Newlands became the leading backer of Roosevelt's conservation measures in Congress. He assiduously forwarded the programs of Roosevelt's Forest Service, against other Western senators, who pleaded special causes, notably that of the cattle industry. Newlands consistently held the view that "the collective ownership of the nation in the public domain, in its vast areas of coal, iron, and oil deposits, in forests and in farms, is a great public trust to be administered in such a way as to secure their highest development in the interest of all the people of present and future generations."[16]

In 1907, Roosevelt responded to the support he had received from Newlands by appointing him to the newly created Inland Waterways Commission. The objective of this commission was the multipurpose development of the nation's rivers, facilitating water transportation, and, as Newlands wrote, "taking into consideration the related questions of forest preservation, of irrigation of arid lands, of reclamation of swamp lands, of bank protection, of clarification of streams, and other kindred questions."[17] Before the year was out, Newlands had presented a bill to Congress to carry out the recommendations of the commission.[18] Calling for a continuing fund of $50 million to finance the program, he argued for a nationally responsible officialdom, which was at the heart of his political theory.

> Large powers and a comparatively free hand should be given to an administrative body of experts in the full development of projects, lest the complexity of the transaction, the time necessary to secure Congressional approval, the difference in view as to purpose or method, may result in indecision and delay. . . . I wish it to handle this capital just as the board of directors of a great corporation would do. . . .[19]

Newlands's measure won strong support from Roosevelt and fatally strong opposition from two other sources: the Corps of Army Engineers and the House Rivers and Harbors Committee. The engineers had been trained to believe that rivers should be developed for navigational purposes only, and they remained loyal to this creed. The Rivers and Harbors Committee was, if possible, more affronted than the engineers. Federally financed rivers and harbors improvements had contributed much toward supplying the pork barrel for congressional districts, and it was therefore natural for the chairman of the House committee to insist that "the specific mode of providing means for improving and promoting navigation should be left to the wisdom of Congress."[20] Against this sentiment, Newlands continued the fight, unavailingly, to his death.

In addition, Newlands believed that the railroads should be brought under unified federal control. In 1905 he called for a national railroad incorporation law, which would have placed the roads under unified control and protected them from the harassments of state legislation, especially in the matter of unfairly high taxation. The increased federal authority under the proposed law would have been handled by the Interstate Commerce Commission.

Railroad consolidation, he argued, was natural and beneficial, and a corresponding centralization of governmental control was also natural and beneficial to the railroads as well as to the public. He did not convince his colleagues on the Commerce Committee, and his proposal died there. Later, however, as war approached, Wilson appointed Newlands chairman of a commission of inquiry into methods of co-ordinating national railroad transportation. There Newlands returned to his idea of national incorporation. He died in the course of the commission's deliberations, but his inquiry led to the creation of the Transportation Act of 1920.

Newlands looked upon the consolidation of industry as being socially useful, provided that its purpose was the conservation of energy and that effective government controls were installed. In 1899 Newlands presented his early views on this matter in a letter to a National Civic Federation conference. He called for a bureau of industry to which all corporations would report their capital stock, bonds, income, transactions, numbers of workers, wages, and other data necessary to guide legislation. Pressure might then be put on the corporations by the bureau through publicity. Newlands believed that the federal government had the constitutional authority to tax corporations, despite the Supreme Court decision of 1894 in the case of *Pollock v. Farmers' Loan and Trust Company*, which invalidated the income-tax law. The new tax would simply be placed on the transactions of the corporation rather than its income.

This federal tax power would have been the key to federal control of the trusts and the means by which the wealthy would have borne their share of the costs of government.

> Accumulated wealth should contribute more than it does to the federal revenue. This is a sufficient reason for commencing immediately with corporations, even if, as is claimed, the evils of unions of capital are imaginary. The machinery being prepared by law, the evils can be taken hold of as they arise, and taxation can be so levied as to restrain, if that only is desirable, or to destroy, if relief is otherwise unobtainable.[21]

He remained opposed to "mere guerrilla warfare upon trusts, which will prove annoying to business generally, and which will be weak and inefficient in operation,"[22] and for those reasons he did not support the antitrust movement.

The day after the dissolution of the Standard Oil Company in 1911, he addressed the Senate on the need for a federal board to control corporations. His personal preference, he said, was the creation of a national holding company under federal jurisdiction, but, he added: "I must admit that, so far as my own party in the Senate is concerned, the views which I entertain upon this subject have not made the headway I could wish."[23]

Although Newlands had once been critical of the Interstate Commerce Commission because it had been given too little power to achieve its purposes, he conceded that it had served a useful function, and eventually he came to view it as the pilot model for good government. It had given an implementation to the Interstate Commerce Act which was entirely lacking in the Sherman Antitrust Act. Accordingly, Newlands introduced a bill that would establish an interstate trade commission and join to it the Bureau of Corporations, which had been organized during Roosevelt's administration in the Department of Commerce and Labor. The commission was to confine its attention to corporations having annual incomes in excess of $5 million, and, in extreme cases, it could have debarred corporations from interstate commerce. Following Wilson's election, Newlands, as chairman of the Senate's committee on interstate commerce, was in a position at last to press successfully for the establishment of the Federal Trade Commission, essentially as he developed it in the Senate bill.

Newlands had never accepted the argument of the late-nineteenth-century liberals that the protective tariff was an unqualified evil that fostered monopoly. He supported Taft in the Payne-Aldrich Tariff, and he was out of sympathy with the majority of his party and the Wilson administration in the debates over the Underwood Tariff. Newlands thought the tariff question too intricate to be decided on the basis of any clear-cut principles, and he believed that the tremendous pressure of economic interests would always prevent Congress from drafting a tariff that would be arrived at scientifically. His solution to the problem was in accord with his main pattern of reform. He wanted an administrative board, similar to the Interstate Commerce Commission, that would be in charge of regulating tariff rates. The Payne-Aldrich Tariff created a Tariff Board, and Newlands supported the bill partly for that reason. The board was dropped under the Democrats, but later re-established during Wilson's administration, at the urging of Newlands.

Throughout his career, Newlands was sympathetic to the demands of organized labor. He argued that so-called labor monopolies helped a large number of workers to increase their shares of the profits derived from production. This, he asserted, worked to the economic advantage of society as a whole; whereas capitalistic combinations strove to depress wages and raise prices, and that this process was, in the long run, self-defeating, even for the owners and managers of industry. Consistent with his political views, however, he emphasized governmental safeguards for labor instead of an increase in union strength.

He always supported such measures as the eight-hour work day for industries with public contracts, and he favored the mediation of labor disputes by a government commission.

Like that of most advanced Progressives, his attitude toward labor was essentially paternalistic. Himself an employer of a large work force on the Comstock, Newlands had remained on good terms with the miners' union, and readily met its demands, unquestionably moved in this regard by the desire for the miners' votes. By the time of his campaign for re-election in 1914 however, his generous paternalism had ceased to be enough: the miners throughout the state voted overwhelmingly for the Socialist ticket.

Compared with other Nevada Senators, Newlands appears to have troubled himself very little about personal requests from his constituents. At the same time, he was always aware of the main interests of his state, and he defended them vigorously in the upper house. The Newlands Act probably brought more benefit to the state than any previous congressional enactment. The mining lawyer-historian Grant Smith, who knew as much about it as anyone did, said that Newlands, despite his absorption in national affairs, did more for Nevada than any of its other representatives in Washington ever did.[24]

Newlands was one of Nevada's most valuable contributions to the nation, a contribution made possible, ironically enough, by the smallness and the corruptibility of the state's population. Newlands was above party, for he had the Nevada State Democratic Central Committee in his pocket. He was permitted a truly national outlook and a spacious independence of mind, which could have been less well afforded by a senator from New York or Ohio or Alabama. Newlands was a Democrat in the Senate for the reason that local circumstances made him a Democrat in Nevada, but he fought against the majority of his party in the Senate on many major issues. Nevertheless, as a member of the party, he advanced steadily in power by virtue of his seniority, hard work, and intelligence.

During Newlands's career in the Senate, the Democratic

Party moved from the states' rights Jeffersonianism of William Jennings Bryan to that thoroughly non-Wilsonian New Nationalism which had come to characterize Wilson's administration by the time the nation entered World War I. More than any other prominent Democrat, Newlands had made it his mission to convert his party from the principles of Jeffersonian states' rights *laissez faire* to a policy of governmental interventionism. Newlands has been generally ignored by historians of the Progressive period, except for his efforts on behalf of conservation; yet he was very likely the single most important advocate in the Democratic Party for the comprehensive transition, which did in fact take place, from the New Freedom of the early Wilson to the New Deal of Franklin D. Roosevelt.

Senator Newlands's career in the upper house, productive as it was, does not constitute an adequate defense for the political oddity of an arbitrarily equal representation of the states in the Senate. Some will argue that Senator Pat McCarran's subsequent crusade for Americanism ought to be cited in defense of the American federal system, and they will have a case to the extent that McCarran, like Newlands, exerted a formative influence upon national affairs. But despite the advantage the seniority system gave to Nevada's senators, none of the others exerted influence that was national in scope except when the interest of Nevada silver was concerned.

Jones and Stewart—both capable men—kept clear of any senatorial responsibility by not serving on any important national committees. Senator Key Pittman beguiled himself into taking a position on the Foreign Relations Committee in 1916, because he thought it might impress Nevadans at a time when Nevada seemed likely to be brought into the war against Germany. The final consequence of this impetuous act was that Pittman found himself saddled with the chairmanship of the Foreign Relations Committee from 1933 to his death in 1940.

Pittman also was a capable man, but he had no stomach for foreign affairs. By being chairman of an important committee at a crucial time, he made an internationally important impact, but it was not a positive one.

IV

Pittman's one important contribution to national affairs was unsurprisingly in the cause of silver. The silver issue had remained comparatively dormant throughout the heyday of Tonopah and Goldfield. The former region produced mainly silver bullion at ever declining prices, and the latter produced chiefly gold, which added to the vast international gold production of the period and so helped to strengthen the nation's faith in its gold standard. Nevada's leading politicians lost all hope for the cause of silver after the passage of the Gold Standard Act in 1900. During the period that followed, silver reached an all time low of $.51 per ounce and a ratio of 36 to 1 with gold.[25]

Then, in 1918, the silver interests had a windfall. Because of World War I Great Britain's trade with Asia increased substantially, especially with India, where silver remained the medium of exchange. Running short of silver, the British government requested the Wilson administration to sell some to it quietly in large amounts so as not to ruin British credit in India, and Wilson gave Pittman the pleasant duty of gaining congressional authorization. Rushed through as an emergency measure, the Pittman Act of 1918 was disguised as legislation that would shore up the nation's gold supply and thereby settle adverse trade balances and stabilize the price of silver.

The measure called for the melting of up to 350 million standard silver dollars, at a value of one dollar per ounce. The Treasury was then to purchase a like amount of American silver at a minimum price of one dollar per ounce. Doubling the price of silver served no international monetary purpose. The price asked was simply the one demanded by the mine owners, who met in convention in Denver while the bill was under discussion in Congress. The Senate, in response to the mine owners' urging, had raised the requested amount of $250 million of silver by an additional $100 million and had passed the bill without opposition. In that form it was quickly approved by the House against disorganized opposition.

The mine owners looked forward to a high-priced market for the next decade, but silver production increased significantly in response to the act, the Treasury did not find the need to melt down the maximum amount of silver, and the end abruptly came into sight in 1923. Senator William A. King of Utah attempted to meet the crisis with a bill that would force the Treasury to sell the maximum amount and thus create a market for an additional $90 million. Instead of going to the Mines and Mining Committee, however, King's bill went to the Banking and Currency Committee, where it died.

When the Treasury purchases were within three months of completion, Pittman was appointed as a one-man subcommittee of the newly formed Commission of Gold and Silver Inquiry to investigate the administration of the act, and he concluded that the Treasury was $14.5 million short in its estimate of the amount it was legally bound to buy. When the Treasury refused to accept his argument, Pittman presented a bill in 1924 that would force the additional purchase. The bill passed the Senate and died in the House both in 1924 and in 1925. At Pittman's suggestion, the silver producers tried to serve a writ of mandamus against the Secretary of the Treasury and the Director of the Mint, but a federal court dismissed their petition.

By that time the silver senators were as of old. When the

House refused to take part in a joint committee to investigate conditions in the silver industry, the Senate created the Commission of Gold and Silver Inquiry in 1923, with Senator Oddie as chairman and Senator Pittman, vice-chairman. The commission invited all silver producers to a meeting in Reno in September. There Oddie and Pittman recommended that they should form an association to look out for their interests in a political way. "I personally cannot take any office in this," Oddie explained to the members of the meeting, "because I am a member of the Senate Commission, but I will entertain a motion for the nomination of some one as chairman."[26]

The American Silver Producers' Association was then formed, but nobody knew what to do, because the commission had already told the mine owners it would be hopeless to fight for the old free-silver issue, or even for bimetallism on any basis. Pittman, in that situation, put forth a four-point program, which called for a government-sponsored silver export program and also for that $14.5 million. The Association later failed in both efforts and fell into desuetude.

The silver situation continued to worsen. India was launched upon a program of gradual demonetization and the price of silver dropped from $.65 in 1926 to $.56 in 1929. Then came the crash, and the price of silver fell to the record low of $.3075. But the miners kept on producing the metal in large quantities, because by the twenties it was primarily a biproduct of the lead, zinc, and copper industries.

In 1930 a subcommittee of the Foreign Relations Committee was created, with Pittman as chairman, for the purpose of improving Sino-American trade relations by raising the price of silver, ". . . by reason of our continuous friendship for her people and our sympathy for them in their poverty."[27] Pittman suggested holding an international conference to achieve this end, and when the World Monetary and Economic Conference was held in London, Pittman was appointed chairman of a subcommittee on silver. The conference adopted a resolution he drew up, which called for the stabilization of the world price of silver, for the substitution of silver for low-value paper money, and for the rejection of any legislation that would further debase the value of the metal.

In a purported effort to achieve price stability, purchasing agreements were drawn up by eight nations, which each signed on its own terms. In effect, none of the countries would change its practices, except the United States, which, with a current annual production of 21.4 million ounces of silver, would now purchase 24 million ounces annually. It was the one notable accomplishment of a generally disastrous conference, and it was hailed in America as a great milestone in international co-operation. The American agreement became law by presidential proclamation in December 1933.

Until the depression, the silverites, always powerful in the Senate, had been frustrated by opposition and indifference in the House of Representatives. After the onset of the depression, however, agrarian radicals returned to the glory days of "Bryan Bryan, Bryan," and congressmen came up with radical silver bills which were designed to inflate farm prices. The Thomas Amendment to the Farm Relief bill, which created the Agricultural Adjustment Administration, was the most important legislation of this kind proposed during the first Hundred Days of the Roosevelt administration. The amendment, revised by Pittman to meet administration objections, empowered the President to place the United States on a free-silver basis.

For the silverites, 1934 was the banner year. Within the course of a few weeks, eleven silver bills were introduced in the House and three in the Senate. In January, Senator Burton K. Wheeler of Montana introduced an amendment to the Gold Reserve bill which called for the purchase of not less than 50 million ounces of silver per month—twice the amount of the national production—until one billion ounces would have been added to the Treasury. When the Wheeler amendment was narrowly defeated, at the personal request of Roosevelt, Pittman succeeded in passing a substitute amendment, after which the bill went through without debate. The Pittman amendment authorized the President to raise the seigniorage charges on foreign silver and to reduce the weight of the standard silver dollar.

Pittman then approached Secretary of the Treasury Henry Morgenthau with a plan to treble silver deposits in order to raise prices, especially those of farm products. He argued that, if it did not work, the President would have the power to reverse the program on his own authority. He would probably have been unable to do so with any inflationary enactment Congress might contrive. Unable to persuade Morgenthau to undertake this program, Pittman pressed successfully for the Silver Purchase Act of 1934, which incorporated the suggestions he had made to Morgenthau and which became the basic silver program of the New Deal. The act provided for a government silver-purchasing program, "with the ultimate objective of having and maintaining one-fourth of the monetary value of such stocks in silver," in the Treasury. The Treasury was given the authority to determine the price it would pay for the metal.

By the time of the Silver Purchase Act, Pittman had established himself, not only as the leading spokesman for the silver cause in Congress, but also as the mediator between the administration and the neo-Populists from the farm regions. When the silver program failed to produce the inflationary effect anticipated however, the farmers' support for silver fell away and, with it, support from the House of Representatives. Thereafter, Pittman was obliged to rely upon the power of silver in the Senate and upon his personal power as chairman of the Foreign Relations Committee to prevent repeal of the Silver Purchase Act and to force Roosevelt to keep the price of silver high. In this cause, Pittman did not scruple to trade his support of critical foreign affairs measures for the President's compliance with his silver demands.

With Pittman's death in 1940, the mantle of leadership in the silver cause fell to Pittman's junior colleague from Nevada, Senator Pat McCarran, who wasted no time in letting the administration feel the loss of the comparatively statesmanlike Pittman. McCarran made it his mission throughout World War II to prevent the government, so far as possible, from using its stock of silver for industrial purposes and to relieve the shortages in metals, notably copper. Legally, Morgenthau was in a position to lend about one third of the government's silver stocks to the Defense Plant Corporation for non-consumer uses, but McCarran fought his efforts to lend out more. McCarran's alternative proposal was to increase the supply of silver by giving the silver producers top priority for mining machinery and by raising the price of the metal.

During the war, the silverites met the organized opposition of another vested interest for the first time in the history of the silver cause. The war, together with the purchasing program, had cut off the supply of silver for commercial purposes. Accordingly, jewelers and silverware manufacturers organized the Silver Users Emergency Committee and found their capable champion in Senator Theodore Green of Rhode Island. He introduced a bill to place all government silver at the disposal of commercial users as well as the war industry, and he managed to place his bill in the Banking and Currency Committee rather than the Silver Committee.

When the committee gave a favorable report on Green's bill, McCarran attempted to amend it out of existence. Failing in this, he prevented its passage during that session by filibustering. When the Senate convened again Green and McCarran returned with rival measures. The final result was a diluted version of Green's measure; the government's silver stocks were to be contributed to the war effort, leaving the newly mined silver available for commercial purposes. At the same time, the price for silver for commercial purposes was pegged at 71.11 cents per ounce; whereas formerly the price paid by the silver users for imported silver had been 45 cents per ounce. As was to be expected. McCarran was widely execrated for hobbling the war effort in the interests of the silver producers, and the loss of Pittman's statesmanship was lamented. Although Pittman would not have displayed quite the avarice of his successor, he had been a Nevadan first and last, and had been as willing as McCarran to trade the nation's security for added profits for Nevada's silver producers.

V

Pittman became the first Nevadan to represent the Sagebrush State in foreign affairs when he attended the London Economic Conference in 1933, to "do something for silver."[28] Then, as earlier, his statesmanship was highly successful, and was carried on in a Wild Western manner which must have been remembered long afterwards by London Bobbies. Arriving in England, Pittman got drunk and stayed that way through much of the conference. He had brought his gun with him, and at times, when he was drinking, he would let his spirits loose by popping out the London streetlights with his six-shooter. He had also brought a bowie knife, and when one technical advisor gave him trouble on the silver matter, Pittman took after him with his knife and chased him through the corridors of the Claridge Hotel.

The senior senator's behavior disturbed the American delegation, and a leading member of it reported with evident disapproval: "The day Pittman was to bring in his silver proposal to the plenary session, he was completely out of working order. The previous evening, he had entertained two 'ladies' who were later ejected by the hotel. . . ."[29] Pittman arrived at the meeting forty-five minutes late, just as a hastily chosen substitute was preparing to state his proposal. After Pittman introduced it for consideration, he continued with a rambling speech which was characterized as "an utter disgrace." Still, he achieved everything he wanted, which was probably more than anybody else at the conference could say.

As chairman of the Foreign Relations Committee, Pittman saw himself in the role of mediator between the administration and the Senate. His primary duty was to draft legislation in accord with the wishes of the administration, but he was of two minds about this new position: diplomacy held no appeal for him; the distinction of his new chairmanship did. Although he was loath to call meetings to discuss foreign matters, he was insistent that he retain the full authority that went with the office. His handling of a proposal for limited association with the World Court made Roosevelt aware of the trouble that was in store for the administration. He delayed summoning his committee for several weeks, pleading that he was too busy attending other important meetings. When the committee reported favorably on the bill, he presented no defense for it, although he voted affirmatively. The bill lost by a narrow margin.

In 1935 Pittman delayed consideration of proposed neutrality legislation, which had been inspired by the Nye Committee investigations of bankers and munitions makers for allegedly having involved the United States in World War I. In April, however, Pittman got down to business when the State Department informed him that Senator Nye was planning his own neutrality bill. After warning the State Department to withhold information from Nye, Pittman summoned his committee, which presented two bills to the Senate in July, neither of them written by him. One bill prohibited loans or any extension of credit to belligerents; the other regulated passports for Americans in wartime. Members of the administration had requested Pittman to kill both of these proposals, and they thought that he had agreed to do so.

To head off the committee proposals, the administration drew up its own measure, giving the President discretionary powers to apply embargoes. When Pittman argued that the Senate would never grant the President this power, the administration withdrew its measure, and Pittman received authorization from his committee to draft his own. When Pittman did not arrive on the Senate floor to present his proposal, the committee members went out to look for him and found him drunk. He had not yet drafted the proposal. After he sobered up, he worked out a draft together with the ranking minority member of the committee, William Borah, and they finished it by 6 p.m.

The proposal was faulty in many respects, such as the granting of discretionary power to the President, which Pittman had included by mistake, but Roosevelt agreed to accept it, as long as it expired in February 1936. It passed in the Senate, 79 to 2, as a distinctly temporary measure. In January 1936, Pittman offered to the Senate, a bill written by the administration, while an identical one was being presented on the floor of the House. A bitter debate followed for six weeks, after which the measure passed with minor alterations. It was in force for a fourteen-month period.

When Congress met in 1937 during the Spanish Civil War, Pittman presented a special proposal from the administration for placing an embargo on shipments to Spain. The neutrality legislation of the previous two years was not applicable to civil conflicts. Pittman insisted upon adding a vague preamble, to which Roosevelt consented after his diplomatic advisors told him that it didn't mean anything. When the measure was discussed in the Senate, this preamble became the chief target of criticism; and when Pittman eliminated it, as a "compromise move," the resolution passed and was sent to the House.

Shortly afterward, Pittman drew up his own resolution on neutrality and presented it to the Senate. The State Department indicated its general approval and then rewrote it. The distinctive feature of Pittman's resolution, which was retained in the State Department's version, was a "cash and carry" provision: Belligerents might buy munitions in the United States, so long as they came for them themselves and paid the bill in full before leaving. In that form, the Pittman measure went before the Senate, which passed it in March, 63 to 6. It had been, Pittman wrote, "the most active and most tedious session that I have experienced."[30]

In March 1939, as a European war appeared imminent, Pittman and Hull came to an agreement on another neutrality bill, which, in case of general war, would work to the advantage of England and France. A week later, however, Pittman changed his mind: "The situation in Europe does not seem to induce any urgent action on neutrality legislation." The Foreign Relations Committee failed to reach agreement and the resolution was not reported out of committee. Pittman advised Roosevelt to "keep quiet" so that Hitler would "be left in doubt as to what our Government would do" in case of war.[31] For his own part, he was busy with plans to raise the price of silver, which had been lowered from 77.57 cents per ounce to 64.5 cents on the very day that the Senate Foreign Relations Committee had begun its deliberation on neutrality legislation.

Pittman appears to have considered the question of neutrality in 1939 almost entirely in the light of the silver issue; whereas Roosevelt was inclined to view it just as one-sidedly in relation to the European crisis. What Roosevelt wanted was the immediate repeal of the mandatory arms-embargo provision of the existing legislation on neutrality. According to Morgenthau, Roosevelt asked Pittman whether he would withhold his support from the administration's measure if the price of silver was not raised, and Pittman replied: "We have got 18 votes—and what are you going to do about it?"[32] Roosevelt raised the price of silver to 71 cents an ounce, and Pittman took the administration's measure to the Senate, where he defended it vigorously. After interminable debate, during which World War II broke out in Europe, the Senate passed the bill, 63 to 30. The House followed quickly, and Roosevelt signed it into law in November.

Once war was declared in Europe, Roosevelt assumed direct leadership in foreign affairs, which he had not been in a position to do before, and he dropped his former tactic of currying favor with the chairman of the Foreign Relations Committee. When Pittman, on his own authority, proposed a thirty-day truce in the war in order to straighten out the differences, Roosevelt told a close friend of the chairman's to inform Pittman that his suggestion was asinine.

Pittman must have known that his death was approaching. He grew thinner and weaker and remained drunk for longer periods; also, he began to make maudlin and irresponsible statements. In November 1940, he died in the land he loved, after being admitted to Washoe Hospital in Reno shortly before his landslide election to a sixth term in the upper house. In the eyes of Nevadans, he was a sterling patriot, who had served his state as faultlessly in the world as in the nation. Roosevelt, in one of his last letters to Pittman, struck off the perfect parody of this spirit of Nevadan internationalism. "Scrugham," he wrote, referring to the congressman from Nevada, "tells me they have found a manganese process and that at the next session we will pass a bill demonetizing silver and substituting manganese. That will give variety to our currency and a nationwide political issue! Not only will the United States Treasury be saved but so will Brazil. That is why the Chairman of the Foreign Relations Committee will introduce it and call it 'The Pittman World Currency Act of 1939.' "[33]

V

It had been Mimosa Pittman's ambition for her husband, when he won his seat in the Senate, that he would become the greatest national statesman, but Pittman had demonstrated neither the capacity nor the inclination for such a role. This was not true of Senator Patrick A. McCarran. His capacity to fill the role might be questioned by many, but his inclination to do so could be doubted by none.

From the beginning of his career, McCarran thought of himself as a statesman rather than as a politician. A lonely childhood prepared him for a lonely political career devoid of the back-slapping, drink-treating, and favor-swapping which had always been taken for granted in Nevada politics. A short, fat man, who suffered throughout his career from high blood pressure and ulcers, McCarran had a superbly senatorial head on his shoulders, and he set it off with a great mane of flowing white hair. He was a born orator for whom ordinary conversation was probably impossible and certainly unpalatable. "I have been a lone wolf all my life," he was fond of saying in his later years, "and it has always paid off."[34]

The bitter fact was that, until he entered the Senate at the age of 57, it had paid in rather poor coin. Never one of the boys, McCarran was hated, despised, and rebuffed by the leading figures in his own party. He had managed to become chief justice of the Nevada supreme court, but in his own mind that was a small achievement. He wanted a seat in the

United States Senate. He made his first lunge for it in 1904, and for twenty-nine years thereafter he suffered the miseries of Job, sustained by none of Job's patience, before he achieved his ambition. Those long years in the political sagebrush probably contributed something toward the nurture of the ornery old mustang who entered the Senate finally in 1933.

Nor was even that victory as sweet for McCarran as it ought to have been. Until Pittman died in 1940, McCarran was obliged to remain the junior colleague of his most hated rival in the Democratic Party of Nevada. Pittman, who gloried in the soubriquet of "Silver Key," was the nationally acknowledged leader of the silver forces, and he had sworn he would fight McCarran every time he ran for any office. When Pittman finally succumbed, McCarran grasped the banner of the silver cause, only to be repaid for his valor by violent abuse in the national press.[35] By that time, however, McCarran was in a position where names could never hurt him. What he knew in 1945 as the nation did not, was that he had already fashioned the basis for a nationwide political power, unlike that possessed by any other Nevada politician except Newlands and Pittman.

McCarran trailed far behind his ticket in Nevada in the Democratic year of 1932, but once elected to the Senate, he immediately outran all other United States senators who had been elected for the first time that year. While newly elected senators around the country were resting on their laurels, breathing heavily after hard campaigns, McCarran rushed to Washington and gained for himself seats on the Judiciary Committee and the Appropriations Committee from Senate majority leader "Uncle Joe" Robinson. These acquisitions laid the foundation for his later power, and his eventual rise was threatened only by his constituency, his ulcers, and his bad heart.[36]

McCarran had been dragged into office on Roosevelt's coattails, with the slogan, "A New Deal for America: Roosevelt, Garner, and McCarran." It is not unlikely that his choice committee assignments were made possible also by his pro-New Deal campaign. Once in possession of the office, and of those assignments, which in the Senate are virtually irrevocable, the lone wolf quickly removed the fleecy disguise. Brushing aside the rule that freshman senators should be seen and not heard, McCarran delivered his first speech during his third day in the Senate and attacked the administration's Economy Bill on the ground that it had been presented on the Senate floor without prior examination by the Senate Judiciary Committee. He thus neatly combined the two principles which were to lift him to the heights of his power: unremitting opposition to the party of his choice and wily manipulation of the club rules of the Senate.[37]

Capture of those two key committee positions assured him of power, but only if he stayed in the Senate long enough for seniority to work its magic. His basic concern, therefore, was the campaign of 1938, and his principal obstacle was Pittman. McCarran did not present the favorable public image to Nevadans that Pittman did. Pittman was a two-fisted drinker with an itchy trigger finger; the junior senator was a pudgy little man, obliged to subsist on baby food because of his ulcers.

It appears that McCarran was spared defeat in 1938 only because the undependable Pittman's resolution was not equal to his hatred. Probably McCarran's attack upon the New Deal, climaxed by his leadership in the fight against the Supreme Court packing scheme, helped him win. At any rate, he won the Democratic nomination without serious opposition and was re-elected. Six years later, following his victory in the primaries against Key Pittman's brother Vail, he became unbeatable, and, by the Senate rules of seniority, his power grew day by day.

In 1947 the determined old man survived a heart attack. At the time of his death, in spite of the long delay in his admission to the Senate, he was the fourth oldest member of the club in point of senatorial tenure; and, grandly sounding the themes of Communist subversion from within and racial subversion from without, he had become one of the most powerful members of the Senate, perhaps for a time second only to the upstart from Wisconsin, Joseph McCarthy.

The climax of McCarran's power came with the triumph of Truman in the election of 1948, accompanied by Democratic majorities in Congress. The Truman-baiting McCarran was at last presented with the chairmanships of the committees on which he had formerly served as the ranking member of the minority party. He became chairman of the Committee on the Judiciary, chairman of the State Department subcommittee of the Committee on Appropriations, chairman of the "watch dog" committee on foreign aid, and chairman of the Senate Internal Security Committee. At the same time, he held positions on several other committees, concerned with irrigation, silver, reclamation, wildlife, and the like, and he kept his hand in on all of them.

Nobody has explained the power of a chairman of a Senate committee more clearly than McCarran: "The chairman of a committee or a subcommittee cannot always assure passage of a bill which has been referred to his group, but he can almost always kill the bill if he wishes to do so."[38] The Judiciary Committee receives about forty per cent of all bills introduced into the Senate, and, in McCarran's words, it controls all legislation on "immigration and naturalization matters, patent law, all private money claims against the government, federal court procedures, constitutional amendments, appointments of federal judges, marshals, and U. S. attorneys, and all laws which would apply to the public generally—like a national divorce law."[39]

By the time the elections of 1948 had returned the Senate to Democratic control, McCarran had discovered a cause in support of which he would be the savior of the nation: the crusade against Communism. In 1946 McCarran attached to an appropriation bill a rider that would give the State Department "absolute discretion" to discharge any employee whose retention it considered harmful to the national interest. In foreign affairs, he called for the heavy subsidization of what he considered to be the world's two most redoubtable bastions of anti-Communism: Chiang Kai-shek's Nationalist China and Francisco Franco's Falangist Spain. At the same time, he favored reducing appropriations to Western Europe, where Communist parties were permitted to flourish freely.

As chairman of the Judiciary Committee, McCarran drew up the Subversive Activities Control Act, which Congress passed over Truman's veto by large majorities. The main provision of the act was the exclusion of aliens who advocated "the economic, international, and governmental doctrines of world communism or the economic and governmental doctrines of any other form of totalitarianism" or who, for any other reason, might, upon entry, engage in activity "subversive to the national security."[40]

The effect of the act was to deny visas to all former members of Communist, Nazi, and Fascist parties (the Spanish Falangists not being included in this last category), regardless of the current political views of the applicants. This caused much embarrassment in America and a good deal of mirth abroad when literary and scientific figures such as Graham Greene and Ernest B. Chain were bound and gagged by governmental red tape in their efforts to make brief visits to the United States. Consequently, in 1951 Congress amended this McCarran Act, to exempt ex-Communists and ex-Fascists from its provisions.

To McCarran, this was hardly more than a divertisement in

his main crusade to protect America, not only from Communist penetration, but from all un-American infiltrations of any description. His main efforts in the four years he controlled his committees were those which resulted in the McCarran-Walter Immigration Act of 1952, the crowning achievement of his career.

Revision of the nation's immigration policies, as laid down by the National Origins Act of 1924, was made imperative at the close of the war by the critical problem of displaced persons in Europe. The Displaced Persons Act was passed to allow displaced persons to enter the United States. In 1949 a more liberal measure, the Celler bill, had passed the House and was already before the Senate. In the winter and spring of 1949, however, McCarran counterattacked vigorously, blocking all action while he held a lengthy series of hearings. For his witnesses, he drew heavily upon veterans' organizations and patriotic societies, and the weight of testimony was therefore against any revision of the existing law. The loudest and lengthiest testifying was done by McCarran himself; he attacked especially the Citizens Committee on Displaced Persons, declaring that "there has been disseminated over the length and breadth of this nation a campaign of misrepresentation and falsehood which has misled many public-spirited and well-meaning citizens and organizations."[41]

As long as he remained on guard in the Senate halls, McCarran was successful in resisting all efforts of the supporters of the measure to bypass his committee. Then overconfidence betrayed him, and in September he departed for Europe to make a personal inspection tour of the displaced persons camps. In his absence the Judiciary Committee reported out the bill without recommendation by a vote of 7 to 3. But on the insistence of Senator James Eastland of Mississippi that senatorial courtesy was being violated by acting in McCarran's absence, the Senate returned the bill to committee by a vote of 36 to 30, ending all chances of amending the law that year.

McCarran next attacked the Celler bill by attempting to amend it to death. The Senate, though, defeated all of McCarran's amendments and passed the measure in April 1950 by a vote of 58 to 15. In McCarran's view, the measure was part of a process by which "the floodgates of the nation are being pried open for the entrance of millions of aliens, from the turbulent populations of the entire world, who are seeking admission into the United States under the guise of displaced persons."[42] Still, the new law would be in effect for only two years, and McCarran was meanwhile busily at work perfecting his own permanent immigration law. In January 1951 McCarran submitted his measure to the Senate, and Francis Walter proposed a nearly identical one in the House, where a more liberal measure, sponsored by Representative Emanuel Celler, the chairman of the House Judiciary Commitee, was also presented. It was therefore decided to hold joint meetings of the House and Senate Judiciary Committees to consider all three bills simultaneously.

The McCarran measure contained several loftily rhetorical passages stressing its importance to the future of the nation. "Today, as never before," it declared, "a sound immigration and naturalization policy is essential to the preservation of our way of life because that system is the conduit through which a stream of humanity flows into the fabric of our society."[43] McCarran was not opposed to the idea of this stream constantly wetting the American fabric, but he was determined to control the stream so as to preserve the ethnic purity of America, such as it was. This was to be achieved by retention of the quota system, established as law in 1924, through which the number of immigrants admitted from each country was supposed to correspond proportionally to the ethnic origins of the American people as a whole. McCarran could talk about his bill all day without alluding to racist theories (less skilled supporters were unable to do this), but the main idea of his bill was to keep America, so far as possible, Anglo-Saxon, Teutonic, and, of course, Celtic.

To achieve this goal, the bill, beyond retaining the quota system, rejected the pooling system of the 1924 law, of which southern and eastern Europeans had been able to take advantage. During the life of the National Origins Act of 1924, England had had the largest quota of any European nation, based on the high percentage of Americans of English origin; at the same time, the idea of settling in the United States had probably been less appealing to Englishmen than to the citizens of other European nations. The consequence had been that some quotas, such as the English, had not been filled, and at the end of the year, these had been lumped together and made available to the nationals of small-quota nations such as Italy or Greece. The anti-restrictionists in Congress had concluded that, given McCarran's influence, a fight against the quota system would be hopeless. They therefore accepted the quota system in the Celler bill and fought to retain the pooling provision.

Senator Hubert Humphrey supported the liberal measure on the ground that "The key and heart of the democratic philosophy is recognition of the dignity of the human kind, and of the brotherhood and fraternity of man,"[44] but he must have been aware that his mixed metaphors and double synonyms would avail him nothing against those of the chairman of the Senate Judiciary Committee. After the McCarran-Walter bill passed in the House by a vote of 206 to 68, the Senate went along with it by voice vote, with only a dozen members present to say "aye." Truman's blistering veto gave the anti-restrictionists heart, and, after the House had passed the measure again, they arrived full force on the Senate floor, only to be defeated, 57 to 26.

McCarran had won his last battle in the cause of "Americanism." When he died in 1954, he was eulogized in a commemorative ceremony in New York by Westbrook Pegler and other leading Americanists. Senator Joseph McCarthy, although he sent a telegram, was unable to attend, and Pegler had occasion to comment ruefully that, if Eleanor Roosevelt had been talking in that auditorium that evening, she would have attracted a lot more people.[45] It turned out that McCarran, after all, had failed in his ambition to become a nationally recognized statesman like Clay or Calhoun, if not Washington or Lincoln. He *was* so recognized in his native Nevada, however, as the McCarran Room in the Nevada Historical Museum testifies. There a statue of him stands, surrounded by his law books and by various presentations made him during his lifetime by grateful groups. In the view of influential Nevadans he was the finest contribution which Nevadaism had made to the perhaps greater area of Americanism.

CHAPTER VII

States' Rights Enterprise

James Madison was aware that "possible mischiefs" might arise from the quality of representation in the Senate. He hazarded the further opinion, in *The Federalist*, that greater troubles were likely to occur as a result of the powers which had been retained by the states than as a result of those which had been conferred upon the national government. "A local spirit," he wrote, "will infallibly prevail much more in the members of Congress, than a national spirit will prevail in the legislatures of the particular states."[1]

By 1787 there already had been abundant evidence to support this view in the irresponsible fiscal policies of states such as Rhode Island and the selfishly anti-national tariff programs of states such as New York. To guard against such manifestations of "local spirit" the Constitutional Convention had been called, and the founding fathers had struck down these specific practices without dissent. What neither Madison nor the other founders foresaw, living in the relatively Arcadian world of eighteenth-century America, was the increased range of mischiefs which would result from the industrial and transportation revolutions. Among the states of the nation, Nevada has been the busiest in availing itself of the advantages of these legal mischiefs made possible by the federal system.

Although the greatest profits to Nevada from states'-rights enterprise proved to be mainly in the areas of marriage, divorce, and legalized gambling, other lines of activity were not neglected. At the turn of the twentieth century, the Sagebrush State decided to do what it could to establish the little town of Reno as the national capital for corporate enterprise, and there was nothing especially presumptuous about it. Little Delaware, as well as New Jersey, had already pioneered in this area of states' rights economics with lax incorporation laws, and such Western states as Arizona had quickly followed suit.

According to the Delaware law, corporations, no matter where they were physically located, could make Delaware their legal residence by paying a fee and sharing an office and a resident agent in the state with other similarly inclined companies. Conveniently located for Eastern businesses which wished to avoid restrictions imposed upon corporations by states such as New York or Pennsylvania, Delaware in the twentieth century became the home of more than 28,000 corporations, paying taxes of more than $5 million a year.[2]

An observer of the American political system who was unfamiliar with the oddities of American federalism, might be surprised that one state could legally usurp authority, as well as tax money, from another state in this manner. He might find it equally surprising that a nationwide monopoly such as the Standard Oil Company could incorporate on a state-wide basis and then could move its legal place of residence arbitrarily from Ohio to New Jersey without having to move any of the business itself. To tell the truth, a good many Americans themselves were surprised by the ease with which Standard Oil accomplished this transformation at the end of the nineteenth century, making itself magically invulnerable to the supreme court of Ohio, which had ordered its dissolution. It was shortly after this much publicized escape from peril by Standard Oil that Nevada, along with other states, hopefully developed its own legal sanctuary.

Amid so much competition, Nevada was obliged to content itself with battening mainly on California, which was the only nearby state with enough business life to make it worthwhile. It is true that a Boston corporation would have suffered little disadvantage in incorporating in Nevada rather than in New Jersey, but it appears that, with few legal advantages to choose between, the corporations usually made their mythical settlements close to home.

Nevada passed its cut-rate general incorporation law in 1903, and the incorporation agents, who immediately sprang into being, were at once deluged with inquiries from corporate enterprises all over the country, existing corporations as well as contemplated ones. There was, of course, a great deal of comparison shopping. "I have just completed an examination of your general incorporation law," an enterpriser wrote from Indianapolis, ". . . and believe it a better law than New Jersey or Arizona, although it is somewhat cheaper in the latter. . . ."[3] The trouble for Nevada was that there were other states, such as Arizona, that wanted to get in on a good thing.

One of the leading agencies in Nevada for incorporating businesses from other states was the State Agent and Transfer Syndicate, Inc. This firm was troubled during the early years of the incorporation law because it did not know what the law meant; nor did its customers. The main points of the law were understood, however, for they were simple. As a company official explained to an inquirer:

> "There is no annual tax on corporations nor is there any supervision over the conduct of the business other than a general compliance with the corporation law. The principal requirements are that a principal office must be established

> and maintained, in which office there must be an oppointed agent to receive any legal service; in said principal office there shall be filed a copy of the articles, a copy of the By-Laws and also be kept on file a duplicate stock ledger; which said ledger is a confidential service as the ledger is not open for inspection save as set forth in the General Corporation Law."[4]

As for costs, the state required twenty cents per $1,000 of capitalization and a minimum of $50; additional fees included $2.50 for notarization and twenty-five cents for filing.[5]

Many of the companies incorporated in Nevada under the new act were fly-by-night operations, much like the promotional mining companies with which Nevada was long familiar. At the same time, the state registered blue-chip organizations, such as the California Standard Oil Company, a customer of the State Agent and Transfer Syndicate, organized to operate in South America as a subsidiary of the Standard Oil Company of California. How a business went about sending its sword to the marriage in such cases is to be seen in the instructions from Standard Oil to the State Agent and Transfer Syndicate:

> We will appreciate it if you will organize with persons from your office, and upon completing the organization, have the board of your directors resign, and call a stockholders' meeting, at which the following directors should be elected . . .[6]

A board was elected and then persuaded to resign, and a stockholders' meeting was held to elect the officers suggested by the legal firm which was handling the affairs of the California Standard Oil Company.[7]

Nevada's old enemy, California, passed a law in 1917 which virtually prohibited the sale in California of stocks of Nevada corporations which did not meet California's legal requirements for incorporation.[8] That Blue Sky Law knocked the bottom out of a growing business, but Nevada continued to operate a modest incorporation activity. However, after the passage of that law, the Nevada legislature began, more and more, to employ the lure of tax benefits, rather than that of corporate benefits, in its effort to siphon off some of the growing wealth of the Golden State.

The obvious key to Nevada's program of tax reform was the fact that the resident population was small and the tourist population growing. The shift of the tax burden from the former to the latter was most successfully accomplished through the gasoline tax. By this means the highways returned the largest share of Nevada's taxes just as the railroads had been obliged to do a generation earlier. In 1955 the income from state and county gasoline taxes was more than $7.3 million; whereas the income from gambling taxes was only $4.75 million.[9]

It might be argued that this tax was justified by the fact that there were more miles of highway per capita in Nevada than elsewhere and that out-of-state users could reasonably be expected to bear their share in the costs of construction and upkeep. They were, however, already doing so. According to the terms of the Oddie-Colton Act of 1927, the federal government was given the authority to increase the federal highway funds available to states that include a large share of the public domain. Consequently, the federal government has put up about eighty per cent of the money to finance Nevada's highways. During the year ending June 30, 1952, Nevada received approximately $6 million of federal money for highway construction.[10]

By the mid-thirties, the Nevada legislature had eliminated all taxes which would seriously affect residents. There was no income tax, no inheritance or death taxes, and no transfer, sales, or gift taxes.[11] The removal of sales and gift taxes was designed to encourage Californians to buy expensive items in

Nevada to escape the sales tax levied in their own state. To facilitate further the development of Nevada into a busy distribution center, its cities were maintained as free ports. Manufacturers were allowed to ship goods into the state and store them indefinitely in warehouses without being taxed; only a few other states permitted this.[12] California retaliated, however, with a use tax on goods imported into the state, and Nevada had to reintroduce the sales tax.[13]

To attract wealthy men to the state, the inheritance tax, instituted in the Progressive reform year of 1913, was repealed in 1925. Consequently, when a wealthy Los Angeles businessman died in 1928, his estate was exempt from the California inheritance tax because he had established his legal residence in Nevada through owning a summer cottage on the Nevada side of Lake Tahoe. The publicity which greeted this novel aspect of his death brought other millionaires legally to Nevada and encouraged the legislature to make further tax reforms in their behalf. In 1936 it limited taxes on personal property and real estate to five cents on the dollar, and in 1939 it reduced real and personal property taxes still further. At the same time, it launched a nationwide campaign to lure rich men and businesses to a state that had few taxes and no labor problems.[14]

The campaign has been at least modestly successful in bringing into the state a wealthy class known contemptuously to the old Nevadans as "the tax dodgers." A key figure in this affluent immigration has been Norman Biltz, a Los Angeles salesman who became a Nevada real estate promoter in the 1920s, concentrating especially on the Tahoe region.[15]

In the search for methods of public finance which would not involve taxation of its citizens, the Nevada legislature returned every now and then to the idea of a state lottery, for which hundreds of thousands of tickets would be sold illegally at great profit in other states. Such a scheme finally passed the legislature in 1937. It required a constitutional amendment, however, which in turn required the affirmative vote of the people, and it was voted down. The opposition to it had been effectively organized by the gambling interests in the state, who, naturally, opposed any proposal in which the state competed with what was rapidly becoming its leading private industry.[16] (The gambling interests were also successful in outlawing bank night in the motion-picture theaters of Reno.[17])

II

Nevadans can hardly deny that their taxes have been structured for the purpose of obtaining money from foreigners and especially Californians; nor, probably would they wish to deny it. From the time of the Comstock Lode to the period of the partially successful attacks by Progressives on railroad-rate discrimination, Nevada was economically a California colony, ruthlessly plundered to enrich San Francisco's entrepreneurs. Every good Nevadan believes that his state has a lot coming to it from California, and this attitude is undoubtedly responsible for much of the support given to the gambling interests by Nevadans who otherwise disapprove of them.

Nevadans are apt to take umbrage when accused of enacting easy divorce laws and legalized gambling only for the purpose of milking strangers. They will argue that this legal laxity in the Sagebrush State is simply an honest expression of that Western individualism which leaves every man free to go to the devil any way he wishes. Unquestionably there is a good deal to this argument. Nevada obviously is not economically motivated in allowing everybody to drive as fast as he likes on its highways, with never a thought of a state speed limit. The absence of a speed limit is in harmony with the generally libertarian outlook of a state devoted almost exclusively to mining and cattle-raising during most of its history.

Legalized prostitution is a more colorful example of Nevada's adherence to the moral code of the old West for sentimental, rather than economic, reasons. Moral forces succeeded in outlawing prostitution in 1923, but it soon returned, by public demand, under police supervision and with mandatory registration and medical inspection. The red-light areas were severely limited, and no soliciting was permitted on the streets. In Las Vegas there was Block 16, a row of shacks just a few blocks from the main thoroughfare. In Reno the "Stockade" or "Bull Pen" was somewhat more removed from the center of town but still accessible. It operated more as a public convenience than as a vested interest: a girl rented one of eighty cribs for two dollars per day and pocketed all of her take.[18]

With the coming of World War II, the Armed Forces brought pressure on the communities of western Nevada to close up their brothels, and open prostitution came to an end in Reno and Las Vegas, as it had a generation earlier during World War I in New Orleans. Since the second world war, prostitution has been, in practice, subject to local option, legally suppressed in the two main centers of population, but somewhat covertly permitted in other towns of the state. (State law, however, prohibits the establishment of a bordello within 400 yards of a church or schoolhouse.)[19] It is not likely that prostitution is looked upon with favor by the gambling interests, for it diverts customers from the tables and is out of harmony with the note of innocent good fun to which the gambling casinos are profitably keyed. That it continues to exist openly in some areas is testimony to an existing public opinion opposed to all sumptuary legislation as a matter of principle.

The easy divorce law, like prostitution and gambling, was inherited from Nevada's frontier past long before it came to be exploited to lure foreign dollars into the state. In 1861 the territorial government established a six-months'-residence divorce law, and this law was retained when Nevada became a state. The period of six months corresponded to the six-month period required for state citizenship. Throughout the nineteenth century, only Nevadans availed themselves of their law, and there were few divorces in the state, because few women lived in it.[20]

The new era opened in 1906 with the lavishly publicized Reno divorce of Laura Corey. Laura's husband William was president of U. S. Steel and, at the age of forty, a leading Eastern financial figure. Corey lost his heart to a singing actress, Mabelle Gilman, and deserted his wife in 1905. A year later, the sorrowing Laura arrived in Reno, amid a prodigious fanfare of national public indignation, and took up residence to receive the most avidly followed divorce of the day. Corey waited nine months and then married his Mabelle, and Reno became almost overnight the divorce capital of the nation.

Because California had passed a law in 1903 requiring a year's wait after a divorce before issuance of the final decree, it soon became the chief source of Reno's new prosperity. However, Nevada's lawyers advertised widely in the East and drew many cases from that area also. By 1910 the number of Nevada divorces had risen to about 300 a year. Nevada's lapse into moral order followed in 1913, during the climax of Progressivism, when it prohibited gambling and instituted an inheritance tax. That year the legislature passed a law requiring a year of residence for at least one of the parties in any divorce suit. Consequently, Reno suffered a severe business slump accompanied by a sharp falling off in church attendance, so in 1915 the state returned to the six-month residence period.

In 1920 Mary Pickford divorced the movie actor Owen

Moore to marry Douglas Fairbanks, and this aided the resurgence of the divorce business. Then, in 1927, faced with growing competition from Mexico and France, and threatened by the possibility that Wyoming might adopt a three-month's residence divorce law, Nevada lowered the period from six months to three. The year 1930 saw the granting of 3,000 divorces in Reno, which then had a permanent population of only 18,000; the estimated profit to the town was $3 million. In 1931 Nevada lowered the residence period to six weeks, and Reno divorces rose to 4,745. That, however, proved to be the high water mark. Idaho and Florida also reduced residence requirements to six weeks, but the Nevada legislature was dissuaded from lowering its requirements from thirty days by lawyers who feared that such divorces might be invalidated by the courts in other states. Divorces then dropped to 2,854 in 1934 and to about 2,000 in 1940. By the latter date, however, the business was still providing the main support for 180 lawyers in Reno, with the side result that Nevada politics has been dominated by bench and bar to an unusual extent.

The marriage business in Nevada also moved briskly, and California provided even greater profits from this than from divorces after it passed a law, in 1940, requiring a blood test and a three-day waiting period after issuance of a marriage certificate. Nevada offered instant marriage, around the clock, at a cost of only two dollars for a marriage license and a small donation to the justice of the peace or minister. Richard Lillard, the historian of Nevada, noted that the competition for the office of justice of the peace in Reno during the 1930s was every bit as furious as the competition for sheriff had been during prohibition. In 1932 in Nevada, 7,088 marriages were performed, compared with 3,989 divorces.

. . .

III

Legalized gambling, like easy divorce in Nevada, was the consequence of both the old libertarian Western tradition and the new states' rights avarice. A prohibitionary gambling law of 1909 was unsatisfactory from the beginning. Underworld figures infiltrated the state, and police bribery became a scandal. Then in 1912 the law was liberalized to permit "social games" such as poker and whist, provided that winnings were paid off in merchandise instead of in money. In 1913 gambling was again prohibited, but two years later the resulting discontent and corruption again forced the state to moderate the prohibition. Gambling operators were licensed, and card games legalized, so long as the game was not banked by the operator. This law was observed mainly in the breach until its repeal in 1931.[21]

The Great Depression hit Nevada hard, perhaps harder than it did most other states, and at the same time the prosperity of the divorce mills of Reno was being threatened by the passage of easy-divorce legislation in competing states. The liquor prohibition law had placed Reno under gangster rule—although apparently a rather easy-going one—and the gambling casinos were operating almost as openly as the speakeasies.[22] Most Nevadans probably had as little respect for the one law as for the other, and it would have been quite natural for the state legislature to have repealed the anti-gambling law, solely in response to the wishes of the constituents. At the same time, the 1931 act that completely legalized gambling again was looked upon as a recovery measure, for it was designed to bring outside money into the state.

Nevada gambling establishments celebrated the passage of the law, but they were remarkably slow in adjusting to the new order of things. Professional gamblers, like saloonkeepers, are essentially a deeply conservative class of people. Their rituals have long been prescribed and, quite aside from economic benefits deriving from their observance, tend to remain controlling factors. An extreme version of this conservatism may be seen today in almost any of the "horse parlors" in Nevada. The Turf Club in Reno, for instance, famous for its Chicago-style kosher pastrami sandwiches, maintains the dignified, studious, atmosphere of a Christian Science reading room. Elderly gentlemen peruse the racing forms and follow the results of races as they are marked up on the blackboard in quiet surroundings, undisturbed by the clatter of slot machines and the jingle of juke boxes which assail the ear in the coffee shops and drug stores throughout the Biggest Little City in the World.

Most Nevada gamblers continued the dear old ways throughout the thirties. They operated in darkened and secluded halls, the dealers in shirtsleeves and green eyeshades, dealing to the same customers as in former days. The idea of advertising their places of business apparently occurred to them no more than it did, at that time, to banking establishments. Their business, no doubt, increased, especially with out-of-state customers, as a consequence of their newly won legality. In Reno, the Bank Club, especially, became more prosperous. The real revolution in modern gambling, however, did not begin until the arrival of an ex-carnival man, Raymond Smith, and his sons, Harold and Raymond, Jr., who, with no professional gambling experience behind them, introduced the basic innovations in the business which characterize it today.[23]

Smith left the West Coast in the middle of the depression with a little capital and opened a small gambling casino on Virginia Street in Reno, which he named Harolds Club after his son. From the first, Smith advertised as widely as his resources permitted, and by the end of the decade his billboard advertisements were scattered across half the nation. To attract customers from among those whose incomes had been reduced by the depression, he introduced penny roulette, and to gain publicity, he introduced such gimmicks as mouse roulette, where the winning number was selected by a live mouse. Smith prospered and expanded rapidly.

Smith's basic purpose was to democratize gambling as Henry Ford had democratized the automobile. The older casinos not only catered chiefly to experienced male gamblers, but, so far as possible, they concentrated their efforts on the "high rollers"—fellow professionals whose big bets during an hour or so determined a casino's profit or loss for the evening. Smith always remained true to his penny-roulette beginnings, catering to the common man, with the result that his profits increased over that of his competitors, while his risk was reduced to the vanishing point.

Smith sought the patronage of the common woman even more assiduously than he pursued that of the common man, and with even greater success. Harolds Club was located on the main street of Reno, its row of glass doors opening twenty-four hours a day onto its brightly lighted bars and gambling tables. He substituted female dealers for men at the twenty-one tables, and also employed female shills, inexpensively acquired and quickly trained from the floating population of divorcees. The female dealers operated according to a fixed set of rules, without choice as to whether they would hit or stick, so that they never pitted themselves against the players. To the contrary, they were instructed to help the customers out by giving them counsel, if requested, on the best possible lines of play. Under this kind of friendly tutelage, women warmed to twenty-one, as well as to craps and roulette, so that they now probably contribute at least as much, and perhaps more, to Nevada's profits from gambling, than men do.

In other ways as well, Smith brought an atmosphere of respectability to his gaming place. He instituted a baby-sitting service, so that children would not be left alone in motels, while their mothers were cranking the handles on the slot machines. He installed a museum of western Americana for the edification as well as the entertainment of his customers, and he contributed many large scholarships to deserving students attending the University of Nevada, which is a little more than a mile up the street. Everywhere there were signs reminding customers that they should not spend more than they could afford. If, as sometimes happened, these admonitions were ignored in the heat of play, Harolds Club readily lent funds for the trip home.

When they finally became convinced that they could not beat Smith, the professional operators in the other casinos grudgingly adopted some of his ways. After the war, new casinos were situated as close as possible to Harolds Club, and they copied it as faithfully as they could. The ex-Detroit gambler Lincoln Fitzgerald built the Nevada Club, departing from the model of Harolds Club by building into his casino a private apartment, from which he seldom emerged onto the street.

The Nevada Club has become, probably, the second most successful of the half-dozen or so direct imitations of Harolds Club in Reno. The most successful has been Harrahs Club, located next door to Smith's establishment, which it resembles in almost all respects. Luckily for the proprietor of the new casino, his name was William Harrah; so nothing could be done about his cashing in on the all but transcontinental billboard advertising of his rival. Like Smith, Harrah came from California with no experience as a professional gambler but with that of an operator of legal games of chance—in his case, bingo—carried on in a carnival atmosphere. These two men, with this common experience, did better than any of the professional gamblers, who operated virtually all of the other large casinos in the state.

IV

At the time that gambling was legalized once again in 1931, Reno was the nearest thing to a center of population which Nevada contained, and the only town in the state which was nationally known. Las Vegas was only a dot on the map, a railroad division point on the line from Los Angeles to Chicago. At the time gambling was legalized, Las Vegas was just beginning to show life, with the construction of neighboring Hoover Dam, authorized by Congress in 1928. It is typical of Nevada statesmanship that this vast project, crucially important to the development of southern Nevada, was sponsored by two Californians, in the Swing-Johnson Bill, while Nevada's Senators were mainly busying themselves on behalf of the silver interests.

Boulder City was created as a government-owned community near Las Vegas, bringing a permanent population to the area, as well as a transient group of construction workers. Because Boulder City was absolutely dry, Las Vegas received the custom of the construction workers, whose historic mission proved to be not only to create Lake Mead and to irrigate the Southwest but to prime the pump for the subsequent torrent of gambling and allied tourist business in Las Vegas, which has increased continually since then.

Except for legalized gambling, Las Vegas has less economic reason for being than Reno, which remains an important distribution point for a large area. Las Vegas, however, draws its customers from the metropolitan areas of Los Angeles and San Diego, more populous and more rapidly growing than the San Francisco Bay region. Consequently, Las Vegas has far outdistanced the rest of the state in its rate of growth. In 1959 the population of Clark County, where Las Vegas is situated, was 122,000, while that of Washoe County was 83,000. Total population of the state stood at 280,000.[24] Nevada prides itself on being the most rapidly growing state in the nation, but outside these two gambling centers, the population has made only modest gains over the past generation.

Initially Las Vegas developed its gambling activities after the pattern established in Reno, but on a smaller scale, its casinos concentrated within a few blocks on Fremont Street in the center of town. Until the close of World War II it was distinctly small-time, compared with the older city to the north. Its first big casino, the Golden Nugget, was built in 1946, under the direction of Guy McAfee, a retired captain of police, and it repaid its original investment in nine months.[25] The Golden Nugget remains the main downtown casino, but it was rapidly overshadowed by developments outside the town along what came to be known as "the Strip."

In 1947 Marion Hicks, a local construction and hotel man, in cooperation with Lieutenant Governor Clifford Jones, built the Thunderbird, which was to be a model for the more lavish hotel-resort-casinos to follow on the Strip. In 1950 Wilbur Clark built the Desert Inn for $4.5 million. The Sahara was completed in 1952 for $5.5 million, followed by the Sands, Showboat, Royal Nevada, Riviera, Moulin Rouge, Dunes, Stardust, Martinique (at a cost of $15 million), Tropicana, Continental, Trade Winds, Vegas Plasa, Casa Blanca, San Souci, Horizon, and others.[26]

With the development of the Strip, Las Vegas asserted its independence of Reno and enthusiastically submitted to the influence of Hollywood. The Desert Inn was a typical Strip operation, employing a manager and two assistants, eighty-five dealers, eighteen pit bosses and box men, seven change girls, and three slot machine supervisors in its casino. In the mid-fifties it kept $2 million on hand for an average day and up to $3 million on weekends.[27] Where the Desert Inn and its more luxurious counterparts departed from Reno hotel-casinos—the Riverside, the Mapes, and the Holiday—was in its lavishness of decor and of free entertainment. In 1954 the Strip hotels paid $8 million for entertainment, in 1955 the outlay rose to $20 million, and it has increased continually since then.[28] The Reno and Lake Tahoe casinos began, then, to imitate those of the Strip, but they have not kept pace.

The palaces on the Strip are calculated to attract the big spenders, leaving the dollar-ante crowd to the downtown casinos. The high rollers from Texas and Los Angeles continue to be an important part of the play on the Strip. However, the big shows are as attractive to the small spenders as to the high rollers, so that the little man and his wife have begun to leave downtown for the Strip, as evidenced by boarded-up casinos on Fremont Street. As in the case of Reno, gambling is de-emphasized in the promotional literature of Paradise, as the unincorporated area which includes the Strip is named. The advertisements instead proclaim the wealth of free entertainment and "fun in the sun." Special airline and hotel rates put a vacation in Las Vegas within the reach of families of modest means throughout the nation, providing the casinos are avoided. However, the promoters expect that the casinos will not be avoided either by these vacationers or by the highly paid entertainers.

In the mid-fifties, at a time when there were only ten resort hotels on the Strip, the Las Vegas area supported thirty-five commercial hotels and 250 motels. The total money left in Las Vegas by tourists in 1955 was computed to be $164,325,-992.50, a little more than $3,650 for every living man, woman, and child in the town.[29] Since then, the number of resort hotels has more than doubled, outrunning the rapidly increasing population, and it may be supposed that the profits from "tourism" have at least kept pace with the expansion of the community. Reno has been cut off from such expansion by the booming Lake Tahoe development, and it therefore retains a good deal of its original natural beauty, which one may find only a few blocks away from the "Alley," where Harolds, Harrahs, and the other clubs keep up the action around the clock every day in the week.

Nevadans, who welcomed legal gambling in the midst of the depression, have mixed emotions about the current state of affairs. One old Nevadan commented recently that "The Nevadans don't like it, and one day they may vote it out. But in the meantime, they have it under control. The Nevadans don't go to these places, and they don't associate with divorcees. And many people coming into the state don't like this either." Some Nevadans evidently continue to look upon themselves as belonging to a mining and cattle state which permits gambling because cattlemen and miners have always engaged in it, but it has long been obvious that this is no longer the case.

In 1958 the personal income derived from ranching comprised 1.2 per cent of the total state income; that from mining, 2.5 per cent. Wholesale and retail trade were more important, at 12.1 per cent; while the income of government workers was increasing and stood at 15.6 per cent. The biggest share, however, came from amusement, recreation, and services, which contributed 29.1 per cent of the state's payroll. In terms of percentage of the work force employed in 1959, mining and agriculture accounted for 10 per cent, as compared with 29 per cent for "services and miscellany" largely gambling and attendant activities. Government accounted for 17.7 per cent and wholesale and retail, for 19.3.[30] The state is dependent upon gambling as upon no other line of business. Since gambling does much to support Nevada's retail trade, its nearest competitors as employers of Nevadans are the federal, state, and local governments. In the area of free enterprise, the gamblers control the economy; they know it and the politicians know it.

V

Down to World War II, gambling in Nevada, centered in Reno, was regarded as a home-operated industry. Raymond Smith, of Harolds Club, the leading operator in the field, was, to be sure, an outsider, but he was devoid of out-of-state gambling connections, and he was making Nevada his home. Following the war, however, only the most guileless of Nevadans could fail to observe that professional gamblers had moved in from out of state to take over the casinos. They were, after all, the people most qualified for the positions. Raymond Smith was unusual in having succeeded in the field without prior experience. He commented once, however, that it had cost him about a million dollars in losses through cheating before he had ironed out the wrinkles.[31]

In 1946 Benjamin "Bugsy" Siegel built the Flamingo Hotel —one of the first on the Strip—with $1 million of his own and $6 million of borrowed money.[32] It has been said that Siegel, as a notorious underworld figure, was not welcomed in the community. At the time he went into business, however, all that was required to receive a gambling license was the making of an application to the city or county commissioners, and no investigation was made of the criminal record of the applicant. Even after 1949, when such investigations began to be made, imprisonment for a gambling offense elsewhere was not counted against the applicant, because gambling was legal in Nevada.[33] Siegel, moreover, held the whip hand over other gambling houses in the area by his control of the racing wire service of the Al Capone mob which was used in all of the larger casinos.

In 1947 Siegel was the spectacular victim of a gangland murder in his home in Los Angeles, and his assassination drew national attention to the possibility of gangster control of Nevada gambling. Then Harry Sherwood was shot in his Lake Tahoe resort, Louis Strauss was arrested and identified as "Russian Louis" of the Eastern underworld, and Benny Binion, indicted in Texas for operating a numbers racket, was questioned concerning the murder of Herbert "the Cat" Noble.[34] The likelihood that these happenings indicated widespread criminal infiltration of Nevada was widely discussed, but the official line in Nevada appears to have been that only Siegel, among the nation's gang leaders, had been seriously involved in Nevada affairs, and that the slate had been wiped clean by his death.[35]

However, in 1950–1 the Senate investigating committee, headed by Estes Kefauver of Tennessee, put an entirely different face on the matter. Siegel, the committee found, had carried on gaming operations in California and elsewhere before coming to Nevada and had been associated with Charles "Lucky" Luciano, Frank Costello, Joe Adonis, Meyer Lansky, and other Eastern mob leaders. Among them, Lansky had become an important Las Vegas operator. Siegel had controlled the Las Vegas racing wire service since 1942, through Moe Sedway, a convicted gambler and former Eastern mobster. After Siegel's death, the Flamingo had been taken over by another gambler with a long record of arrests, Sanford Adler, and his associates. Adler had later sold out his interests to other hoodlums and had removed to the Reno and Lake Tahoe areas to continue his operations there.[36]

The committee found the Desert Inn to be operated by Wilbur Clark, an old-time gambler who had once worked the gambling boats off California, and whose business associates were identified as gamblers and bootleggers from the Middle West and elsewhere.[37] It also learned that the Bank Club in Reno

> . . . is owned and operated by William Graham and James McKay, who were convicted of mail fraud in New York, but who returned to Nevada after the expiration of their prison terms. . . . Also operating in Reno are Mert Wertheimer, a big-time Michigan gambler who has been in partnership in Florida with such notorious gangsters as Joe Adonis, the Lanskys, and Frank Erickson, and with Lincoln Fitzgerald and Daniel Sullivan, members of the Michigan gambling syndicate.[38]

Kefauver elicited from Lieutenant Governor Clifford Jones and State Tax Commissioner William J. Moore the fact that prior to 1949 little or no effort had been made to screen the applicants for gambling licenses. After that time some effort was made to deny them to undesirables, but those already holding licenses were not disturbed, and gambling convictions were not held against new applicants. It was the conclusion of the Kefauver Committee that,

> . . . too many of the men running gambling operations in Nevada are either members of existing out-of-state gambling syndicates or have had histories of close association with the underworld characters who operate those syndicates. The licensing system which is in effect in the state has not resulted in excluding the undesirables from the State but has merely served to give their activities a seeming cloak of respectability.[39]

The committee concluded that two major national crime syndicates existed, and that both of them were operating in Nevada, or at least had associates operating there.

Jones and Moore, despite their responsible positions in the state with respect to controlling gambling, were financially involved in the gaming business. Moore, who was on the commission directly responsible for gaining control, was part owner of the Last Frontier, and he had recently received a wire service deal which, in the opinion of the committee, gave him a considerable financial advantage over his competitors. Jones was part owner of the Thunderbird and holder of a small share in the Pioneer Club, which had been sold to him for $5000 and had regularly returned $14,000 annually to him thereafter. Jones's law partner, the committee further pointed out, was the district attorney of Clark County.[40]

It was not until 1955 that the first real efforts were made to bring Nevada gambling under actual governmental control. In that year the Thunderbird's gambling license was suspended until Marion Hicks and former Lieutenant Governor Jones divested themselves of their interests. The New Frontier's license was delayed pending an investigation, and the motion picture actor George Raft was denied the right to purchase two per cent of the Flamingo because of his long association with such mobsters as Mickey Cohen and "Bugsy" Siegel. Tony Cornero Stralla was denied a license for his $6.5 million Stardust, because he had been convicted as a rum-rummer and had operated gambling ships off the coast of California.[41]

Governor Charles H. Russell, in the course of his efforts to reform Nevada gambling in 1955, conceded that the state's leading industry had been infiltrated by elements of Murder, Incorporated, and by hoodlums from New York, Chicago, St. Louis, Miami, and Detroit. He declared, however: "I am determined that Nevada's licensed gambling shall not be invaded by hoodlums or organized crime."[42] To this end, a ninety-day moratorium was imposed on new gambling licenses, except those which were already pending. A three-man commission was organized with authority over gambling throughout the state and with the power to impound casino records and to compel the attendance of witnesses at hearings. Their control over state gambling is subject to request by the tax commission for the reopening of any licensing case.

The Gaming Commission has listed men believed to be leading figures in the national crime syndicates, and has told state gambling interests not to associate with them in any way. In October 1963 the Commission revoked the gambling license of Frank Sinatra because he had permitted a black-listed hoodlum to stay at the Cal-Neva Lodge at Lake Tahoe. The effect of this was to force Sinatra to sell his 50 per cent interest in the Cal-Neva and his 9 per cent interest in the Sands Hotel in Las Vegas, holdings valued at an estimated $3.5 million.[43] These efforts to assert governmental authority over Nevada gambling were begun only after a decade of virtually unopposed infiltration by gangsters, and it does not appear that anything is seriously contemplated that would divorce gambling from those gangsters who are already entrenched in the business.

VI

"Among the many unlooked-for treasures that are bound up and hidden away in the depths of Sierra solitudes," wrote the naturalist John Muir, "none more surely charm and surprise all kinds of travelers than the glacier lakes." Muir supposed that there were not less than 1,500 of these, but the undoubted queen among them was Lake Tahoe.

> Lake Tahoe, 22 miles long by 10 wide, and from 500 to over 1600 feet in depth, is the largest of all the Sierra lakes. . . . Its forested shores go curving in and out around many an emerald bay and pinecrowned promontory, and its waters are everywhere as keenly pure as any to be found among the highest mountains.[44]

Mark Twain walked up from Carson City to Lake Tahoe in the early sixties and camped there for several weeks, and like Muir, he was most struck by the lake's "keenly pure" waters:

> The forest above us was dense and cool, the sky above us was cloudless and brilliant with sunshine, the broad lake before us was glassy and clear, or rippled and breezy, or black and storm-tossed, according to Nature's mood. . . . The view was always fascinating, bewitching, entrancing. . . . So singularly clear was the water that where it was only twenty or thirty feet deep the bottom was so perfectly distinct that the boat seemed floating in the air! Yes, where it was even *eighty* feet deep. Every little pebble was distinct, every speckled trout, every hand's-breadth of sand. . . . Down through the transparency of these great depths the water was not *merely* transparent, but dazzlingly, brilliantly so. All objects seen through it had a bright, strong vividness, not only of outline, but of every minute detail, which they would not have had when seen simply through the same depth of atmosphere.[45]

Today travelers coming upon Lake Tahoe from the south side by Highway 50 may well be surprised at what they see, but they will not be charmed. They will come, first of all, upon a dirty beach, one of several around that great, high lake, which are maintained for the public, complete with life-guard and hot-dog stand. The lake will be there to see, but it will take several more miles of driving before it is framed for them above by the dense, cool forests. They must, of course, drive past Stateline; past Harrahs and Harolds and Harveys and so on, and after that they must find a place, between the private cottages and smaller casinos, where they can go down to the water.

Some might wonder why Lake Tahoe was not set aside as a national park long before the real-estate promoters came and cut it into private lots. It might be supposed that Francis G. Newlands, Nevada's most distinguished senator and the leading conservationist in Congress, might have made some effort to preserve this part of his state. That was not the kind of conservationist that Newlands was, however, nor was this the kind of conservation which appealed especially to his Progressive colleagues. He and they looked upon conservation less as the preserving of nature than as the putting of nature to intelligent use for the benefit of society. Newlands, as he wrote the Nevada *State Journal* in 1909,[46] saw Lake Tahoe as a source of water power and as a navigable waterway, even though, from a navigational point of view, it is difficult to see that Lake Tahoe had much to offer. The Progressive movement was good but not beautiful.

Lake Tahoe was left mainly to the real-estate promoters, and on the Nevada side they appealed to the well-to-do summer-cottage crowd, to the winter-sports enthusiasts, and, in ever greater numbers, to the "tax dodgers." There were also coffee shops and bars which had slot machines, but the real potential of Lake Tahoe was not understood until William Harrah moved in, in the 1950s.

It appears that, during the fifties, Harrah took up where the Smiths had left off in the development of gambling operational methods in Reno. During the late forties and early fifties, Harolds Club suffered from the fact that one of the owners, Harold himself, went on a ten-year drinking bout, consuming according to his own accounts, as much as four quarts of whiskey in a day. During that period, he gambled away his money in rival casinos to the point where it was feared that other operators might gain influence in the Smith organization. Harold Smith finally got a grip on himself and made a vow to the "Big Gent Upstairs," as he puts it, and he became president of the organization.[47] In the meantime, the gaunt, grey, austere, efficient William Harrah moved methodically ahead to become the state's leading operator of gambling establishments.

Incredible as it may seem, Harrah was the first big-time Nevada operator to reason that the state line at Lake Tahoe, as the closest point to California customers, was strategically located for a gambling casino. It was urged against this idea, that a casino in that area would have to close during the winter and that in other seasons there would be no place for customers to stay overnight. Nevertheless, Harrah bought up the acres adjoining the California border and built two large casinos and a spacious parking lot. Since it was an inconvenient trip for San Franciscans to make in one day—almost five hours each way—Harrah started bus lines.

Characteristically scientific in his business operations, Harrah paid the non-profit, tax-exempt Stanford Research Institute $16,000 to tell him how he could get customers around the clock by bus. The resulting monograph, entitled *An Investigation of Factors Influencing Bus Scheduling*, concluded that his typical client would be "elderly, in low occupational status, unmarried, a renter rather than home owner, and without a car," and that such persons comprised "an unusual segment of the total population."[48] It was also a segment of the population which had relatively little money, but what money it did have Harrah went after. Accepting the conclusions of the monograph, he advertised for this segment in Stockton, Manteca, Oakland, and elsewhere.

Following the advice of the Stanford Research Institute, Harrah wrung such a fortune from these marginal economic groups that similar operations were set up by rivals. The number of motels in the area increased from ten to 375, and customers began driving in as well as coming by bus. The casinos vied with one another for big-name, million-dollar entertainment, the highway became an all-weather route, and Lake Tahoe was well on its way toward eclipsing its parent town, Reno, as the gambling center of northern Nevada.

The new development posed new problems, and one of them was sewage. Lake Tahoe is in a great basin surrounded by forested mountains. Its one outlet is the Truckee River, which serves Reno. With thousands of people coming into the area, an effluvium problem arose which was temporarily solved by treating the sewage and then spraying it on the surrounding forests. This was the least expensive method possible, except for dumping the sewage directly into the lake or into the Truckee River. In the opinion of experts, however, this spraying of the forests, if continued, would pollute the lake irrevocably. Meanwhile, the gambling center at Stateline continued to develop, and a number of new building applications were approved, including a twenty-nine story addition to Harrahs, (estimated to produce an additional 200,000 gallons of effluvium daily) and Del Webb's Sahara-Tahoe casino-restaurant-hotel (estimated to produce an additional 240,000 gallons daily). Smaller approved projects were, of course, expected to produce lesser amounts of additional effluvium.[49]

As an interstate lake, Tahoe is clearly a concern of the national government. Accordingly, the President's Water Pollution Control Advisory Board convened with representatives from California and Nevada in September 1963. Experts testified at the meeting that Lake Tahoe would be ruined by a continuance of the existing sewage-disposal system, which would cause algae to develop in it, eventually turning it from its crystal purity to a scummy, murky green; and that such algae had already been found in the lake, which showed that its ruination had begun. The experts concluded that the sewage would have to be removed from the area altogether and that the best method would be to purify it and send it down the Truckee River.

Presumably this could have been done hygienically, or the experts would not have recommended the method, but politically it was out of the question. Governor Grant Sawyer of Nevada turned it down. The spraying of sewage would therefore continue, unless Governor Edmund G. Brown of California called upon the federal government to intervene, which he was clearly invited to do. Brown had a good deal to say against the gambling developments on the Nevada shore of Lake Tahoe, but he refrained from asking the national government to intercede.

Nevada has a Bureau of Environmental Health. The director of this bureau, W. W. White, attended the Water Pollution Control meeting, and in connection with the spraying of sewage he confessed that "there isn't much land left. I don't believe we have capacity for our sewage here more than three or four years." He had no positive solution to the problem, but he said that he would at least halt construction in the area "until we find some answers or it gets too hot."[50] It got too hot immediately. White's statement was made on September 27, 1963. On October 3, White said that he was now ready to approve permits to put an additional 650,000 gallons of sewage a day into the Lake Tahoe treatment plant. Asked why he had changed his mind, he answered that permission for this additional sewage was necessary to the plans of the casino enterprisers—Harrah, Del Webb, and the smaller ones —who were planning to build in the area in the next six months.[51]

The Lake Tahoe sewage plant failed to function properly, for some reason, early in October, so signs had to be put up along streams in Eldorado County, California; they read: "Warning. Do Not Drink, Fish, Swim, or Wade in this Water. By Order of the Eldorado County Health Department."[52] There remained the problem of what to do with a putatively sovereign state, where, as Hugo Fisher, the administrator of the California Resources Agency, said: "powerful local interests appear to be stronger than the State jurisdictions in effect."[53]

A meeting between Governors Brown and Sawyer in November did nothing to clear up the problem, so, naturally, Governor Brown felt called upon to defend himself in a subsequent speech before a conference of the Resources Agency of California. He was certain, he said, that Nevada gamblers would turn their side of the lake into a "neon jungle of high-rise buildings." He saw that the consequence might well be the polluting of Lake Tahoe past redemption, "so that multimillionaire gambling interests can get a little fatter from the profits of the slot machines and crap tables." He then defended his own role in the controversy, by pointing out that one governor cannot tell another what to do.[54]

* * *

In 1787 the American Constitution provided for the first federal republic in the history of the world. None of the leagues or confederations of Europe, ancient or contemporary, constituted a true precedent for the design of the founders, and none exerted any significant influence as an example for the delegates to the Constitutional Convention, who discovered acceptable precedents only in their own state constitutions and in the Articles of Confederation. The government which resulted has provided the classic example of federalism from the time it was established to the present, and *The Federalist*, its best contemporary defense, is recognized to be the most authoritative treatise on federalism.

The Federalist presented the best arguments which the authors were able to make for a particular Constitution which none of them entirely endorsed privately. Of the three writers of the *Federalist* papers, Madison was perhaps the most favorably disposed toward the Constitution, for he, more truly than any other man, was the document's author. As has been seen, however, Madison had some private doubts, especially about the upper house of the legislature, while his co-author, Hamilton, basically disbelieved in the whole federal principle.

If these defenders of the system held such reservations, it is probable that reservations were common in the nation, even though its citizens agreed, after much bitter debate, to reconstitute it under the new federal system.

This spirit of suspicious and tentative acceptance continued through the first generation of the new government until the age of nationalism which abruptly followed the War of 1812. What resulted from that war was irrevocable acceptance of the Constitution by almost all Americans, who believed that it provided the most nearly perfect form of government devised by man.

During the early nineteenth century prominent New England Federalists felt free to denounce the Constitution, especially its provision for admitting new Western states into the Union, at a time when they could not even have conceived of such an outlandish state as Nevada. In the period following the War of 1812, however, even the impeccably orthodox Boston Federalist Edward Everett came to assert that "by the wise and happy partition between the national and state governments, in virtue of which the national government is relieved from all the odium of internal administration, and the state governments are spared the conflicts of foreign policies,"[55] the limitless expansion of the nation was possible in full accordance with republican principles. The Civil War was, among other things, the result of a failure of the Constitution to work, but the war did not indicate that the Constitution was any less universally accepted, for both sides fought to uphold it as they understood it.

During the late nineteenth and early twentieth centuries, after the Union was reconstituted, the American federal system came to be viewed by European liberals as the master plan for libertarian government, to a greater extent, probably, than in the pre-Civil War days of Alexis de Tocqueville's *Democracy in America.* Accordingly, the great historian Lord Acton chose to conclude his *Lectures on Modern His-*

tory with a historical account of the American Revolution and Constitution, as though the true course for his own generation had been revealed by these events.

He made this point explicit in his concluding paragraphs, observing that under the American system only certain powers are delegated to the federal government, whereas all other powers are reserved to the states. He further noted the Great Compromise, through which the lower house had been based upon the principle of representation proportional to population, and the upper house upon equality of representation among the states. In the last sentence of his final lecture, he concluded that the United States, "by the principle of Federalism . . . has produced a community more powerful, more prosperous, more intelligent, and more free than any other which the world has ever known."[56]

America today is much more powerful and prosperous than it was at the opening of the century, when Acton spoke those flattering lines, and—although this cannot be so readily demonstrated—it is possibly also more intelligent and free. To the extent that these attributes resulted from the federal system embodied in the Constitution, Madison, as the document's chief architect, stands vindicated today as never before. However, the gamblers' recent take-over of Nevada's economy provides strong evidence supporting his chief criticism of the Constitution: the "possible mischiefs" which small states might get into under its provisions.

By authority of the powers reserved to the states, Nevada was able to rebuild its economy on the foundations of the gambling industry and place that industry at the disposal of ex-convicts from other states. Then, through its spokesmen in the United States Senate, it was able to protect its new basic industry from federal harassments, such as the prohibition of slot machines in interstate commerce or the crippling of the gambling industry by taxes.

What will result eventually from this burgeoning business

may hardly be guessed at, because the industry, as a legitimate one, is new and developing rapidly, and because Congress would probably be able to suppress gambling, if it ever decided to do so. A lesser question, to all but nature lovers, is whether "keenly pure" Lake Tahoe will be turned a murky green by the effluents from the rising gambling city of Stateline. If that greatest of the glacier lakes *does* turn green through the seepage of Stateline sewage, it will become an appropriate symbol of twentieth-century Nevada states' rights enterprise, especially since most of the lake is on the California side.

Bibliographical Note

The manuscript sources available for research on the history of Nevada are more extensive than one might suppose, if one considers the meagerness of its history and the lack of interest the state has itself shown in preserving the records of its past. The most important collections of papers are widely scattered, including those of Senator Francis G. Newlands in the Yale University Library, Senator Key Pittman in the Library of Congress, Senators Tasker L. Oddie and John P. Jones in the Huntington Library, Senator William M. Stewart in the Nevada Historical Society Library at Reno, and Senator Pat McCarran in the Nevada Museum at Carson City.

Among these, the Oddie and Jones collections are rather small but valuable. The McCarran collection is extensive for the period after 1940 but contains little about his early career or about Nevada politics. A large addition to this collection is expected presently. The Stewart collection consists of letterbooks and scrapbooks that cover mainly the period of his second senatorial career. Both the Pittman and Newlands collections are voluminous and extremely rich in information on both national affairs and local politics throughout the careers of the two men.

By far the most important repository of manuscript material

dealing with Nevada is the Bancroft Library at Berkeley, and the Y. M. Yerington papers are its most important Nevada collection. As the superintendent of the Virginia & Truckee Railroad and a leading political figure in Nevada, Yerington year after year wrote letters dealing with politics, business, labor problems, newspapers, and personalities, covering the last quarter of the nineteenth century, a period for which no reliable historical account of Nevada has been written. Despite Yerington's obvious prejudices and his incorrigibly wishful thinking, his correspondence is the one major source for this period of Nevada history.

Also of great value is the Bancroft Library's collection of Grant Smith papers. A mining lawyer and native of Virginia City, Smith was by all odds the best authority on the history of the Comstock. At the time of his death, Smith had completed and was revising an extensive manuscript on the life and times of John W. Mackay, the greatest and most successful of all the Comstock miners. The manuscript, together with annotated newspaper clippings and Smith's notes, carefully typed and arranged, make up the main part of this collection.

In addition, the Bancroft Library possesses numerous smaller collections covering the period down through the rise of Tonopah, the most important of which are cited here in the footnotes, and the best collection of Nevada newspapers. The business records of most of the major Comstock mines are housed in the Mackay School of Mines at the University of Nevada.

The romantic period of the Comstock Lode, from 1859 to 1879, has naturally attracted the interest of writers much more than any subsequent period of Nevada history has, except, perhaps, the gambling era of modern times. Many valuable accounts might be cited for this period, but the three most informative and reliable are Myron Angel, ed., *History of Nevada* (1881), Eliot Lord, *Comstock Mining and Miners* (1883), and Grant Smith, *The History of the Comstock Lode, 1850–1920* (1943). The first of these contains essays on all aspects of early Nevada life and gives the best account of the early political history of the territory and state. The second, although it deals broadly with developments on the Comstock, is at its best in its discussions of the technological history of the lode and the history of the early litigation. The third is a brief general account of the Comstock Lode drawn from Smith's manuscript biography of Mackay.

Both Lord and Smith include San Francisco banking and stock-market activities in their books. For a fuller account of the City during that period, the best work is John S. Hittell, *A History of the City of San Francisco* . . . (1878). There are also two good biographies of Ralston and one of Sutro: Julian Dana, *The Man Who Built San Francisco* (1936), Cecil G. Tilton, *William Chapman Ralston, Courageous Builder* (1937), and Robert E. Stewart, Jr., and Mary Frances Stewart, *Adolph Sutro, A Biography* (1962). W. Turrentine Jackson's *Treasure Hill, Portrait of a Silver Mining Camp* (1963) is a detailed account of one of the peripheral mining regions during the Comstock era, solidly based upon local newspaper reports and mining records.

The nearest approach to a general account of the period following the decline of the Comstock is Sam. P. Davis, ed., *The History of Nevada*, 2 vols. (1913), which contains fragmentary and unreliable tales about political happenings. The history of Tonopah is chronicled more fully, although not much more reliably, in Carl B. Glasscock, *Gold in Them Hills* (1932). Less comprehensive but more scholarly is Francis C. Lincoln, *Mining Districts and Mineral Resources of Nevada* . . . (1923). Two good University of California, Berkeley, theses are Russell Elliot, "The Tonopah-Goldfield-Bullfrog Mining Districts, 1900–1915," (Ph.D., 1946) and Byrd W. Sawyer, "The Gold and Silver Rushes of Nevada, 1900–1910," (M.A., 1931).

Richard Lillard's *Desert Challenge* (1942) is the only general historical discussion there is of Nevada in the twentieth century, and it is a comprehensive, informative, and interesting account. Since the Second World War, Nevada has attracted wide attention again by emerging as the gambling center of the nation. A spate of writings has resulted, much of it apparently based upon the gossip of bartenders, pit bosses, and twenty-one dealers. Among these writings, probably the most trustworthy account of Reno gambling is Oscar Lewis's *Sagebrush Casinos* (1953) and of Las Vegas gambling, *Las Vegas* (1955) by Katharine Best and

Katharine Hillyer. A valuable repository of printed material on contemporary Nevada is the Nevada Room of the University of Nevada library.

The leading political figures of twentieth-century Nevada are discussed in two good secondary works. Arthur B. Darling, ed., *The Public Papers of Francis G. Newlands*, 2 vols. (1932), is a well-edited collection, which gives a full account of Newlands's political philosophy and political record. *Nevada's Key Pittman* (1963) by Fred L. Israel is the most scholarly published biography ever accorded a Nevadan.

CHAPTER I

Notes

1. H. L. Slosson, Jr.: *Deep Mining on the Comstock* (1909), p. 3.
2. Claims to earlier discovery are based upon dubious evidence. See Grant Smith: *The History of the Comstock Lode, 1850–1920* (1943), pp. 1–7.
3. For a recent comparison of California and Nevada mining methods, see Rodman W. Paul: *Mining Frontiers of the Far West, 1848–1880* (1963). For a clear, expert contemporary account of California mining methods, see J. Ross Browne: *United States Mineral Resources for 1866* (1867).
4. Paul: *Mining Frontiers,* p. 32.
5. *Mining and Scientific Press,* Feb. 20, 1875.
6. Thomas A. Rickard: *A History of American Mining* (1932), pp. 32–3.
7. H. H. Bancroft: *Works* (1883–1890), XXXVIII, 208.
8. Grant Smith: *Papers,* Bancroft Library, Berkeley: Box I, Vol. 4.
9. Smith: *Comstock Lode,* p. 45; Rickard: *American Mining,* p. 102; Eliot Lord, *Comstock Mining and Miners* (1883). The following discussion is based primarily on Lord's account. See Rickard: *American Mining,* p. 101, for a brief, clear explanation of the "Washoe Process," which the Comstock mills finally perfected.
10. Duane L. Bliss: "Data Concerning the Virginia & Truckee Railroad," Bancroft Library Manuscripts, Berkeley.
11. William H. Brewer: *Up and Down California, 1860–1864* (1931), p. 552; George F. Becker: *Geology of the Comstock Lode and the Washoe District* (1882), p. 3.
12. *Alta California,* July 8, 1870.
13. Smith: *Papers,* Box II, Vol. 1b (Mackay biography, p. 131).
14. *Mining and Scientific Press,* Feb. 20, 1875, in Smith: *Papers,* Box I, Vol. 4.

15. Henry DeGroat: "Sketches of Washoe Silver Mines," typescript in Smith *Papers,* Box I, Vol. 1.
16. Myron Angel (ed.): *History of Nevada* (1881), pp. 414–15, 449, 462, 476, 502; Smith: *Papers,* Box II, Vol. 1, Box II, Vol. 1b (Mackay biography, pp. 204, 363); Lester W. Mills: *A Sagebrush Saga* (1956), pp. 24–9.
17. Smith: *Comstock Lode,* p. 27.
18. Smith: *Papers,* Box I, Vol. 1.
19. Browne: *U.S. Mineral Resources for 1866,* pp. 30–1.
20. Joseph L. King: *History of the San Francisco Stock Exchange Board* (1910) is an extensive, although not very informative, account by an insider.
21. May 2, 1885.
22. Smith: *Papers,* Box I, Vol. 3, Box I, Vol. 6.
23. Ibid., Box I, Vol. 6.
24. Ibid., Box I, Vol. 6.
25. Smith: *Comstock,* p. 237.
26. Bancroft: *Works,* XXXVIII, 208.
27. Smith: *Papers,* Box I, Vols. 3, 4.
28. Charles H. Shinn: *The Story of the Mines* (1896), p. 125.
29. Effie M. Mack: "William M. Stewart," (Ph.D., University of California, Berkeley, 1931), *passim.*
30. Feb. 16, 1867, quoted in Lord: *Comstock Miners,* p. 178.
31. The story of the discovery of the Comstock Lode has been the subject of a great deal of imaginative writing. Probably the most authoritative account is that printed in the Virginia *Daily Union,* Oct. 9, 1863, and reprinted in the San Francisco *Bulletin,* Oct. 14, 1863, based upon notes provided by Almarin B. Paul, the leading quartz-mill operator on the Comstock in the early period, and C. C. Stevenson, a mining superintendent who later became Governor of Nevada. Both men were among the earliest arrivals on the lode, and both were well acquainted with the men involved.
32. J. P. Jones: *Ms.,* Huntington Library, "Gold Hill Mining Records —edited typescript."
33. Smith: *Papers,* Box I, Vol. 2.
34. Lord: *Comstock Mining,* pp. 411–13; Angel: *Nevada,* p. 622.
35. Smith: *Papers,* Box I, Vol. 1.
36. J. P. Jones: *Ms.,* "Gold Hill Mining Records—edited typescript."
37. Ibid.

38. *Roughing It* (1872), Chapter 29.
39. "Star District, Humboldt County, Recorder's Book, 1861–1867," Nevada Historical Society.
40. Quoted in Lord: *Comstock Mining*, p. 52.
41. Lord: *Comstock Mining*, presents the fullest account of the Comstock litigation, and it is the basis for the following discussion, except where otherwise indicated.
42. Smith: *Papers*, Box IV, Vol. 2.
43. Ibid., Box I, Vol. 8; Virginia *Evening Bulletin*, Aug. 5, 1863.
44. Charles De Long to John R. De Long, Sept. 2, 1863, printed in California Historical Society *Quarterly*, Vol. XI, No. 1 (Mar., 1932), p. 6.
45. Mack: "Stewart"; J. P. O'Brien: *The Bench and Bar in Nevada* (1913), p. 30.
46. William M. Stewart: *Reminiscences of William Morris Stewart* (1907), pp. 130–1.
47. Samuel P. Davis (ed.): *The History of Nevada*, 2 vols., (1913) I, 393.
48. Stewart: *Reminiscences*, p. 160.
49. John W. North: *Ms.*, typescript in Bancroft Library, North to George Loomis, Nov. 29, 1863.
50. Ibid.
51. Ibid., to George Loomis, Feb. 7, 1864.
52. Ibid., "North-Stewart Award of Arbitration."
53. Stewart: *Reminiscences*, p. 153.
54. Davis: *History of Nevada*, I, 393.
55. Rickard: *American Mining*, p. 113; Mack: "Stewart," p. 108.
56. The question of why Nevada was admitted to the Union is discussed in Effie M. Mack: *A History of Nevada* (1943), pp. 254–5; F. Lauiston Bullard: "Abraham Lincoln and the Statehood of Nevada," American Bar Association *Journal*, March, April, 1940, pp. 210–12, 313–17; and Earl S. Pomeroy: "Lincoln, the Thirteenth Amendment and the Admission of Nevada," *Pacific Historical Review*, XII (1943), 362.
57. Angel: *Nevada*, pp. 75–86, probably the best account of Nevada's territorial government.
58. *Roughing It*, Ch. 25.
59. Ibid.
60. Angel: *Nevada*, p. 82; Bancroft, *Works*, XXV, 117–79.
61. Dec. 13, 1863. Quoted in Angel: *Nevada*, p. 82.

CHAPTER II

Notes

1. There are a number of extensive accounts of Ralston's career, notably Julian Dana: *The Man who Built San Francisco* (1936); Cecil G. Tilton: *William Chapman Ralston, Courageous Builder* (1937); and George D. Lyman: *Ralston's Ring* (1937). Tilton's biography is the most extensive of these and is footnoted.
2. Tilton: *Ralston*, p. 99.
3. Ira B. Cross: *History of Banking in California*, 4 vols., (1925), I, 259.
4. Quoted in Dana: *Man Who Built San Francisco*, p. 379.
5. John S. Hittell: *A History of the City of San Francisco . . .* (1878), pp. 211–22, is a good account of the business world of San Francisco at the time of Ralston's arrival.
6. Ibid., pp. 218–22.
7. Ibid., pp. 218–19. Copy in Bancroft Library.
8. Tilton: *Ralston*, p. 103.
9. A. J. Ralston: "Biography of W. C. Ralston," Bancroft *Ms.*, Bancroft Library.
10. Asbury Harpingden: *The Great Diamond Hoax . . .* (1913), p. 13.
11. Notes for Sharon biography, Bancroft *Ms.*
12. Smith: *Comstock*, p. 131.
13. Quoted in Tilton: *Ralston*, p. 29.
14. Cross: *Banking in California*, I, 260; Notes for Ralston biography, Bancroft: *Ms.*; Lord: *Comstock Mining*, pp. 245 ff.
15. Gilbert H. Kneiss: *Bonanza Railroads* (1941), pp. 57–63; Smith: *Papers*, Box II, Vol. 1c (Mackay biography, pp. 494–5).
16. Adolph Sutro: . . . *The Mystery Explained* (1873), p. 5.
17. *Alta California*, Oct. 29, 1863.
18. Smith: *Papers*, Box II, Vol. 1b (Mackay biography, p. 387).
19. Ibid.
20. Smith: *Comstock*, p. 129; Lord: *Comstock Mining*, pp. 280–5; San Francisco *Chronicle*, May 19, 1872.
21. Harpingden: *Diamond Hoax* is a detailed, although inaccurate,

account by an insider; Smith: *Papers,* Box I, Vol. 4, from San Francisco *Call,* Dec. 28, 1875.

22. Smith: *Papers,* Unpublished biography of John W. Mackay *passim;* Lord: *Comstock Mining,* p. 302.
23. Smith: *Papers,* Box II, Vol. 1c, for this account of the four partners. See San Francisco *Examiner,* Dec. 30, 1894, for detailed and malicious Fair obituary.
24. Lord: *Comstock Mining,* p. 323.
25. Rickard: *American Mining,* p. 107; Shinn: *Story of the Mine,* p. 179.
26. Smith: *Comstock Lode,* pp. 158n., 230.
27. Ibid., p. 263.
28. Kneiss: *Bonanza Railroads,* p. 68.
29. The accounts of the circumstances of the bank failure are in substantial agreement, although differing in many small details. See the accounts in Tilton, Dana, Lyman, Cross, and Harpingden.
30. Dana: *Man Who Built San Francisco,* p. 386.
31. The settlement is fully recounted in Tilton and in Dana. Smith: *Comstock,* p. 131; Dana: *Man Who Built San Francisco,* p. 363.
32. Except for a single quotation and a six cent sales figure, all of the following material is to be found in Robert E. Stewart, Jr., and Mary Frances Stewart: *Adolph Sutro, A Biography* (1962), an admiring portrait, which, nevertheless, conscientiously presents all of the damaging evidence against Sutro, including much that is too tenuous to be considered here. Sutro also bulks large in the works of Smith, Lord, and Angel.
33. Smith: *Comstock,* p. 107.
34. Joseph Aron: *History of a Great Work . . .* no date, p. 19. Copy in Bancroft Library.
35. Turner: *The Frontier in American History* (1921), p. 258.
36. Grant: *Papers,* Box I, Vol. 4.
37. H. M. Yerington: *Ms.,* Bancroft Library, Yerington to D. O. Mills, Sept. 30, 1876 (not sent).
38. See below, Chapter III.
39. Smith: *Papers,* Box II, Vol. 1b (Mackay biography, p. 387).
40. Davis: *Nevada,* II, 421.
41. Yerington: *Ms.,* to D. O. Mills, Nov. 6, 1888.
42. Davis: *Nevada,* I, 421.
43. Smith: *Papers,* Box II, Vol. 1c; Bancroft: *Works,* XXV, 182.
44. Yerington: *Ms.,* to D. O. Mills, Nov. 9, 1876.

45. Bancroft: *Ms.*, materials for Fair biography.
46. Davis: *Nevada*, I, 422; Smith: *Papers*, Box II, Vol. 1d (Mackay biography, p. 607), and numbers of letters from Yerington: *Ms.* during the period.
47. Davis: *Nevada*, I, 422; Smith *Comstock*, p. 112.
48. Smith: *Papers*, Box II, Vol. 1d (Mackay biography, p. 607).
49. Ibid.
50. Ibid., Box II, Vol. 1d (Mackay biography, p. 609).
51. Yerington: *Ms.*, to D. O. Mills, Oct. 31, 1880.
52. Smith: *Papers*, Box II, Vol. 1d, (Mackay biography, p. 607).
53. Yerington: *Ms.*, to D. O. Mills, no date.

CHAPTER III

Notes

1. Huntington: *Ms.*, Huntington Library, Huntington to Stanford, Jan. 25, 1875.
2. John D. Galloway: *The First Transcontinental Railroad* (1950) is the source for the discussion of the building of the railroad, except where otherwise indicated.
3. Bancroft: *Ms.*, Material for biography of Charles Crocker.
4. Galloway: *Transcontinental Railroad*, p. 98.
5. Ibid., pp. 98–9.
6. Stuart Daggett: *Chapters on the History of the Southern Pacific* (1922), p. 365.
7. Smith: *Comstock*, p. 297.
8. Ibid., p. 285.
9. Yerington: *Ms.*, to D. O. Mills, April 24, 1888; Yerington to F. G. Newlands, Oct. 6, 1888.
10. Smith: *Comstock*, p. 297.
11. Ibid., p. 286.
12. Robert B. Merrivale: "Nevada, 1859–1881: The Impact of an Advanced Technological Society upon a Frontier Area," (Ph.D., University of Chicago, 1957), p. 49n.
13. Mills: *Sagebrush Saga*, pp. 80, 83.
14. Ibid., pp. 83–4.

15. Richard Lillard: *Desert Challenge* (1942), p. 54.
16. Mills: *Sagebrush Saga,* p. 85.
17. James S. Scrugham (ed.): *Nevada, a Narrative of the Conquest of a Frontier Land,* 3 vols. (1935), I, 296.
18. Yerington: *Ms.,* Yerington to D. O. Mills, April 12, 1873.
19. Scrugham (ed.): *Nevada,* I, 296, 311.
20. Mills: *Sagebrush Saga,* p. 82.
21. Effie M. Mack, Idel Anderson, and Beulah E. Singleton: *Nevada Government* (1953), p. 295.
22. Angel: *Nevada,* p. 277.
23. Rollin Daggett: *Railroad Wrongs* (1891), p. 10.
24. Ibid, p. 25.
25. Yerington: *Ms.,* to A. C. Cleveland, Sept. 18, 1878.
26. Davis: *Nevada,* I, 441.
27. Ibid.
28. Smith: *Papers,* Box II, Vol. 1d (Mackay biography, p. 608).
29. Yerington: *Ms.,* to Mills, Feb. 21, 1881.
30. Ibid., to Mills, June 11, 1878 and June 29, 1878.
31. Ibid., to Mills, March 5, 1881.
32. Yerington: *Ms.,* to Mills, Mar. 5, 1881.
33. Ibid., to Mills, Feb. 11, 1881.
34. Ibid., to Mills, Feb. 21, 1881.
35. Huntington: *Ms.,* Crocker to Sharon, Jan. 25, 1879.
36. Yerington: *Ms.,* to Mills, Dec. 17, 1880.
37. Daggett: *Southern Pacific,* pp. 370–394, for the history of the Thurman Act.
38. Huntington: *Ms.,* Huntington to Crocker, May 30, 1870.
39. Ibid., Huntington to Crocker, Dec. 6, 1867.
40. Ibid., Huntington to Crocker, Oct. 29, 1867.
41. Ibid., Huntington to Hopkins, April 28, 1869.
42. San Francisco *Bulletin,* July 22, 1879.
43. Huntington: *Ms.,* Huntington to Colton, Feb. 8, 1875.
44. Ibid., Huntington to Stanford, Jan. 25, 1875.
45. Ibid., Hopkins to Huntington, Feb. 20, 1873.
46. San Francisco *Chronicle,* Dec. 23, 1883.
47. Ibid.

• • •

CHAPTER IV

Notes

1. The discussion of bimetallism is based upon J. Laurence Laughlin: *The History of Bimetallism in the United States* (1896).
2. W. H. Harvey: *Coin's Financial School* (1894), p. 20.
3. Elmer Ellis: *Henry Moore Teller, Defender of the West* (1941), pp. 185–228, for a general history of the silver controversy.
4. Smith: *Ms.*, Box II, Vol. 1b (Mackay biography, p. 387).
5. Smith: *Ms.*, Box II, Vol. 1d (Mackay biography, p. 616).
6. Stewart: *Ms.*, Nevada Historical Society, Stewart to Huntington, Nov. 30, 1893, to Herrin, Dec. 22, 1893, to Wm. D. Baldwin, Mar. 23, 1890 and other letters.
7. Stewart: *Reminiscences*, p. 265.
8. Stewart: *Ms.*, Sept. 18, 1888.
9. Ibid., to Maxwell Evarts, March 16, 1905.
10. Ibid., Dec. 1, 1893.
11. Mack: "Stewart," p. 191.
12. Stewart: *Ms.*, Sept. 16, 1893.
13. John D. Hicks: *The Populist Revolt* (1931), p. 309. For a recent brief account which supports the views of Hicks concerning the nature of Populism, see Norman Pollack: *The Populist Response to Industrial America* (1962).
14. Pollack: *Populist Response*, p. 135; Hicks: *Populist Revolt*, p. 316.
15. Ellis: *Teller*, pp. 185–228; Hicks: *Populist Revolt*, pp. 313–18, Mack: "Stewart," p. 247.
16. Hicks: *Populist Revolt*, p. 319.
17. Newlands: *Ms.*, Yale University Library, to Herrin, undated, gives an extensive account of the formation of the Silver party and its history. Among the histories of Nevada, the best account is to be found in Davis: *Nevada*.
18. Newlands: *Ms.*, C. D. Van Duzer to Newlands, May 29, 1900.
19. Smith: *Ms.*, Box II, Vol. 1d (Mackay biography), p. 608.
20. Scrugham: *Nevada*, p. 365.
21. Newlands: *Ms.*, typescript in folder entitled "Politics, 1908."
22. Smith: *Ms.*, Box II, Vol. 1d (Mackay biography, p. 610).

23. The only fairly good published account of this struggle, although biased and inaccurate, is in Sam Davis: *Nevada.*
24. Yerington: *Ms.*, to Gilman, Oct. 25, 1890.
25. Davis: *Nevada,* I, 427.
26. Yerington: *Ms.*, to Mills, Oct. 27, 1893.
27. Ibid., to D. J. Colton, Oct. 4, 1894.
28. Ibid., Mar. 9, 1895.
29. Ibid., to Whitelaw Reid, Mar. 11, 1897.
30. Newlands: *Ms.*, Feb. 19, 1898.
31. Ibid., from William Sharon, June 6, 1898; Yerington: *Ms.*, Oct. 24, 1898.
32. Yerington: *Ms.*, to Mills, Nov. 17, 1898.
33. Newlands: *Ms.*, to Herrin, undated.
34. Davis, *Nevada,* I, 429–32.
35. Yerington: *Ms.*, to Mills, Feb. 16, 1899.
36. Newlands: *Ms.*, Mar. 16, 1899.
37. Ibid., undated.
38. Ibid., from Clarence Van Duzer, Sept. 10, 1900.
39. Yerington: *Ms.*, to Mills, Aug. 6, 1902.
40. Newlands: *Ms.*, to William F. Sheehan, Sept. 17, 1904.
41. Yerington: *Ms.*, to Mills, Nov. 7, 1902.
42. Newlands: *Ms.*, to William F. Sheehan, Sept. 17, 1904.
43. Ibid.
44. Angel: *Nevada*, p. 291.
45. Wells Drury: *An Editor on the Comstock Lode* (1936), p. 182.
46. San Francisco *Chronicle,* Nov. 10, 1874.
47. Yerington: *Ms.*, to Mills, Aug. 9, 1882.
48. Drury: *Editor*, p. 187.
49. G. C. Goodwin: *As I Remember Them* (1913), pp. 185–91.
50. Yerington: *Ms.*, to Mills, Jan. 8, 1881.
51. Ibid., to Mills, Jan. 22 and Feb. 4, 1881.
52. Huntington: *Ms.*, Huntington to Hopkins, Mar. 31, 1876.
53. Jan. 13, 1877, quoted in Smith: *Papers,* Box II, Vol 1c.
54. Smith: *Papers,* Box II, Vol. 1c, (Mackay biography, pp. 414, 497).
55. Newlands: *Ms.*, List of Nevada Newspapers, Sept. 1912.
56. Yerington: *Ms.*, Aug. 24, 1880.
57. Ibid., Oct. 14, 1886.
58. Pittman: *Ms.*, Library of Congress, Pittman to Vail Pittman, April 26, 1916.

• • •

CHAPTER V

Notes

1. In contrast to the Comstock, the Tonopah-Goldfield region attracted little attention from historians and other observers. Carl B. Glasscock: *Gold in Them Hills* (1932) is a popular and fairly detailed account, which, however, relies heavily on the shaky authority of interviews with old-timers long after the event. See also Francis C. Lincoln: *Mining Districts and Mineral Resources of Nevada* . . . (1923) and two University of California dissertations: Russell Elliott: "The Tonopah-Goldfield–Bullfrog Mining Districts, 1900–1915" (Ph.D., 1946) and Byrd W. Sawyer, "The Gold and Silver Rushes of Nevada, 1900–1910" (M.A., 1931).
2. Glasscock: *Gold in Hills,* pp. 21–2; 28–30.
3. Yerington: *Ms.,* to Mills, Dec. 28, 1903.
4. Glasscock: *Gold in Hills,* p. 174.
5. Goldfield Mining *Ms.,* The Bancroft Library, Berkeley, J. S. Ewen to Watson, Van Dyck & Company, June 21, 1904.
6. Goldfield Mining *Ms.,* unsigned letter to Max R. McColloms, Oct. 6, 1905.
7. *Mining and Scientific Press,* Oct. 22, 1910.
8. Glasscock: *Gold in Hills,* p. 127.
9. *The New West,* Oct. 1912.
10. Yerington: *Ms.,* to Mills, April 11, 1908.
11. Glasscock: *Gold in Hills,* pp. 60, 132, 135.
12. Ibid., p. 314.
13. Ibid., p. 42; Sawyer: "Rushes in Nevada," p. 44.
14. Lincoln: *Mining Districts,* p. 267.
15. Newlands: *Ms.,* C. D. Van Duzer to Newlands, Nov. 1, 1899.
16. Sawyer: "Rushes in Nevada," pp. 68–9; Glasscock: *Gold in Hills,* pp. 241–4.
17. Ibid., pp. 309–11.
18. Sawyer: "Rushes in Nevada," p. 135.
19. Fred L. Israel: *Nevada's Key Pittman* (1963), p. 23.
20. Newlands: *Ms.,* to William Herrin, 1900 (otherwise undated).

21. Boyd Moore: *Nevada and Nevadans* (1950), p. 14.
22. Moore: *Nevadans*, p. 32.
23. Sacramento *Bee*, Jan. 3, 1934.
24. Ibid., p. 32.
25. Pittman: *Ms.*, to A. B. Gray, Jan. 8, 1912.
26. Ibid., from Woodburn, May 18, 1928.
27. Mack, et al.: *Nevada Government*, p. 295.
28. Newlands: *Ms.*, to Franklin K. Lane, Nov. 29, 1914.
29. Pittman: *Ms.*, to J. W. Babcock, Jan. 8, 1912.
30. Israel: *Pittman*, Ch. I, for Pittman's early career.
31. Ibid., p. 42.
32. Ibid., p. 132.
33. Ibid., p. 15.
34. Pittman: *Ms.*, to J. C. Humphreys, July 6, 1902.
35. Ibid., to Thomas Warburton, July 7, 1902.
36. Israel: *Pittman*, p. 34.
37. Ibid., p. 22.
38. Pittman: *Ms.*, Campaign Letter, Nov. 1, 1910.
39. Pittman: *Ms.*, to C. S. Rosener, Nov. 18, 1910.
40. Ibid., to J. F. Haley, July 24, 1910.
41. Ibid., to Zeb Ray, Nov. 18, 1910.
42. Davis: *Nevada*, vol. I, p. 434.
43. Israel: *Pittman*, *passim.*
44. Ibid., p. 49.
45. Ibid., p. 173.
46. Pittman: *Ms.*, from Woodburn, Oct. 16, 1922.
47. Newlands: *Ms.*, to William Woodburn, Sr., Sept. 20, 1899; to William Woodburn, Jr., in various letters in 1906.
48. Pittman: *Ms.*, from Sam Davis, April 4, 1915.
49. Ibid., from Woodburn, June 13, 1922.
50. Israel, *Pittman*, p. 28.
51. Ibid., pp. 121–3; 127.
52. Ibid., p. 3.
53. Ibid., p. 63.
54. Ibid., p. 4.
55. Tasker L. Oddie: *Ms.*, Huntington Library. See repeated letters referring to his financial difficulties during 1910 especially.
56. Ibid.
57. Ibid., C. M. Smith to Oddie, Sept. 16, 1910.
58. Ibid., from American Adjusting Association, Mar. 4, 1913, and

from Francis G. Luke, Merchants Protective Association, Nov. 24, 1913.

59. Ibid., to Mark G. Bradshaw, July 7, 1911.
60. Moore: *Nevadans*, p. 18.
61. Pittman: *Ms.*, to Sam Davis, Aug. 15, 1908; Newlands: *Ms.*, from Clay Tallman, April 10, 1914.
62. Israel: *Pittman*, p. 32.
63. Pittman: *Ms.*, Bartlett to Metson, July 20, 1916.
64. Pittman: *Ms.*, to Woodburn, Oct. 24, 1933.
65. Ibid., "Wingfield Offer in Compromise, July 3, 1935."
66. Israel: *Pittman*, p. 111
67. Pittman: *Ms.*, to Vail Pittman, Feb. 14, 1940.
68. Ibid., to Vail Pittman, June 12, 1940.
69. Pat McCarran: *Ms.*, Nevada Historical Museum, McCarran to Mike Dowd, Sept. 9, 1944.
70. Israel: *Pittman*, pp. 125–126.
71. *The Reporter*, June 9, 1953, an article by Tom Mechling about his campaign; *New Republic*, Dec. 22, 1952; *Nation*, Sept. 13, 1952.
72. *The Reporter*, Ibid.
73. Ibid.
74. *Time* Magazine, May 19, 1958; Sept. 15, 1958.

CHAPTER VI

Notes

1. Except where otherwise noted, this discussion of the Constitutional Convention is based upon Max Farrand: *The Framing of the Constitution of the United States* (1913).
2. Farrand: *Constitution*, p. 92.
3. James Madison: *Journal of the Federal Convention*, E. H. Scott (ed.), (1898), p. 126.
4. Farrand: *Constitution*, p. 99.
5. *Federalist Papers*, #62.
6. Adrienne Koch: *Jefferson and Madison, The Great Collaboration* (1950), p. 40.

7. Correa M. Walsh: *The Political Science of John Adams* (1915), p. 357.
8. Paul Dolan: *The Government and Administration of Delaware* (1956), p. 299.
9. Robert G. Whittemore, Jr.: "Problems of Federal Land Policy in Nevada Mining," (M.A., University of California, Berkeley, 1949), p. 49. Whittemore's thesis is the source for the discussion of the Mining Law of 1866 which follows. Other detailed accounts of the subject are to be found in Beulah Hershiser, "The Influence of Nevada on the National Mining Legislation of 1866," (M.A., University of California, Berkeley, 1912), and Mack: "Stewart."
10. Whittemore, "Problems . . . ," pp. 50–1.
11. Ibid., p. 58.
12. *Mining and Scientific Press,* July 12, 1902.
13. Smith: *Ms.,* Box II, Vol. 1d (Mackay biography, p. 608).
14. Arthur B. Darling (ed.): *The Public Papers of Francis G. Newlands,* 2 vols. (1932) presents a full account of Newlands' political ideas. Unless otherwise indicated the following discussion of his ideas is based on this source.
15. George Wharton James: *Reclaiming the Arid West* (1917), pp. 14–20; 217–33.
16. Darling (ed.): *Newlands Papers,* I, 111.
17. Ibid., II, 189.
18. Samuel P. Hays: *Conservation and the Gospel of Efficiency* (1959), p. 109.
19. Ibid., p. 110.
20. Ibid., p. 113.
21. Darling (ed.): *Newlands Papers,* vol. I, p. 395.
22. Ibid., I, 401.
23. Ibid., I, 410.
24. Smith: *Ms.,* Box II, Vol. ld (Mackay biography, p. 608).
25. The following discussion of silver politics is based upon Everett L. Cooley: "Silver Policies in the United States, 1918–1946," (Ph.D., University of California, Berkeley, 1951).
26. Ibid., p. 45.
27. Ibid., p. 56.
28. Israel: *Pittman,* p. 90. The following discussion of Pittman's career as chairman of the Foreign Relations Committee is based upon Israel's biography.

29. Ibid., p. 92.
30. Ibid., p. 154.
31. Ibid., p. 163.
32. Ibid., p. 167.
33. Ibid., p. 118.
34. Alfred Steinberg: "McCarran, Lone Wolf of the Senate," *Harpers Magazine*, November, 1950.
35. Cooley: "Silver Policies," pp. 192–3.
36. Steinberg: "McCarran."
37. Ibid.
38. New York *Times*, Sept. 17, 1952; *Current Biography*, 1957.
39. Steinberg: "McCarran."
40. Milton R. Konvitz: *Civil Rights in Immigration* (1953), pp. 30–1.
41. Robert A. Divine: *American Immigration Policy, 1924–1952* (1957), p. 136. The following discussion of the McCarran-Walter Act is based on Divine's monograph.
42. Ibid., p. 137.
43. Ibid., p. 175.
44. Ibid., p. 181.
45. New York *Times*, September 30, 1954.

CHAPTER VII

Notes

1. *The Federalist*, #46.
2. Paul Dolan: *The Government and Administration of Delaware* (1956), p. 300.
3. P. B. Ellis: *Ms.*, The Bancroft Library. Lewis T. Coleman, Indianapolis, to J. D. Torreyson, Carson City, Nov. 28, 1903.
4. Ibid., Ellis to L. J. Clarke, Feb. 3, 1919.
5. Ibid., Ellis to W. B. Ames, May 31, 1917.
6. Ibid., Oscar Sutro, of Pillsbury, Madison & Sutro, to State Agent and Transfer Syndicate, Inc., Aug. 5, 1922.
7. Ibid., State Agent and Transfer Syndicate, Inc. to Pillsbury, Madison and Sutro, Aug. 8, 1922.

8. Ibid., from Automatic Electric Faucet Company, April 24, 1917.
9. Nevada Tax Commission *Report* (1955), p. 7.
10. Mack, et al.: *Nevada Government*, p. 218.
11. Lillard: *Desert Challenge*, p. 87.
12. Mack, et al.: *Nevada Government*, p. 122.
13. Lillard: *Desert Challenge*, p. 82.
14. Ibid., pp. 82, 86.
15. Moore: *Nevadans*, p. 98.
16. Lillard: *Desert Challenge*, p. 93.
17. Ibid., p. 86.
18. Ibid., pp. 327–9.
19. *Nevada Compiled Laws*, Section 10193.
20. The following discussion of Nevada divorce and marriage law is based on Lillard: *Desert Challenge*, pp. 335–68.
21. Except where otherwise indicated, the discussion of Nevada gambling is based on Oscar Lewis: *Sagebrush Casinos* (1953).
22. Lillard: *Desert Challenge*, p. 320.
23. See Harold Smith: *I Want to Quit Winners* (1961).
24. R. A. Zubrov, R. L. Decker, E. H. Plank: *Financing State and Local Government in Nevada* (1960), p. 5.
25. Paul Ralli: *Viva Vegas* (1953), pp. 53–4.
26. Katharine Best and Katharine Hillyer: *Las Vegas* (1955), p. 65.
27. Ibid., p. 18.
28. Ibid., p. 98.
29. Alfred M. Smith: "A Study of the Natural and Industrial Resources of Clark County, Nevada," (mimeographed report, 1956), p. 17.
30. Zubrov, Decker, Plank: *Financing in Nevada*, p. 7.
31. Lewis: *Sagebrush Casinos*, p. 132.
32. Best and Hillyer: *Las Vegas*, p. 63.
33. U. S. Senate: *Hearings Before the Special Committee to Investigate Organized Crime in Interstate Commerce* (Kefauver Committee) (1951), Part 10, p. 24.
34. Best and Hillyer: *Las Vegas*, p. 79.
35. See Ralli: *Viva Vegas*, p. 2.
36. Kefauver Committee *Hearings*, Part 10, p. 91.
37. Ibid., Part 10, p. 92.
38. Ibid.
39. Ibid., Part 10, p. 93.
40. Ibid.

41. Best and Hillyer: *Las Vegas*, p. 83.
42. Ibid., p. 82.
43. S. F. *Chronicle*, Oct. 23, 1963.
44. *The Mountains of California* (1894), pp. 98, 100.
45. *Roughing It*, Ch. 23.
46. Darling (ed.): *Newlands Papers*, I, 81–2.
47. Smith, *I Want to Quit Winners*, pp. 104, 18.
48. Keith Monroe, "The New Gambling King and the Social Sciences," *Harpers*, January 1962, is the source for this account of Harrah's Lake Tahoe enterprise.
49. S. F. *Chronicle*, Sept. 28, 1963.
50. Ibid.
51. Ibid., Oct. 4, 1963.
52. Ibid., Oct. 9, 1963.
53. Ibid.
54. Ibid., Nov. 16, 1963.
55. Quoted in Albert K. Weinberg: *Manifest Destiny* (1935), p. 106.
56. J. E. E. Dalbert, Lord Acton: *Lectures on Modern History* (1906), p. 314.

Index

Index

Index

Index

A NOTE ABOUT THE AUTHOR

Gilman M. Ostrander was born in San Francisco, California, in 1923. He received his A.B. from Columbia University in 1946; his M.A. from the University of California, Berkeley, in 1947; and his Ph.D. from the latter university in 1953. With the exception of a brief stint as a reporter for the San Francisco *Chronicle*, Mr. Ostrander has devoted his professional life to the teaching of American history, with an emphasis on American intellectual history. He taught at Reed College, Ohio State University, and the University of Missouri. Since 1959 he has been associate professor of history at Michigan State University. Mr. Ostrander is the author of *The Prohibition Movement in California, 1848–1933* (1957), *The Rights of Man in America, 1606–1861* (1960), and *A Profile History of the United States* (1964).

January 1966

A NOTE ON THE TYPE

The text of this book was set on the Linotype in Janson, a recutting made direct from type cast from matrices long thought to have been made by the Dutchman Anton Janson, who was a practicing type founder in Leipzig during the years 1668–87. However, it has been conclusively demonstrated that these types are actually the work of Nicholas Kis (1650–1702), a Hungarian, who most probably learned his trade from the master Dutch type founder Dirk Voskens. The type is an excellent example of the influential and sturdy Dutch types that prevailed in England up to the time William Caslon developed his own incomparable designs from these Dutch faces.

Composed, printed, and bound by
The Haddon Craftsmen, Inc., Scranton, Pa.
Typography and Binding by Albert Burkhardt